TYPES OF MODERN THEOLOGY

TYPES OF
MODERN THEOLOGY
Schleiermacher to Barth

by

HUGH ROSS MACKINTOSH
D.Phil., D.D., D.Th.
LATE PROFESSOR OF CHRISTIAN DOGMATICS
NEW COLLEGE, UNIVERSITY OF EDINBURGH

LONDON: NISBET AND CO. LTD.
22 BERNERS STREET W.1

First published in 1937
Reprinted · July 1937
Reprinted · April 1942
Reprinted · May 1945
Reprinted January 1947
Reprinted September 1949
Reprinted · March 1952

Made and Printed in Great Britain

CONTENTS

v

PREFACE

THIS BOOK represents in an expanded form the lectures delivered under the Croall Trust by Professor Mackintosh in the autumn of 1933. With the exception of part of Chapter VIII, the contents were revised by him for publication before his lamented death on June 8, 1936. For the closing pages (from page 306 onwards) use has been made of a manuscript which was to form the basis of the final version. To Chapter VIII the author devoted a great deal of thought, for he held Professor Karl Barth in high esteem, and was anxious to do full justice to the changing phases of his theological work.

This is not the place to attempt an appreciation of the life, character and numerous writings of Professor Mackintosh. To know him was both to admire the erudite scholar and to love the man. He was indeed ἀνὴρ ἀγαθὸς καὶ πλήρης Πνεύματος Ἁγίου καὶ πίστεως.

In preparing the book for publication the Editor wishes to acknowledge gratefully the invaluable help he has received from the Rev. Oswald B. Milligan, M.C., T.D., B.D., Corstorphine, the Rev. Professor D. M. Baillie, D.D., St. Andrews, and the Publishers.

A. B. MACAULAY

EDINBURGH, 1937.

I

INTRODUCTORY

§ 1. CHARACTER OF THE MODERN PERIOD

THE PERIOD of theological history, some aspects of which are to be studied in the following pages, is one of the most notable ever traversed by the Christian Church. The nineteenth century—this, with some extension into the twentieth, forms, roughly speaking, the area of our subject—exhibits a confluence of various streams, issuing in a complexity of ideas, a fascinating yet confusing absence of uniformity, which is very unlike the theology of three hundred years ago, but on the other hand recalls the life of the early Church. In the Patristic era, if a divine was orthodox on the Person of Christ he received, or at all events he claimed, a certain latitude with regard to some other doctrinal topics, such as the atonement or eschatology. By degrees this freedom was withdrawn ; in the Middle Ages tradition had more than begun to weave its bonds ; and by the seventeenth century both Roman and Protestant writers had become pretty closely tied up by the detail of their creeds. The difference is clear once the nineteenth century has begun. For the last three or four generations men have been working out fresh interpretations. The result has in some good ways been to quicken interest and banish stagnation. It has been said with point that hardly one of the great German or Swiss theologians of the last hundred years—Schleiermacher, Biedermann, Lipsius, Rothe, or Ritschl—would have been able to survive an appeal for the exercise of Presbyterian discipline.

In theology we cannot well make experiments, and in that case we should be all the more careful to use observation. It is perhaps from thinkers of the modern period that a man derives most help or warning in the formation of his own theology. Only as it evokes or clarifies our personal convictions does the historical study of theology yield a positive gain, for in this field the historian's besetting temptation is so to subtilize and refine that he becomes nearly incapable of recognizing truth or affirming it with the ring of persuasion. Happily our minds—at all events if they have been touched by Christian faith—are so made that it is all but impossible to take or keep that unmoving posture of perfectly balanced and sustained impartiality to which certain ideals of history would confine us. To know what others have believed, or where their thought-forms came from, is not enough. "Were the knowledge of religion historical only," writes Hegel, "we should have to regard theologians as resembling the bank-clerk who enters in his ledger large sums of money belonging to other people, yet acquires little of his own." To use history as a cushion to ward off the necessity for personal decision is to misuse it.

One striking feature of modern theology is its swiftness of movement. As in the political history of France, the student can watch a tendency working itself out in a comparatively brief period. It is in its development that the implications of an idea or a system come to light. Schiller's aphorism, which declares that the world's history is the world's judgment, holds true in a special degree of ideas ; for what comes out of them demonstrates what in fact was in them. The nemesis of a one-sided or unwholesome theological principle may be looked for in its life-story. The new concept will receive its certification of value only through the arbitrament of later inquiry.

To a patriotic Briton there may appear to be some humiliation in the fact that throughout a study like the present nothing, or next to nothing, is said regarding our native contribution to doctrinal history, or even regarding Anglo-Saxon thought in the wider sense. As in the neighbouring field of philosophy, most of the time is spent in recording movements of opinion on the Continent. The air is mostly filled with German names. In 1857 Mark Pattison put the facts with an emphasis which would doubtless have to be moderated to-day, yet which was not unjust to his own time.

It must not be supposed, [he wrote] that German Theology is some obscure national product, the concern exclusively of the country which has given it birth. It is no insulated phenomenon. Though generated in Germany, it belongs to Christendom. It is the theological movement of the age. It is only because there is fuller intellectual life in Germany than elsewhere—only because it so happens that, at present, European speculation is transacted by Germans, as our financial affairs are by Jews—that German characteristics are impressed on the substance of the Christian science. The capital of learning is in the hands of Germans, and theirs has been the enterprise which has directed it into theological channels.

This we may accept as roughly true, even though before our inquiry has ended we may see much reason to doubt whether German nineteenth-century " speculation " has always moved within the limits of authentic Christian faith, and whether the grave charge Professor Karl Barth has made against it of having substituted the word of man for the Word of God is not more than half justified.[1]

In any case, what gave German theology its relative pre-eminence in the last century may be traced to three outstanding circumstances, two of these more extraneous, the third profound and permanent in influence. (1) The larger numbers engaged. Something like twenty-five fully staffed Faculties of theology have been at work in Germany alone, apart from German Switzerland, " each ",

[1] One defect of German academic theology as a whole has been its lack of vital contact with the life of the worshipping Church.

as Sanday once put it, "watching all the rest, and all throwing their knowledge into a common stock". (2) The enjoyment of a wider doctrinal freedom. Contrary to a not unfamiliar view, close relations to the State have not actually gone to keep the Church orthodox. Fear of the Church's disciplinary action has not, as with us, retarded the movement of individual thought. No doubt such action has its uses, but at times an excessively high price is paid for it. (3) The love of thorough and exact knowledge characteristic of the German mind—what may be called its *Gründlichkeit*. Their writers are perpetually moving on. No sooner does a definite result appear to have been gained, than new questions begin to be asked. In large measure this is owing to the fact that German theologians have the advantage over us of taking part in a continuous debate. The writer of each new book or article has his immediate predecessors in view. From all this it certainly does not follow that we are to go on our knees to German theology. The Anglo-Saxon mind on the average has considerably less learning; but very often, I think, it exhibits a much sounder judgment. But we must not impeach the nature of human life and thought. These types of mind are both essential. The German type is prone to advance in a zigzag manner, tacking from one extreme to another, enveloping all in a fierce spirit of party, equipping each new school with the penetrating power of a one-sided fervour as well as with the practically effective slogan which calls men round a newly erected banner. Our type keeps more steadily to the middle of the road, but is so much the less apt to initiate new movements.

With the work of Schleiermacher, theology may be said to have entered on a new phase. Unless the impulses given by him, for good or ill, be studied with some care, the present position and prospects of theology will largely remain mysterious. At the outset of his activity, Schleiermacher found himself confronted by a definite situation which can only be understood in the light of its antecedents. What is known as the law of cause and effect cannot operate in the spiritual or intellectual world precisely as it does in the world of physics, since in the former case the forces at work are reasons or motives that persuade or attract ; still, it operates, and this must be allowed for by the historian.   In the physical realm things go by mechanical necessity ; in history, the domain of specifically human life, causal connexion takes the form of a free acceptance of influence, or, quite as often, free reaction against it. Here causality becomes motivation.   Yet this fact, that conditioned freedom but not caprice obtains in history and imparts to it its own distinctive quality, must not be interpreted as reducing the past to a chapter of accidents. There is a moral though not a mechanically ordered sequence of events ; stage is linked to stage, and phase to phase.   " If history proves nothing, and predicts nothing ", it has been said, " yet, rightly used, it will suggest a great deal ".   Moreover, it is clear that the historian must himself be a man of personal faith if he is to perceive the magnitude of the issues out of which the greater controversies of the theological past have risen. There can be no more superficial blunder than to suppose that these major doctrinal conflicts centred on points devoid of real importance, and might reasonably have been compromised by a little give-and-take.   Over and over again the Gospel itself has been in the balance.

In earlier years, [wrote Froude of Carlyle] he had spoken contemptuously of the Athanasian controversy, of the Christian world torn in pieces over a diphthong, and he would ring the changes in broad Annandale on the Homoousion and the Homoiousion.   He told me now that he perceived Christianity itself to have been at stake.   If the Arians had won, it would have dwindled away into a legend.

§ 2. REFORMATION AND POST-REFORMATION THOUGHT

It hardly needs saying that the great precursor of modern evangelical theology is the Reformation. Modernist writers have long been wont to urge that by their radical criticism of all received dogmas they are only carrying to its logical conclusion the basal principle of Reformation thought. They wish to be thoroughgoing in the use of critical ideas which, though no doubt implicitly asserted in the sixteenth century, had not then been applied with any full consciousness of their real meaning. The Reformers left their work half done, and the neglected portions must now be overtaken.[1]

There is plainly some truth in this. Like all revivals, the Reformation had a profound effect on theology. It is misleading to say that the secret and inspiration of the new evangelical message was the right of private judgment, which is in no sense a distinctively religious idea ; nor is this secret to be found, either, in the affirmation of the immediate access of the soul to God, which can hardly be denied to great saints like St. Bernard. Actually it lay in a new thought of the intrinsic authority belonging to God's revelation of Himself. It was the discovery that unless Jesus Christ attests Himself to the soul in whom His Word has been made living and powerful by the Holy Spirit, the Christian religion cannot begin to live. In consequence the Reformers taught that, the believer being face to face with God, his convictions are reached by responsible decision, in the spontaneous act of faith. They are the Spirit-prompted response of his mind and heart to the Word. They are convictions which God leaves *him* no option but to hold. From the outset, accordingly, evangelical Protestantism had its honourable risks. It was at least possible that the personal beliefs held by

[1] Eighteenth-century Pietism first struck this note, though with some hesitation.

evangelical Christians might differ, as they were less likely
to do in the Roman Church, though in point of fact we
much exaggerate the agreement of Roman thinkers. But
more : there existed a danger lest the Reformers' protest
against a legally prescribed system of dogma should get
beyond control, and—perhaps by imperceptible degrees
—change into a positive assault on the central facts of
Christianity. Not seldom, as all men know, the right of
private judgment has been taken to legitimize this equally
into other more positive forms of opinion. It has been
construed as meaning that every one is entitled to think
as he likes. But this is merely Protestantism in caricature.
No sane man thinks just as he likes ; he thinks, at least
by intention, in accordance with fact. None the less,
a new principle for theology had been introduced, viz.,
that truth revealed in Christ admits of no external proof,
but is made the inward possession of the believing mind
by the convincing power of the Holy Spirit. To perceive
and affirm this called for a real choice between alternatives ; personal judgment comes in, forming finally its
own conclusions, and standing by them in the sight of
God, whether it stands in a great company or stands alone.
It is not a faith any man or Church can make for you. If
it be said that this invitation to think at the level of
freedom is perilous, the only reply is that apart from such
perils there can be no such thing as true personal faith.
And it was because, under God, Luther had revived faith
that inevitably he revived the life and spirit of theology.
It dawned upon him that there was theological material
in the living experience of Christian souls. Dogmas which
seemed to have lost vitality and to have become the mere
dead tools of intellectual discipline, filled again with life
when their lost religious interest had been seized anew.[1]

Great ideas too often are vulgarized in the second gener-

[1] See especially Lindsay, *History of the Reformation*, Vol. I,
Chap. VIII.

ation. " The original impulse weakens as it spreads ; the living passion petrifies in codes and creeds ; the revelation becomes a commonplace ; and so the religion that began in vision ends in orthodoxy." Thus it was with the profound doctrines put forth at the Reformation. In the seventeenth century began the ascendancy of what is known as Protestant Scholasticism, a mood or spirit of theological rigour, consequent upon and more or less keeping pace with the fierce conflicts of Lutheran and Calvinist. It was an age of vast dogmatic systems, often spoken of in tones of condescending patronage as ignorant as it is absurd. Doubtless it is hard not to grow impatient with the harshnesses and limitations of an age which developed to an extreme point the sub-Christian doctrine of the Verbal Inspiration of Scripture as well as a rigidly penal and quantitative theory of the atonement.

But in justice two things must be remembered. In the first place, the chief purpose of great seventeenth-century divines was to impress the thought of their own time, not of ours ; and if they enclosed the kernel of religious truth in a thick husk, this was meant by way of protection. Secondly, if we may refer to such dubious entities as " laws of history ", [1] it appears to be something like a " law " that on any great creative movement, such as the Reformation, there should follow a period of diminished originality but of larger discursive power, in which the gains of the larger time are, so to speak, catalogued, arranged, and valued. The mine having been opened by the Reformers, it became a duty to get out the ore and smelt it. In the process traditional orthodoxy emerged —a distinct historical phenomenon, characterized by the

[1] Ed. Meyer, the famous historian, puts the matter very plainly : " During a long course of historical enquiry, I have never myself discovered a law of history, nor have I ever met with one in the mind of any other. It may be taken as agreed that laws of history have, so far, no existence except as postulates " (*Zur Theorie und Methodik der Geschichte*).

fatal tendency to attach an absolute value to dogmatic formulas, to consider faith and assent to creed as virtually one and the same thing, to harp upon the language of confession or catechism without at each point getting back behind the form of sound words to truth as truth is in Jesus. These writers overlooked the cardinal fact that, as it has been put, " the vast mass of the most important truths are known to us and communicated to others under the form of symbols with a penumbra of indefinable suggestion ". As we study works of this type, we are prepared to agree cordially with the counsel lately given to dogmatic theologians to read more poetry.

Along with this insensitiveness to the symbolic nature of religious thought went an assumption of something very like omniscience in spiritual things. Minds of this cast have the appearance of knowing more concerning the ways of God with man than we can easily believe to be within the compass of the most instructed Christian. All this brought on a strong inclination to get rid of open questions, or to find a solution of hard problems in misplaced rational logic—for example, in the two-edged doctrine of pre-destination to life and to death [1]—or in the violent use of Biblical proof-texts. Scholasticism, the name by which this period of Protestant theology goes, essentially means an intellectual temper which may invade any subject in any age ; in religion, it is the spirit of law overbearing the spirit of the Gospel. Theological stagnation was the result, not least in the fields of Biblical Exegesis and Church History, where it is safe to say men can work to little purpose if they work in chains. Also the ascendancy of the doctrinal polemic was fostered ; and the activity of the polemic, still more his popularity, has an all but fatal effect on the sense for truth. What is wanted is

[1] It is only fair to recollect that to a very large extent Calvin's teaching on Election and Reprobation simply repeats that of St. Thomas Aquinas.

powder and shot for controversy ; the champion goes out
to kill his man rather than to convince him. Thus by the
end of the seventeenth century forces making for ossifi-
cation had got the upper hand. It is impossible to
beget life or maintain it by mechanism. But, of course,
the most vigilant precautions against free thought prove
self-defeating. The seventeenth century made way for the
eighteenth ; and when traditional orthodoxy had done its
work, Butler could write, in the advertisement to the
first edition of his *Analogy*, issued in 1736 : " It is come,
I know not how, to be taken for granted by many persons
that Christianity is not so much a subject for enquiry,
but that it is now at length discovered to be fictitious."

A more than ordinarily hurtful feature in traditional
orthodoxy, it can now be seen, was the restored predominance of Aristotelianism in Christian theology. The
great philosopher has been called, not without point, the
prophet of the natural man. Luther had declared, with
justifiable vehemence, that the assumptions of Aristotelian
philosophy, particularly with regard to the nature of God,
were an incubus on living faith. He cast them out as the
figments of pagan metaphysic. But as the tide of new
life ebbed, the old incongruous presuppositions rose into
power again. Aristotle was once more permitted to dictate
conclusions at war with the meaning of the Bible, and the
truth of Christ's transcendent revelation was yet again
diluted to the prescription of non-Christian philosophy.
By a natural consequence men more and more grew blind
to the wonder of the New Testament message. Christianity
came in many quarters to be represented as no more
than the confirmation of truths which had long been the
possession of natural reason. The Gospel did but set forth
" what oft was thought, but ne'er so well expressed ".
" Christianity as old as Creation " and " Christianity not
Mysterious "—such are the titles of two influential and
characteristic publications of the time. Christ is suffici-

ently acknowledged, it is suggested, if we say that He
gave His imprimatur to certain beliefs universally held
by intelligent persons.   On such terms, all the romance
and glory of the Gospel fade out.   The triumphant certain=
ties of the Apostolic faith lapse into rational and necessary
axioms, so commonplace and decent that to acquiesce in
them is hardly worth a sinner's while.

§ 3.   PIETISM

The main forces of a theological kind bearing on the
mind of the eighteenth century were Pietism and the
Rationalism of the *Aufklärung* or Enlightenment.   We
must glance briefly at these before devoting what can
be no more than a few pages to the great philosophical
renascence with which the nineteenth century opened.

Pietism at its best was a recoil of living faith from
a dead and rigid orthodoxy.   It followed on a time which
had contented itself in large measure with the acceptance
of dogmatic formulas and the practice of ecclesiastical
usage.   The standard work on Pietism was for long a three-
volume history by Ritschl published in the 'eighties of
last century ;   though once regarded as authoritative, if
not final, it now carries somewhat less weight.   Certainly
he had no love for the Pietists ;   he found in them to
a noxious degree the spirit of separatism, and in particular
he accused them of having betrayed the cardinal doctrine
of the Reformation, justification by faith.   Yet Ritschl's
temperament—that of a sturdy moralism—gravely unfitted
him for dealing justly with a movement calculated, perhaps,
like no other to evoke his characteristic antipathies.   While
nothing was further from the intention of Pietist leaders
than any disloyalty of the sort charged upon them, it
must be admitted that the watchword of Pietistic teaching
came to be the New Life, viewed as a subjective process,
rather than Justification, which is the act of God.

The purpose which men like Spener and Francke had in their mind was not so much to remodel doctrine as to quicken spiritual life. They fought the worldliness and apathy of the Church. Like the Methodists in England, they urged the necessity for a deeper devotional acquaintance with Scripture, and with this in view they encouraged the formation of private circles for Bible study, the tone of which should be devout rather than scientific. In addition, they called upon Christian people to be separate from the world and give up its ways. These principles were recommended by the establishment of noble philanthropic institutions, some of which persist to this day.

But the weaker men who followed in their train were apt to turn principle into narrow and bitter prejudice. Attendance at private Bible-circles came to be regarded as of more importance than Church fellowship. A meagre and utilitarian idea of doctrine tended to become a favourite ; nothing could pass muster except that which yielded immediate edification ; and the rank and file soon forgot that there is such a thing as the study of Christian truth for its own sake. Again, the demand was frequently made that every believer must have undergone a certain prescribed series of conversion-experiences, in a prescribed order—so much in the way of legal terrors, so much new-found joy. Nor, as we might expect, was it long before certain representatives of the Pietistic school began to use expressions, imprudent or worse, which meant that these subjective experiences of the convert are the real ground of his acceptance with God. This was plainly the thin end of the legalistic wedge. It taught men to look inward, not upward, and threatened to silence that open declaration of the free and undeserved grace of God without which the preached Gospel has lost its savour.

All this goes to prove that in character the positive message of Pietism was more ethical than theological. Such an estimate remains broadly true, even although it must be admitted that the Pietistic contention, that the value of Christian doctrines can in a real degree be measured by their significance for practical religious life, was itself an insistence on a theological principle thoroughly definite in kind, and, apart from extravagances, wholesomely spiritual. The real achievement of Pietism in the field of theology consists in its having broken the power of Protestant Scholasticism. It persuaded men, at least in some measure, that dogmas having no relation to the life of trust and obedience are worthless. Zinzendorf gave help at this point by his concentration of faith, and its convictions, on the Person of Jesus ; and Bengel helped by his all-pervasive Biblicism. It was largely owing to Pietism that when the tides of negation flowed in later, submerging Christian belief and self-sacrifice, so much of vital religion outlasted the deluge.

§ 4.   THE RATIONALISM OF THE ENLIGHTENMENT

The other factor of chief importance in the theology of the eighteenth century was the Rationalism associated more or less closely with the *Aufklärung* or Enlightenment. This influential movement, which apart from religion left a deep mark on science, philosophy and philanthropy, may in its theological aspects be set forth historically in three main stages ; and these, in a broad way, may be thus distinguished. Let it be premised that for the thinkers of the *Aufklärung*, as for English Deists, reason and understanding mean pretty much the same thing. First, then, comes the stage at which it was said : We can defend the orthodox creed by reason, and we ought to. Christian truth is all the better for having its foundations in the universal laws of thought made clear, or at all events for proof that it is not out of harmony with the rest of our ordinary knowledge. In the next place, men proceeded to make distinctions between the orthodox faith

which might legitimately be professed in public, and the
private views cherished by the initiated few. This is
a position favoured by Semler, one of the pioneers of New
Testament criticism. It is, of course, a fatal theory. Men
cannot keep a naturalistic version of Christianity for the
study and a supernatural one for the pulpit. Truth will
not thus be divided into two types ; and if naturalistic
beliefs in religion are too paralysing or ineffectual to be
brought out into the open, the only reasonable inference
is that they are false ; while, on the other hand, if Church
doctrines will not bear inspection, must not the only
ground of this be that they have no defensible hold on
facts ? Nothing could eventually be meant except that
none but the private views were credible, whereas doctrines
got up for popular consumption possessed only what may
be called diplomatic value.

The third stage is that which puts reason—conceived
not as embracing all man's cognitive powers but as the
mere understanding that operates with common sense or
rule-of-thumb logic—on the seat of judgment, and insists
that every Christian doctrine must undergo trial in the
court of reason thus defined. Only what is rational can
be accepted. We are bound to reduce the creed to
dimensions that will satisfy the familiar rules of argumentation. This third stage is Rationalism proper ; it is, to
put it so, Rationalism at its full height and completely
conscious of itself. The doctrines of the divinity of Christ,
of original sin, of forgiveness mediated by the Cross, of
sacraments and miracles were put aside, at times con-
descendingly, but probably much more often with a
perfectly honest feeling of mystification. The New Testament itself, it was urged, had never meant us to take
these things seriously. Leading thinkers of this complexion were guided by a maxim which, roughly but not
unfairly, may be formulated thus : " I will believe nothing
I cannot understand, and I understand only what conforms

to the acknowledged rules of logic and can be explained to anyone of normal intelligence." The newer physics itself would have caused no little difficulty to all who thus held that real knowledge is limited to what can be rationally conceived.

One thing, apparently, was to be left intact—the Teaching of Jesus. Yet not even this *corpus* of doctrine could be accepted just as it stood ; some alien accretions and obscurities, due indirectly to Rabbinism or Greek philosophy, must be eliminated. St. Paul was the real culprit. In his mind the simple ethical precepts of Jesus had to an unfortunate extent become adulterated with Jewish theologumena. At a later point Platonism had come in with the Gnostics ; Neo-platonism, too, through the unconscious influence of thinkers to whom Gnosticism was anathema. Thus by degrees the teaching of Jesus had been lost to sight behind a defensive screen of metaphysics gathered round it by the Church. As in the last quarter of the nineteenth century, the cry went up that at all costs we must get back from faith in Christ to the simple religion of Jesus. His personal beliefs had been no more than the normal dictates of reason. He stood for truth, He inculcated virtue, He promised to virtuous men the reward of immortality.

It is easy to imagine how on these terms the majesty and power of the Christian Gospel vanished. There is little to produce " joy unspeakable and full of glory " in a form of Christianity which, with half a sheet of notepaper and a spare hour, the average man can construct for himself. People naturally ceased to reverence something with which, at a pinch, they could dispense. Sentimental commonplaces are poor enough fare for the penitent, the tempted, the afflicted. It is by no means surprising that the clergy who proclaimed such a message frequently exhibited a keener interest in sport or agriculture than in the cure of souls.

The movement had this curious feature, that though professing to prove everything by reason the Rationalists hardly appear to have raised the question what reason is. The common assumption was that everybody knew. In each human mind, so the theory went, there is to be found an ascertainable outfit of intellectual, moral and religious convictions whose validity is a matter of universal agreement. Reason was taken to be not unanimous merely, but in good working order in the generality of men; for there was nothing the Rationalists so much disliked as the notion of original sin. It was a time of jubilant and all but fatuous optimism, strongly buttressed by faith in the infinite perfectibility of man through education. Not that the reality of sin was denied; but it was explained genetically as due to the senses having started ahead of the spirit. It is a disease of childhood, like measles, which the human race may justly expect to outgrow. If the individual has done his best to improve, what the Church calls " sin " is forgiven as a matter of course. Jesus undoubtedly is our Pattern, yet it is wholly unnecessary on that account to credit Him with attributes of a supernatural order. Paulus, a professor at Heidelberg and the typical exegete of the *Aufklärung*, undertook to explain narratives of miracles without remainder as owing to misunderstandings on the part of the narrators. The Resurrection, for example, was no more than recovery from apparent death ; the feeding of the multitude is erroneously set down as if it implied a marvel, whereas the real facts were much more simple—the crowd, following the lead of Jesus and the disciples, took provisions out of their pockets and handed them round. At the Transfiguration, an unknown friend of Jesus, hidden in the morning mists, called out in the hearing of the apostolic three, " This is my beloved Son ". We need not multiply examples of the vulgar and perfunctory level to which this form of criticism could descend. The feeling grows upon us, as we read on, that humour was far from being the Rationalist's strong suit.

As we have seen, no one took pains to inquire carefully
what reason is. Yet this was the one question worth
asking. The assumption that man's higher consciousness
is a constant quantity, the same in all, is of course gratuitously false. There are savages who cannot count beyond
five, in Australia (as Spencer and Gillen show) beyond
four. Conscience, these writers held, is just reason on its
practical side and therefore identical in all men ; yet
nothing could be more evident than that no two men's
consciences are quite the same. We shall not err grievously
if we say that for Rationalistic thought reason—in its
ethical and religious aspects—stands simply for the
residuum left in man's higher mental life when you have
purged out everything derived from Christianity. Abstract
the Christian ingredients, and you have generic man, man
as he really is. But if there is anything on which virtually
all schools of thought now agree, it is that this so-called
reason—this constant, unvarying, and universally distributed stock of moral and spiritual convictions—is devoid
of real existence. There is in fact no such thing ; otherwise why should we be so much concerned with education
and nurture ? What did most to bring public discredit
upon their views was probably the circumstance that
profounder and more instructed minds than those of the
Rationalists themselves gave a wholly different interpretation of reason, its nature and its capacities. If the
Rationalists held, as a conviction sprung from reason,
that to speak of congenital sinfulness is mere folly, whereas
Kant spoke of human nature as infested with radical evil,
men felt at liberty to choose between them ; and in the
comparison Kant's argument, it is certain, did not suffer.

The *Aufklärung*, with Deism as its English counterpart,
has of course been described here in merely general terms,
and from the foregoing account the inference might colour-

ably be drawn that its effects were wholly bad. But this
would be a grave mistake ; here too the Church owes
much to heretics. Thus it was no matter for regret that
in the eighteenth century clericalism should have had
a severe setback ; if, when thrust into the background,
it too often carried religion along with it, yet religion
might later revive, and clericalism still be deservedly left
in shadow. Again, ethics may too much predominate in
religion, if it be so taught as to exclude grace ; yet it is
of vital importance that responsibility and decision should
be stressed, and to a real extent the Rationalists stressed
them. Also it was good that blind acquiescence in old
custom should be disturbed, even at the risk—inseparable
from all forward movement—that the new temper might
change freedom into license. Lastly, in spite of the
emphasis which has justly been laid on the unhistorical
temper of the *Aufklärung*, it must not be forgotten that
to powerful thinkers within its ranks we owe the first
beginnings of New Testament science. The modern
historical and critical view of the Bible, with its gains
and losses, is in the main an outcome of the Rationalistic
movement, which raised for the first time an astonishing
number of problems not yet completely solved. The
dogma of the universal damnation of the heathen was
called in question ; the persecution of witches was de-
nounced. All these things, even when summed together,
may seem to furnish a poor recompense for the loss of
genuine faith in revelation, in the free and supernatural
action of God, in forgiveness as mediated through Jesus
Christ and specifically through His death ; and with such
a judgment I should have no great quarrel. Yet even
here we cannot forget the saying of a witty French writer
that " God need not grudge even His enemies their
virtues ". A movement or century, like an individual,
is not seldom better than its creed. What is more, among
the Rationalists there were many who lived upon a practical

faith larger and richer by far than their explicit principles
would have justified. The name of Jesus, it has been
said, comes with power wherever it comes ; and He, we
need not doubt, found His own also among them.

§ 5.   THE PHILOSOPHICAL RENASCENCE

There now confronts us the great new outburst of
philosophical Idealism, in one of its most striking forms,
which marked the passage from one century to another,
and in the light of which alone the theological history of
our period becomes intelligible. The famous names are
four : Kant, Fichte, Schelling, Hegel. There is obviously
an approach to absurdity in the very effort to describe
in a few pages the legacy left to the theologian by these
masters of them that know ; yet, with all its shortcomings,
the effort must now be made.

Kant, it is agreed, has become the fruitful and creative
source of philosophy in its most impressive form within
the modern age. Awakened by David Hume from his
dogmatic slumber, he proposed to himself the aim of
vindicating for the principle of causality that universal and
objective necessity which Hume, in his purely empirical
fashion, had explained away as the deposit of mere
non-rational custom. The question about causality, however, widened out before long into the larger one, how
propositions originating not in experience, but in pure
thought can none the less have validity for the world of
objects. The answer reached by Kant is what he called
his " Copernican revolution ". Briefly it amounts to this,
that we have to reverse the relation hitherto supposed to
obtain between the mind and objects. Instead of our
mind, in order to know, adapting itself to the objects,
cognition of which is sought, what actually happens is
that all objects are under the necessity of adapting themselves to our mind. Thus we can know nature *a priori*

—that is, with a cogency that owes nothing to experience
—because nature is in fact more than half the work of
our own intelligence. It submits to the legislation of the
understanding. We are able to employ principles of
apprehension, or, to use his own term, categories, in conformity with which our knowledge must come to us. We
find rationality in nature because we ourselves put it
there. When we inquire further, it is to discover that
this magisterial power of mind over objects is owing to
the fact that, in the last resort, objects are *in* the mind,
and our knowledge, from end to end, is stamped with
mere phenomenality. To quote his own words, we know
" only the mode in which our senses are affected by an
unknown something ". " Supposing us to carry our
empirical perception even to the very highest degree of
clearness, we should not thereby advance one step nearer
to a knowledge of the constitution of objects as things-
in-themselves. For we could only, at best, arrive at a
complete cognition of our own mode of perception, that
is, of our sensibility." And again : " It is incomprehensible
how the perception even of a present object should give
me a knowledge of that thing as it is in itself, seeing that
its properties cannot migrate or wander over into my
presentative faculty." Things in space, then, are simply
my spatially disposed perceptions. As we scrutinize the
various strata to be found in the *Critique of Pure Reason*,
it becomes plain that Kant was himself far from being
satisfied with this form of subjective idealism, in which
he virtually joined hands with Berkeley. But, as has
been said, good intentions cannot be credited in philosophy ;
and, however much against his own better judgment, the
theory of knowledge that issues from his explicit argument
is one that saves the consistency of knowledge at the price
of its objective value. Phenomena are not in themselves
things, Kant declares. " They are nothing but ideas, and
cannot exist at all beyond our minds."

There is a further consequence flowing directly from the Kantian argument, this time connected not with the nature of knowledge but, so to speak, with its permitted range. Categories are valid only within experience, which in a context of this kind means sense-experience ; they have no valid hold upon, or relevance to, objects which are incapable of being presented sensibly. They are, so to say, unable to work in a vacuum from which sense-elements have been withdrawn. What is the effect of this far-reaching consideration ? It means, for one thing, that reason in its theoretical capacity affords no ground of any sort for the statement that God is the cause of the world. Causality, which is a relation obtaining solely between finite objects, and represents a certain specific kind of link between one sensible reality and another, has no bearing on an object which by very nature is infinite. Were God a cause in the normal sense, the mind would immediately be obliged to look upon Him as but one item in a series of causes and effects, and to search back behind Him for the antecedent cause by which in turn He Himself had been caused. But this, if true, means that the basis of the traditional proofs of God's existence has been destroyed at a blow. These proofs are unable to make a start till the argument from causality has been accepted. Not only so ; if, as all are agreed, God cannot be presented to the mind sensibly, there can be no such thing as *know-ledge* of Him, in the Kantian sense of the word. It is of course another question whether the Kantian limitation of knowledge as such to the sense-world can be admitted as anything more than an arbitrary feat of definition. Are, for example, the conclusions of the *Critique* itself to be designated as knowledge ?

It cannot reasonably be doubted that in all this Kant felt himself to be serving a laudably apologetic purpose. In his own famous words, he had removed knowledge to make room for belief. As he passes on to the field of moral experience and its meaning for religious faith, his tone, as it has been put, is that " of one who has dislodged a pretender, and is now engaged in making good the claims of the sovereign ", not at all that of " a defeated general trying another method of assault ". Yet it may well be that this view alternated in his mind with the other, that whatever had been lost in the arena of theory was now to be more than retrieved by way of ethics. At all events, in the second *Critique*, his position briefly put is this, that we are entitled to argue with complete moral confidence from the categorical imperative of duty to the reality of freedom, immortality, and God. He vindicates belief in the existence of God as a " postulate of the moral reason ", i.e. as a venture of faith not merely demanded by, but as it were enacted in, our moral life. The supersensible world is not merely an upper storey in the edifice of reality such that of it, as of the first storey in time and space, we can have a special *a priori* knowledge; it is a world " of whose reality we are convinced by actually entering into it ", and we gain entrance not by argument but by moral action. This, Kant is well assured, is an objective contact with the real which science can neither give nor take away. He to whom the moral law is supreme cannot but hold fast to personal immortality and the existence of a Moral Ruler of the universe.[1]

None the less, over and over again we are warned that the moral certainty we thus obtain is itself far from being certainty of the kind demanded by theoretic reason. It is enough for conviction, but much less than will furnish necessitating proof. Not much in an argumentative point of view is added to this by the suggestion, contained in the third *Critique*, that a kinship exists between the moral

[1] By his attack on the scholastic proofs of God's existence, taken along with his assertion that God is a postulate of the moral consciousness, Kant at least repudiated the view that the idea of God can be arrived at by any purely theoretical path.

spirit in ourselves and the spirit which reveals itself through the beauty and purposiveness of Nature.

On the whole we are led to think that Kant, whether as man or as philosopher, felt comparatively little interest in religion for its own sake, and the gap thus left is scarcely filled by a work published in his extreme old age, under the title *Religion within the Bounds of mere Reason*. In his mind religion plainly was overshadowed by morality. He so feared the intrusion of external constraint into ethics, he held so convincedly that, to avoid what he called heteronomy in morals, we are safe only when we view reason as giving itself its own law, not receiving it from elsewhere, even from above, that the notion of dependence upon God became of such secondary importance for him as to be virtually negligible. Without injustice we may place alongside of Kant's view this extract from the old Chinese religious classic entitled *The Conduct of Life*, with its pure vein of sober common sense : " The ordinance of God is what we call the law of our being ; to fulfil the law of our being is what we call the moral law ; the moral law when reduced to a system is what we call religion." To be religious is to view our duties as divine commands. The fact that the command is divine ought to make no difference to conduct ; if an act is not in any case our duty, it is not made our duty by God's willing it. True as this may be in a provisional though not ultimate sense, the underlying concept of religion obviously has no place for such things as personal fellowship with God, the communion of prayer, or even—such is Kant's moral individualism— the corporate nature of Christian life. God is introduced with deep reverence, yet not for His own sake, but rather as a necessary presupposition of the moral system. He enters to effect a reconciliation between duty and happiness, becoming, in Herder's felicitous phrase, " a nail to hold together a morality that was falling to pieces ".

Kant, whose life no one can read without being stirred

to deep personal regard, has not seldom although quite
inaccurately been styled " the philosopher of Protestantism ".   In point of fact he is much more like Erasmus than
Luther, and a too close reliance on the Kantian ethic has
done as much as anything to hide from many a nineteenth-
century theologian the real meaning and glory of the
Gospel.   For the man after Kant's own heart, be it remembered, is one whose confidence in his powers of moral
self-discipline and triumph more than half renders him
deaf to the call to penitence and the message of pardoning
mercy.   The frequency with which the significant word
" merit " occurs on some of the most crucial pages of his
latest work on religion is enough to show where in the last
resort he takes his stand.   He was blind to the inexorable
fact that, just in proportion as we adopt the right and
good as our supreme maxim, our eyes open—if the holiness
of God has once been perceived—to our hopeless inward
guilt.   Our willing acknowledgment of the right and its
claim upon us really does not convince us that by this
very fact we are one with God ; on the contrary, it con-
victs us of a deep inward antagonism to God, and of our
complete inability, as of ourselves, to keep His law.   This
is why Kant has nothing to say that matters concerning
the Mediatorship of Christ.   In the ultimate sense one
who is prepared to take charge of his own moral life needs
no mediator.

The significance of Kant for the modern period of
theology largely consists in the two-fold fact that in him
the *Aufklärung* utters its last word, while yet his philosophy
essentially faced towards the future and laid down certain
important guiding lines for the very different era that
followed.   It was an immense gain for theological method
that he should have distinguished so firmly between pure
and practical reason, and (not without satisfaction) have
reached the finding that we cannot demonstrate the being
of God, in any sense which has an interest for faith, by

theoretic argumentation. His doctrine of the autonomy
of the moral consciousness still needed to be deepened into
harmony with Luther's new and profounder evangelical
reading of what duty means ; yet it was and remains a
moving expression of a piety that derives its characteristic
tone from manly reverence. His view of the categorical
imperative of duty has the moral grandeur of the Old
Testament. He makes a clean sweep of the comfortable
moral optimism of the Enlightenment by his infinitely
grave doctrine of the radical evil in man.[1] " We call it,"
he writes, " a natural propensity to evil, and since man
must nevertheless always bear the blame of it, it may
actually be styled a radical badness in human nature,
innate, but none the less drawn upon us by ourselves."
In fact he teaches that moral corruption has its seat in
human reason itself. In view of this it has become more
difficult than ever for theology to develop a shallow
doctrine of sin ; modern tendencies to Pelagianism have
felt themselves steadily confronted by this dark, uncompromising and consciously paradoxical view that sin is
rooted in man's inmost and native disposition, while yet
we cannot but view ourselves as responsible for it. Kant
inclines, as we have seen, to regard religion as the handmaid of morality. Still, as has been remarked, " he brings
out all the more for that reason the importance of the office
of the moral consciousness in the criticism of the religious
tradition, in discharging which it becomes the principal
agent in the progressive development of religion ". And
in a real sense this holds true, even if we add, as we must,
that the " moral consciousness " in question has owed its
reforming insight and power to the ever-freshened apprehension in religious faith of God as revealed in Christ.

---

[1] See especially Brunner, *The Mediator*, Chap. VI. Brunner,
however, points out that in spite of Kant's profound insight into
the doctrine of the radical evil in man, he implicitly abandons it
in the end, to save our moral autonomy.

It has already been shown that Kant's theory of knowledge is a well-marked form of what is known as subjective idealism, in spite of the realistic elements for which from time to time he strove to find a place. Objects are ultimately the work of our own minds, and of things in themselves we not only are, but must be wholly, ignorant. The next step was taken promptly by Fichte. This outlying fringe of unknowable things in themselves, he argued, is superfluous, and ought forthwith to be cut away. If existence is to be explicable at all, it must all be explained by a single principle; and this can be no other than the self-centred, self-created life of the Ego; for the Ego, within whose circle all things have their being, is the one primary and indubitable fact. In essence all things are forms of the Ego's productive activity. Thus the universal proposition is laid down that the non-self as such owes its being to the Self; and Fichte rests finally in an idealism pure and simple, of a kind which may justly be described as depriving both God and man of real existence. When we say " objects ", we are in reality speaking of the acts of pure thought, of things as posited or created by the Self, whose depths for ultimate reflection are identical with the very Absolute. Thus the point of view for which Fichte stands in the philosophical advance of his time is one which empties all things into the Ego; it is this cardinal doctrine or hypothesis which his successors took as their legacy from his brave and subtle mind, and which they strove logically to deepen and elaborate.

It might seem as if the only issue of such a contention must be Illusionism, for supposedly it is we who make things by thinking them. Fichte, however, who so far had only expounded what he took to be the consistent outcome of Kantian epistemology, gave back substantiality to things by an impressive moral argument for which also, at least in part, he claimed to have Kant's own authority.

The world of things regains its objectivity by way of the absolute law : " Thou shalt." In other words, the world is real as providing the authentic sphere of duty ; and duty, in turn, is the concrete essence of the Self. Nay more : duty is that which identifies us with God. It is in virtue of the necessary self-affirmation of the moral Self that we arrive finally at the affirmation of Deity. It is indeed scarcely too much to say that for Fichte Duty *is* God. St. Paul's words in the eighth chapter of Romans, he tells us, might well be read : " All things work together for good to them that love Duty." The idea of justification found in the New Testament is dismissed as a melancholy and poor-spirited lapse from the heights of speculative self-sufficiency ; we need no Saviour from without, for what saves is not the historical, but the metaphysical alone. To demand faith in Jesus is contrary to the Christian religion. We are summoned, declares Fichte, not to owe our life to another, but with the creative force of will to call the world into being as our *deed*. Thus carrying ethical activism to its limit, Fichte would challenge us to stand erect in God's presence, secure in the moral rectitude that goes hand in hand with manly conviction. It is the highest task of religion to make itself superfluous. " In ordinary life, and in a well-ordered society, religion is not practical but merely an affair of knowledge ; all that it does is to make man perfectly clear and intelligible to himself, and to answer the loftiest questions he can raise." Wordsworth in a memorable phrase declared that poetry is " the impassioned expression which is in the countenance of all Science ". In like manner it may be said that for Fichte religion is the impassioned expression found in the countenance of all morality. Through duty alone can we understand nature ; and nature we know to have real existence, imparted not by a transcendent Creator, but by the moral consciousness as such, because it forms a necessary pre-condition of ethical life.

After Fichte came Schelling, to prolong the line of Spinoza and Goethe. He broke with a certain exuberance through the narrow bounds of the Fichtean idealism, resolved as he was to plant the Ego once more in the midst of a concrete and fruitful world of things. But the tendency of Schelling's thought, whether in his earlier and more positive phase or in his later, is not so much that of sacrificing things outright to the Ego, as Fichte had done, as of submerging both Ego and things in an Absolute which is neither Ego nor things, neither spirit nor nature, but somehow indifferently or identically both at once. Nature, we are told, is visible Spirit, as Spirit is invisible Nature. One and the same Life is struggling up from the depths of the inorganic through the plant and animal kingdoms, till it flowers out into the consciousness of man. In some degree, this philosophy of Identity may be taken as a reversion to the naturalism of Spinoza, on a much lower level, it must be confessed, of speculative power, for Schelling's work too often was intolerably obscure in detail as well as capricious and rhapsodical in language. It is in this light that Hegel views it in some of his sharpest sentences of disapproval; as when he protests that an Absolute, such as hovered before Schelling's cloudy mind, is, in its indistinguishable vagueness, no better than " the night in which all cows are black ". The profound dictum, again, that " everything in philosophy depends on the insight that the Absolute is to be apprehended not as Substance but as Subject ", is chiefly meant for Schelling's profit.

Hutchison Stirling has said, apropos of Schelling's frequent changes of philosophical manner, that " a human being leaping in such a variety of directions, according to the latest goad, is not an edifying spectacle ". It is scarcely to be thought that such a mind could make a serious contribution to the understanding of the Christian Gospel. Suffice it to say that Schelling strove to combine

pantheism and theism in the higher notion of God as at
once free and in subjection to development. There is
only too much reason to think that by this phrase is
meant that in God Himself there exists a dark primordial
ground, a " nature ", a negative principle which has, as
it were, to be worked out of the Divine system, as it
advances from imperfection to perfection, through the
piece-by-piece process of becoming. This idea, that God
traverses an inevitable pathway from the less to the more,
from what is defective to the perfect and complete, seems
to have been a constitutive element in Schelling's thought
from first to last, so far as it took a theological direction.
Per tot casus, per tot discrimina rerum, he fought his way
out to a Gnostic Christianity.

Ideas struck out by Schelling in hours of intuitive
vision were elaborated with vastly greater speculative
power by Hegel. In a later chapter the attempt will be
made to deal more fully with the Hegelian interpretation
of Christianity as a whole, and at present it is needless
to do more than introduce the subject briefly. Hegel's
design, it may be said concisely, was to display as mediated
through difference, both logical and real, that identity of
Spirit and Nature which Schelling had too hastily assumed
as ready-made, or at all events as intelligible apart from
actual process. The secret of reality lies in the *coincidentia
oppositorum*, the living and interactive affinity of contrasts, which it is the business of logical thought to
discover and exhibit in a continuous ascending order.
All existence makes headway first by evoking antagonism,
then capturing this antagonism for a higher unity in
which both lower terms are at once cancelled and absorbed.
In other words, negativity, followed by deeper and more
comprehensive assertion, is the principle by which all
being moves. It may therefore be argued, Hegel suggests,
that even the Absolute is no finished fact, eternally complete ; it also may be viewed as the result, no less than

the ground, of the infinite forward urge. This, as soon as
we come to the particulars of Christian doctrine, is seen
to involve the position that God is constituted, or realizes
Himself, through the phenomena of history and Nature.
" Without the world," Hegel says roundly, " God were
not God."

We shall have to ask whether within this great, or at
least imposing, framework of ideas room can be found
for that personal being of God and man which holds a
central place throughout the whole range of Biblical
thought, and without which the Christian religion can
neither be nor be conceived.

II

THE THEOLOGY OF FEELING (A)

SCHLEIERMACHER'S INTERPRETATION OF RELIGION

§ 1. HIS LIFE AND CHARACTER

" A GREAT MAN," it has been remarked, " condemns the world to the task of explaining him." Of no Christian thinker is the saying more true than of Friedrich Schleiermacher. His time of leadership in Protestant dogmatics may now be over, but his work at the close of the eighteenth century opened a new era not only in theology as a whole but still more definitely in the scientific interpretation of religion. During the last fifty years he has been studied with closer application in Continental circles than anyone except Luther ; and even Brunner, whose recent attack upon his teaching is one of the most formidable, describes him as the only great theologian of the nineteenth century. The breakdown of speculative systems prompted a return to one who ranked as the theologian *par excellence* of Christian experience, and the pressure exerted still later on Ritschlian thought by the progress of Gospel criticism increased his attractiveness. On the other hand, the Barthian school has strongly urged the uncompromising repudiation alike of his method and of his results. Hence, in one way or another, Schleiermacher at the moment is tolerably near the centre of the stage.

The philosophy of Kant, it will be agreed, can be made fairly intelligible to a reader who knows little or nothing of the philosopher's personal career, but the thought of

31

Schleiermacher is luminous only when read in the light of his biography. The salient facts of his life, therefore, ought to be noted briefly.

Schleiermacher was born in Breslau on November 21, 1768, as the son of an army chaplain. Even amidst his classical studies he was troubled at an unusually early age by problems of religion; the fact that he could work out no exact equivalence between the sufferings of Christ and the punishment due to the redeemed, cost him more than one sleepless night. In 1783 he became a pupil in a Moravian school at Niesky, and found a second home among the influences ruling there—piety, education, friendship. What presented itself for imitation was not the grave or bitter soul-conflicts of Pietism, but Zinzendorf's emotional delight in the Saviour's love. Schleiermacher drank deeply of the Moravian spirit. In later years he could say that for him a revised Moravianism ranked as the ideal Christian life. He was a true lover of Jesus, as anyone may see from his Christology.

In 1785, now as it were an adopted child of the Brotherhood, he entered its theological seminary at Barby. But, yielding to the tide of new intellectual life just beginning to flow, he and others of the abler men launched into philosophical discussions which alarmed their teachers, and led to their expulsion. Schleiermacher next made his way to Halle, and plunged into the study of Kant. At this time also he laid the foundation of his wide knowledge of Greek philosophy. His first theological examination was passed in 1790, and he became a preacher of the Reformed or Calvinistic Church. After the fashion of that day, he now took a post as domestic tutor, and in the family of Count Dohna, in West Prussia, found a circle of sympathetic friends, as well as, what he especially valued, the society of cultivated women. There is the fragment of a treatise on " Freedom " dating from this time—an able defence of determinism. He learned to preach, and in the pulpit set forth a strongly moralistic type of Christianity. In 1793 he moved on to a teaching post in Berlin, and in 1796 became regular preacher at the Charity Hospital in the city, a position he continued to hold for six years. About this date he thought it worth while to issue a translation of Blair's " Sermons ".

Now began a new era of his life. Berlin had been the headquarters of the Enlightenment, whose ideas now tended to wear fairly thin ; and the more sensitive minds were by this time listening eagerly to the tender and exquisite tones of Romanticism.[1] Friedrich Schlegel, a clever but erratic leader of the new school, together with the gifted women who surrounded him, became Schleiermacher's intimate companions. He was hungry for life, and explored the new world with zest. Schlegel urged him to write. In 1798 he began work on the *Reden* or " Addresses on Religion to its Cultured Despisers ", and by the next spring the book was finished. It appeared anonymously, the author only revealing his name when the second edition was issued in 1806, though his identity had been guessed long before. The subject of the *Reden* is curiously different from what might have been expected. Ethics had filled Schleiermacher's mind for years, but the

---

[1] Romanticism, which is more a mood or temper than a creed, was a reaction against the predominance of classical norms in literature and art, as well as a revolt against the arid intellectuality of eighteenth-century rationalism. It may be defined as an impassioned return to natural instincts, to life, to freedom, to individual predilection, to the spontaneity of the creative fancy. It looked upon nature and man with eyes full of wonder, and pointed anew to the mystery of life. In its less prudent representatives it appeared to proclaim that the individual was absolute and that the liberated soul must stand for the defiance of authority, the glorification of mere wish. " Be thyself " was its insistent call. Plainly there is something here that might well go to the head of a youthful genius. Of this movement, with the vague splendours and pursuit of the indeterminate which were its lifeblood, Schleiermacher—with reservations—made himself the champion in the religious field.

book has nothing to do with ethics. It is an impassioned treatment of religion, as if the writer meant thereby to make an act of atonement to the early influences which, for a time, he had seemed to forget.

In the early part of 1800 he gave the *Reden* its ethical counterpart. This was the *Monologen*, or " Soliloquies ". Here, again in prophetic style, he set forth the leading thought of his ethics, viz., that each self must grow into an individual and irreplaceable representation of humanity as such. The style, by its exalted and semi-poetic rhythm, is an index of the highly romantic thought.

His next work was less happy. Schlegel had published a novel of doubtful quality, which was severely censured ; and Schleiermacher rushed quixotically to its defence. The incident merely delayed his break with Schlegel. The two had planned a German translation of Plato, but with characteristic selfishness the older man threw the whole burden on the younger. Friends advised him to leave Berlin, and reluctantly he went into what he felt to be exile at Stolpe, where he spent two years as court-preacher. It was a lonely time, during which access to books was difficult, but he used the leisure to perfect himself in theological equipment. Now appeared the first volume of his translation of Plato—this in its complete form was a great gift to Germany—and about the same time, in a series of pamphlets, he began to press for the closer union of Lutherans and Calvinists in Prussia.

At last, in 1804, he was called to a junior professorship in Halle, and eagerly began to lecture. His range was vast ; he appears eventually to have taught, some time or other, every subject in the curriculum but Old Testament, his weakest side. To this Halle period (he became a full professor in 1806) belong the second edition of the *Addresses* or *Speeches*, two volumes of the Plato translation, a brief, more or less romantic, book in dialogue form on the meaning of Christmas, and a critical treatise on

1 Timothy (this, by the way, was the first of his works to be rendered in English). Alongside of all this went his activities as a great preacher and pastor. It is interesting to find that he prepared Bismarck for confirmation.

In the winter of 1807 he once more settled in Berlin, and gave public lectures on Greek philosophy. When the new University opened in 1810, Schleiermacher became one of the first members of the staff. Shortly before that date he had begun to preach regularly from the pulpit of Holy Trinity Church, exercising there for many years the most powerful influence of its kind in the country. He was a patriot of flaming zeal, and during the French occupation was summoned before General Davoust and cautioned for his fiery sermons. In 1814, he was elected Secretary of the philological and historical section of the Academy of Berlin, a post which he held till his death in 1834.

It was Schleiermacher's peculiar gift to unite in an exceptional degree the most passionate religion with the unbending rigour of a scientific thinker. The humane, for him, is one at bottom with the Christian, and the fear perpetually haunted him lest the line of communications between religion and intellectual life should be cut, and piety little by little become synonymous with barbarism. For his own part, he placed religion at the centre of the full human life. A similar universality gave lustre to his character. He liked to think of himself as " an expert in friendship ". He was filled with an insatiable thirst for the communion of mind with mind. " When occupied with inward thought," he writes, " or with observation, or with the enjoyment of what is novel, I need the presence of some loved one, so that on the inner experience there may immediately follow the sharing of it with another." And again : " In solitude, the very springs of my soul dry up, and the course of my thoughts is checked."

Through his nature, undeniably, there ran a strong
vein of sentimentality; but by the time he reached manhood he had mastered himself, and held all his powers
with a firm grasp. His body—short, rather meagre, and
very slightly mis-shapen—was the obedient servant of his
will. As a moralist, we have seen, he rejected the idea
of free self-determination; yet in personal conduct he
displayed it, bravely ignoring ill-health and suppressing
pain. For many years, in addition to writing and preaching, he taught three hours daily in the lecture-room. So
much were his mind and knowledge at command, that a
few moments of quiet sufficed for the preparation of an
address. His well-known liberalism, both in theology and
in politics, gained for him the dark and persistent suspicion of the Governmental authorities, and at one point
he came within an ace of losing his University chair.

§ 2. HIS PHILOSOPHICAL TENDENCIES

The theological work of Schleiermacher revolved round
two cardinal questions : What is Religion ? and What is
Christianity ? The first is the subject of his famous
Addresses, which appeared in 1799; the second, of his
great Dogmatic work, *The Christian Faith, systematically
set forth according to the principles of the Evangelical Church*,
issued in 1821, and in a carefully revised though not perhaps essentially altered form in 1831. Before embarking
on the study of these classical works, it may be convenient
to refer briefly to the hard-won philosophical conclusions
which form the background of his theology proper.

We may here gather all that is needed for our purpose
from two of his volumes—the *Monologues*, already referred
to, and the *Dialectic*, issued posthumously. The *Monologues* expound, in prose of a lyrical order, Schleiermacher's
leading ethical idea that man's highest task is to shape
the self into an individual and, so to say, artistically

satisfying representation of humanity.[1]   The writer revolts
from the Kantian notion of the categorical imperative,
as lacking in justice to the nobility of man.   In morality
we are called not primarily to receive, but to produce,
and this out of our own resources.   Morality, it is argued,
must work itself out not in analogy to public State law
but in analogy to the laws of Nature ; it should not be
juridical in quality but organic.   Thus in the event he
offers what is no more than an anthropological account
of the moral life.   His standards are biological or æsthetic,
not ethical in the proper sense.   The free man is not
under command to submit himself to the moral law ;
his task is to live out his life untrammelled and uncon-
trolled by any authority higher than his own soul—growing, blossoming, ripening as the plants do.   Once he has
understood the task set him of expressing his nature with
spontaneous fulness, nothing must be allowed to impede
his course—not the world, or fate, or God.   We are here
to get out our unique and individual natures into full-
toned and many-sided actuality.   So conceived, the free
man is lord of all things.   But Schleiermacher forgets to
add, as Luther had done, that the free Christian man,
while lord of all, is also the servant of all for Christ's sake.

On these assumptions, freedom can be no more than a
natural phenomenon, explicable in terms of natural causation.   Schleiermacher starts not from the " goodwill ",
but from the actual human will as a psychological force.
So he naturalizes the spirit of man by thrusting aside
the commanding and implicitly transcendent conception of
the " ought ".   As Sigwart puts it :

[1] " Each man is meant to represent humanity in his own way,
combining its elements uniquely. . . .   This thought alone has
uplifted me, and set me apart from everything common and
untransformed in my surroundings ; it has made of me an elect
creation of the Godhead, rejoicing in a unique form and character "
(Eng. trans. of *Schleiermacher's Soliloquies*, by H. N. Friess, p.
317).

Instead of finding in volition, as Kant had done, the self-determination of will by laws and maxims, he reduces volition to the same merely causal relationship between the intellectual and the organic, between thought and being—the same relationship as had previously made its appearance in cognition, only turned the other way round.[1]

" In thine own person body forth humanity uniquely "—this is the message of these " Soliloquies ". We are called to develop our own individuality, not in isolation, but in society as the appointed form of human life. The book has nothing to say concerning moral failure, still less concerning sin. Schleiermacher's reply to the implied censure no doubt would have been that it contained not so much his achievements as his aspirations, and that aspiration inevitably takes on the form of the ideal. He felt that he was bound to be misunderstood, and that much in what he had written would be put down to pride.

In the *Dialectic* is unfolded Schleiermacher's theory of the art of thinking, and for him, as for Plato, the elaboration of such a theory eventually crosses over the line into epistemology and metaphysics. Now thinking is meant to issue in knowledge. But knowledge demands or involves two kinds of correspondence—first, that between thought and the real, secondly, that between the thoughts of different thinkers.

The first of these is only to be explained if we postulate an original or primary interrelation between thought and being. Our thinking has in it the quality of certitude, which means that there must somehow be a fundamental or underlying unity in which are rooted equally the two opposed worlds of ideal and real being, and which thus supplies the condition of the agreement between the two which is called " knowledge ". It is solely in virtue of this common ground that cognition in any sense becomes

[1] Quoted by Brunner, *Die Mystik und das Wort*, p. 343.

possible. To assert the validity of knowledge is in the
last resort a venture, a faith or conviction the truth of
which never can be proved. All we can say is that to
deny it is to deny reason itself. This ultimate or basal
and universal ground we designate by two correlative
names : in one view it is God, in the other the World.

The argument just sketched is obviously one characteristically modern form of the ontological proof of God's
existence. It raises the question whether we are not
obliged to regard as valid a conception which is organically
bound up with the very possibility of knowledge. It
points to the ideal laws of thought on the one hand, and
on the other to the real laws of being, and asks whether
from their actual harmony the mind is not finally carried
back to the reality of Absolute Spirit, manifesting itself
alike in subjective thinking and in objective existence.
Alongside of this Schleiermacher places a similar argument
bearing upon will. If our volition is not to be futile, we
must believe that being is approachable by, and susceptible of, our intentional and formative action. It
would be vain to will, if we could make no impression on
reality. Whence comes the certainty that our act can
tell on the real ? It rests, we are again told, on this
faith in a basal identity or converging ground of thought
and being. Thus from another side we are led to affirm
the Absolute, or, as the religious man prefers to say, God.
Of these two lines of approach, Schleiermacher believes,
the second is better suited to the generality of men, who
have little or no speculative interest. He adds what is a
recurrent thought in his pages—that since the idea of
God is to be postulated for the satisfaction alike of knowledge and of will, its proper home within our consciousness must be in that which precedes and underlies will
and knowledge equally, viz., feeling.

As we saw, it is Schleiermacher's contention that the
fundamental Unity may be designated either God or

World. These two ideas are given only in and with each other. Think the world without God, and it has no bond of union ; think God without the world, and the object of our thought is devoid of content. Yet the one is in no sense identical with the other. The world is the supreme Unity including all antitheses ; God is the supreme Unity excluding all antitheses. Or again, the relation of the two ideas to cognition is wholly different ; for the thought of God is the *terminus a quo*, as the condition which renders knowledge possible, whereas the thought of the world is the *terminus ad quem*, as the goal to which knowledge is ever seeking to approximate. Both ideas are transcendental in the sense that they are presuppositions of all valid knowledge, yet never themselves directly cognizable. They lie beyond the frontier of knowledge strictly understood, but for opposite reasons. God we cannot ever *know*, since this is a conception for which we have no sense data ; nor can we know the world, since here we have an infinite manifold of sense data to which no adequate interpretative conception or category can be applied, for none exists. Already it is plain how grave are the difficulties certain to face Schleiermacher in working out a harmony between these speculative ideas and some cardinal certainties of Biblical faith, such as the Personality of God and His sovereign Creatorship.

We shall find, I think, that there exists a general harmony between the conclusions of the *Dialectic* as just summarized and some positions taken in Schleiermacher's great dogmatic work, *The Christian Faith*. In both books equally it is taught that God is originally presented in feeling ; that we possess no strictly objective cognition of Him (or It, for the use of the personal pronoun in this context is, we are given to understand, hardly admissible) ; perhaps too that objective thought as such, if fully elucidated, leads back necessarily to the underlying reality of God ; and that God is never apprehended as it were nakedly, but always in conjunction with, or mediated by, some finite element of the world.

Schleiermacher was a thinker of real but not first-rate philosophical power. After reading the *Addresses*, Schelling wrote of their author, " I honour him as a mind that we can place nowhere but on a level with the leading original philosophers ". But Schleiermacher took a more modest view of his own claims to speculative eminence. " I shall never be anything but a dilettante in philosophy," are his words. After all, his contemporaries in that field were amongst the greatest thinkers of all time, and might well outshine a merely gifted worker.

There has, however, been long and animated discussion about a question much more important than Schleiermacher's absolute size in metaphysics, viz., whether his philosophy is or is not the true key wherewith to unlock the problems of his theology. Did the speculative thinker in him dictate to the Christian ? Wehrung argues that, especially in the *Dialectic*, we can see the steadily growing predominance of speculative over critical or inductive thinking, as also the tendency of a Philosophy of Identity— in some degree learnt from Schelling—to deflect conclusions that ought to have followed from the argument of the *Addresses on Religion*. Bender wrote at great length to prove that to elicit the real meaning of *The Christian Faith* we must recur to his speculative positions ; and Brunner, in his very able general attack, finds that Schleiermacher's theology was virtually prescribed for him by his semi-pantheistic philosophy.

No doubt his own declarations might make us sceptical in this regard. We have a well-known letter to Jacobi in which he claims to have an equally balanced interest in both disciplines. They are, he says, like the two *foci* of his intellectual ellipse. The two, his philosophy and his Dogmatic, influence and approximate to each other ; but he is unaware of any dependence on either side. In one " Open Letter to Lücke ", he makes a vigorous protest against the notion that his *Christian Faith* was in any sense meant as a philosophical Dogmatic. " I have said repeatedly that Christian doctrine must be set forth in complete independence of each and every philosophical system. . . . I could never allow that my faith in Christ came from philosophy." These deliberate statements show little trace of anxiety to get somehow round an awkward corner ; they leave us in no doubt as to his intention, though they cannot of course be taken as settling the question whether this intention was successfully carried out. To take one instance, it has been plausibly argued that the basis of his certainty of God in the *Dialectic* is found in an *a priori* and universally valid presupposition of every possible consciousness, whereas in *The Christian Faith* the certainty of God rests upon a specific experience, characterized as the feeling of absolute dependence, which is really an extract from the whole Christian experience of redemption. In other words, faith in God is now no necessity of thought as such, but can only be present in one who has been impressed in a definite way by Jesus Christ. However this may be, we ought not to conclude too hastily that to reach his Christian beliefs Schleiermacher felt he had only to develop his theory of knowledge, or at all events must keep sedulously within its limits. Yet we are dealing with a thinker who (it has been said) took both sides on every question ; and in examining details, the reader is only too often compelled to say that the philosopher's speculative preoccupations have had a fatal influence on the theologian's reading of doctrine. A man has only one mind, and one half of it will inevitably colour, or help to colour, the other half. A glaring example is the obstinate attempt Schleiermacher makes, as we shall see, to argue that the will of God and the nexus of natural causation are only two names for the same thing. Because

God is immutable, there can arise in Him no new purpose. As Wendland puts it, interpreting him correctly : " Everything in the world must be traceable to immanent factors, which ultimately, no doubt, do carry us back to the Divine fount of being ; but a new influx of Divine life from a transcendent sphere he nowhere recognizes." What relation, except that of antagonism, does this thought of an immutable cosmic process have to the Biblical view of the world as wholly, and at every moment, in the hand of a God who is free and almighty ? At this point, as at some others, Schleiermacher has lost sight of the Absolute Power that, for prophets and apostles, resides in Absolute Love and Holiness ; and what has hidden it from him is his impersonal philosophy.

§ 3. His Conception of Religion in the *Addresses*

In the famous " Addresses on Religion to its Cultured Despisers " Schleiermacher expounded in classical form what may be called the Romantic or emotional view of religion as such, and its place in human life. Throughout, the writer has before him that enlightened and scornful temper which scarcely regards Christianity as worth the trouble of disproof. In the recent past, it must be remembered, religion had come to be identified with a group of rational and moral doctrines about God and the world, touched with a spirit of petty teleology, while in the austere view of Kant it had virtually been made equivalent to a single aspect of morality. The thinkers had forgotten the human heart and its thirst for the Unseen. Schleiermacher felt that men must be led back to the elementary but life-giving perception that religion is an experience, not given for cold analysis but to be lived in and enjoyed. " You reject," we can hear him say, " the dogmas and propositions of religion. Very well, reject them. They are not in any case the essence of religion itself. Religion

does not need them ; it is only human reflection on the
content of our religious feelings or affections which requires
anything of the kind, or calls it into being. Do you say
that you cannot away with miracles, revelation, inspiration ? You are right ; we are children no longer ; the
time for fairy-tales is past. Only cast off as I do faith in
everything of that sort, and I will show you miracles and
revelations and inspirations of quite another species. To me
everything that has an immediate relation to the Infinite,
the Universe is a miracle ; and everything finite has such
a relation, in so far as I find in it a token or indication
of the Infinite. What is revelation ? Every new and
original communication of the Universe to man ; and
every elemental feeling to me is inspiration. The religion
to which I will lead you demands no blind faith, no
negation of physics and psychology ; it is wholly natural,
and yet again, as the immediate product of the Universe,
it is all of grace.''

From words like these we can infer Schleiermacher's
conception both of his audience and of the message he
sought to bring them. He is setting forth a novel view
of what religion is. Its nature, he declares with passion,
has been misapprehended. It is not science ; it is not
morality ; its seat is not in reason, or conscience, or will.
Since religion is the direct touch of the soul with the
Divine, its home can be nowhere but in *feeling*. As he
puts it, `` Pious contemplation is the immediate consciousness of the universal existence of all finite things
in and through the Infinite, and of all temporal things in
and through the Eternal.'' We must explore the deeper
nature of man if we are to find the point where God
touches man, and man awakes to God. Thus, when
Schleiermacher asks what religion is, his question is not
primarily historical but psychological. He is not out to
ascertain what in the way of convictions, hopes, norms or
usages has remained constant throughout the varied forms

of human worship in the past, but rather to discover the
special psychical function in man which is concerned
wherever and whenever man comes to be in the religious
attitude. This specifically religious function he detects
not in knowledge or will, but in that which forms a third
partner along with knowledge and action—feeling, or
immediate self-consciousness.

In saying this, of course, he is conforming to the " faculty
psychology " of his time ; the view, in other words, that
each essential and primary activity of mind presupposes
a " faculty " out of which the activity springs. He
decides that the particular faculty behind religion is feeling.
And in his defence of religion against the scorners, it is
noticeable how he does not seek to convert them by
bringing forward a convincing demonstration that certain
religious doctrines are *true*, but rather by showing that
religion rises out of a definite faculty of the human spirit,
and thus must be a real element in sound and whole
manhood. Let him only make out this point, and he
regards the argument as complete. He can count on his
readers to acknowledge, as he does, the principle that
whatever is truly human must be received and affirmed.
This psychological inquiry, we shall see, has appended to
it a historical survey.

If we examine his words carefully, we find that Schleiermacher—like Goethe, whose idea of piety much resembles
his, and who in his own person represented the great
background of Romanticism—can put what religion means
for him in all sorts of ways. An anthology of passages
would display a striking variety of phrase. Thus, religion
consists in man's becoming conscious of his own limitations, of the fortuitous nature of his life as his being runs
its course and silently disappears in the Infinite. It is
his giving up all audacious pride, and regarding all
individual things, himself included, as being necessarily
what they are. It is to live in the endless nature of the

Whole, to perceive and divine with quiet reverence the place assigned therein to each and all. It is to have sense and taste for the Infinite, to lie on the bosom of the Universe and feel its boundless life and creative power pulsing within our own. It is to drink in the beauty of the world and be drenched through and through with its spirit. It is devoutly to overhear the All in its expressions and acts, to let oneself be swept away by its influence as we contemplate the wonders of its workings, to discover and love the Spirit pervading the cosmic whole.

In formulating so sharply the element of directness or immediacy in pious feeling, Schleiermacher obviously desires to secure the full independence of piety, as the soul's inner holy of holies, over against knowledge and morality. Quantity of knowledge, as he says, is not quantity of religion. Doubtless religion may take the form of contemplation, and has an open sense for the life of the world. But such contemplation does not view the individual object in the light in which science views it, i.e. as it stands related to other things, but in its character as a revelation of the infinite Unseen. What is specifically religious needs no certificate from knowledge ; it carries with it the evidence of its own truth and shines by its own glow. Ever since, Schleiermacher's critics have naturally been occupied in discussing the question whether he has not made religion " immediate " and " inward " in a sense so narrow and exclusive as to reduce it to a mere emotion. After all, religion, or at least religion with any claim to be called Christian, is concerned with God, not with our own " nice feelings ". In the first edition of the *Addresses* Schleiermacher might be thought beyond the reach of any such criticism, on the ground that in the well-known description he there gives of the process through which the soul passes in having a complete religious experience, he stresses the element of " intuition " equally with that of " feeling ". By " intuition " he clearly means a direct perception of the object confronting the mind, just as by " feeling ", in the same passage, is meant a change in the inner state of the subject. Of this feeling the Universe or the Divine is the cause, but what is felt is the affection or modification of the soul. Yet when this description is cited in proof that Schleiermacher's instinct for objectivity never failed him, one point must be noted. In the first edition of the *Addresses*, intuition had predominated over feeling, but subsequently, in order to stress even more emphatically the radical distinction between religion and knowledge as operating in philosophy or science, Schleiermacher placed the whole weight upon feeling, as the less intellectual of the two, and the better fitted to express the directness or immediacy of the pious relationship. It was a change which, from every point of view, proved singularly unfortunate. It immensely added to the risk that, with whatever injustice, he might be interpreted as deliberately cutting off all relations between the religious mind and its transsubjective Correlate. With the disappearance of intuition, as Kirn remarks, " the one window is shut, through which the subject comes in touch with the objective world ".

We encounter here what is perhaps the most baffling of all problems in the interpretation of Schleiermacher. And it is a problem which becomes not less but more difficult as we pursue it out of his earlier into his later and more mature treatment of Christianity in his Dogmatic, where religion is defined as " the *feeling* of absolute dependence ". What does he mean by feeling ? Are we to regard him as bound literally by his actual language, or ought we to go behind words to that which there seems— at least often—fairly good reason for believing to be his intention ? The truth is, passages can be cited freely for either view. If we go by words, in what is perhaps a minority of cases he is undoubtedly guilty of the psychological subjectivism of which so many critics have accused him, none more vigorously than the Barthian school. From this point of view, neglect of an objective revelation is natural, for in religion our eye is bent inward on ourselves, on the contents of what Schleiermacher calls our "immediate self-consciousness". In the main the soul is absorbed in its own states. If we take the other line, we are justified in holding that for him "feeling" is a mode of objective apprehension, a species of emotional perception or awareness of spiritual things, and God is viewed as confronting the soul in His real and infinite causality. There can be little doubt, I think, that Schleiermacher *intended* "feeling" to be read in this second sense, and we must read it so wherever we can. But his argument often proceeds on the first sense. What is more, it is impossible not to feel that the ambiguity served him well, and that at various points his argument would have broken down irretrievably had the ambiguity been cleared up. A kindred ambiguity, and one equally rich in fallacies, has often in later theologies come to attach to the term "experience", which has the air of setting the religious experient free from all dependence on Divine revelation.

We have seen that by definition Schleiermacher distinguishes religion as sharply from morality as from knowledge. Not that he means to cut it off utterly from contact with practice. Piety is in no sense a direct cause of moral activity and must not be degraded into the mere handmaid of moral purpose ; we ought to do everything with religion but nothing from religion, as he puts it ; yet in actual life it has morality as its unfailing accompaniment. Not only must every religious man be moral, but no one can be moral in the right way without being religious.

Thus in Schleiermacher's hands religion, strictly considered, is isolated from all other human activities. The pious mind as such knows nothing and does nothing. Piety, indeed, may be described as an inward music. No account is taken of the constitutive function of *belief* in religion as we actually know it. " Ideas and principles are all foreign to religion " are his own uncompromising words. He does indeed grant that ideas are connected with religion, and are indispensable when we wish to communicate religion to other minds. But such a connexion is secondary and irrelevant to the intrinsic nature of piety itself. In short, he exemplifies a well-known logical fallacy by arguing that since religion is not *mere* knowledge, we are entitled to deny that it is a whole in which knowledge is a constitutive element. In the event, he saves his theory from purely mystical vagueness by calling in aid the imagination, and conceding that while we are forbidden to make any dogmatic statements concerning the Eternal, yet our nature compels us to represent the Eternal to ourselves by way of images. Thus, by an unconsciously furtive attempt to reintroduce the cognitive element in feeling or faith, he seeks to escape from the view implicit in his presuppositions, construed as he often construes them, that the religious mind is unable to transcend its own states. His error lay in the assumption that because religion is not metaphysics or science, it cannot be, or include, knowledge of any kind. On terms such as his, it is impossible to understand why believers have always exhibited a profound interest in the *truth* of what they believe.

Yet we must not do him injustice. There are plenty of passages in the *Addresses on Religion* where we are given to understand that by piety Schleiermacher does not mean any ecstatic rapture, moving solely within itself, but rather the emotional consciousness of the Infinite awakened through the finite. It is a warm and intimate awareness of an eternal significance in all being and becoming. " Your feeling is piety," he writes, " in so far as it expresses, in the manner described, the being and life common to you and the All. Your feeling is piety

in so far as it is the result of the operation of God in you
by means of the operation of the world upon you." There
is no sensation, he declares, that is not pious ; but later
he is careful to explain (for he disliked owning up to a
change of mind) that by this he meant simply that no
natural or moral feeling, such as wedded love, can be
incompatible with piety. But it is one of the bad effects
of his all but exclusive emphasis on the emotional nature
of man that he is unable to draw any definite distinction
between impressions of a religious and of an æsthetic
kind. After all explanations have been given, a baffling
and incurable ambiguity remains.

§ 4. THE IDEA OF GOD IN THE *ADDRESSES*

We have seen that Schleiermacher's descriptions of
what religion is form a varied series ; this may also be
said of his names for the Object with which pious feeling
is concerned. Here are some of them : the World, the
Universe, the One and Whole, the eternal World, the
Heavenly, the eternal and holy Destiny, the lofty World-
Spirit, the divine Life and Action of the All. At this
point too a marked difference obtains between the first
edition of 1799 and the second edition of 1806. In the
first, the terms usually employed to denote the object of
religion are such as " the Universe " and " the World-
All ". His thought in this phase is strongly marked by
a Spinozistic flavour. " The Universe " is the writer's
favourite designation of that by which the pious sentiment
is touched and awakened—the Universe regarded as
forming, by its endless multiplicity of finite manifestations,
a beautiful and harmonious work of art. We must not
forget that the first edition of the *Addresses* is by far the
most characteristic of the four ; and there his inclination
clearly is to put Pantheism alongside of Theism as a form
of impressionistic piety which has at least as much to

say for itself as the other.   It is even laid down that the idea of God is irrelevant for religion : true faith can dispense with it altogether.   Such early phrases were later explained away.

In the second edition these semi-pantheistic forms of designation, really equivalent in sense to the *natura naturans* of Spinoza, largely made way for others better adjusted to the Christian outlook.   But they do not wholly disappear, and the temper to which they give expression remains.   Thus, describing what is " the source of every religious emotion ", Schleiermacher can still write :

You lie directly on the bosom of the infinite world.   In that moment you are its soul.   Through one part of your nature you feel, as your own, all its powers and its endless life.   In that moment it is your body, you pervade, as your own, its muscles and members, and your thinking and forecasting set its inmost nerves in motion.

All we can say, in delay of judgment, is that Schleiermacher persists in assigning to the finite individual a richer and more substantive life than is compatible with a thorough-going Spinozism.   For him the finite person counts as a unique and irreplaceable embodiment of the Whole.   And by degrees, as the distinction between God and the world stood out more clearly, these earlier appellations were replaced by such terms as " the Divine ", " God " and " the Godhead ".   But neither then nor later did Schleiermacher renounce the right he claimed so firmly to urge that with a personal God outside the world, religion as such has nothing to do.   The struggle between Pantheism and inherited Christian belief lasted all through his life.   At the former point of view, religion appeared to him to be interested not so much in the objective reality of God as in His subjective presence.   Pious feeling, he constantly seems on the verge of affirming, may virtually be said to *be* God.   He was moved by " the speculative impulse to annihilate anthropomorphism in the conception of the Highest Being " ; and when charged on this account with abandoning Theism, his defence consisted in the rejoinder, more dialectical than Christian, that just as belief in the existence of a personal God does not necessarily connote real piety, so belief in an impersonal God does not necessarily exclude it. God he felt to be so close that it was hard, at times impossible, to contemplate Him objectively.

As might have been anticipated, the *Addresses* were widely supposed to be a statement of mystic or romantic Pantheism. If each religious mood or affection springs out of a moment wherein self and Universe are fused together, religious feeling must be conscious and welcomed absorption in the Whole. The criticism might seem unanswerable ; yet it is always possible to argue that the artist wrought in Schleiermacher no less than the mystic, and what the artist seeks is not the universal merely, but the universal as it takes shape in an individual and concrete form—not abstract beauty, but *this* beautiful thing. Thus he pleads that religion does not cancel the Self ; it stands for a certain felt relationship between the one and the All. If a man awaken to the fact that within his single life the Whole is living, that in his personal existence there is beating vividly, vitally, the pulse of the Infinite move-ment, then in that man, Schleiermacher teaches, authentic piety is born.

The best defence of his general method of approach is probably that put forward by Otto. What *can* be said in favour of a writer who, in his description of religion, is willing at least provisionally to dispense even with the idea of God ? Otto's reply would run somewhat on these lines. Schleiermacher, be it remembered, was writing at a time when men were only beginning to learn the needful lesson that the truth of Theism cannot be taken for granted. It is no part of the natural endowment of the human mind.

The world, looked at in the large, does not obviously or on the surface suggest naïve Theism as the one possible interpretation of the facts.   Accordingly, Schleiermacher declines to start simply with a defence of the traditional position.   Rather to his sceptical contemporaries he puts the question :   There is a divine element in things, have you opened your mind to its reality and answered its appeal ?   A sublime and eternal meaning pervades the world, which no human conceptions can ever compass or exhaust :   has your soul bowed before it in reverence ? Am not I right in urging that to the susceptible heart this presence of the infinite and ineffable comes home directly, even as in hours of vision the poet discovers behind and within the greatness and glory of the material universe a diviner greatness and a diviner glory ?   Let this be our initial certainty.   If we first grasp the eternal, in due time we shall discern the Eternal One.   If we awaken to the divine, our opened eyes will presently behold God.

From that position he advances slowly—from the divine to God, from an unchanging order and significance in life to the Unchanging One.   He goes up this path very stumblingly, no doubt, not yet having seen the bearing upon his problem of tragic moral experience, or of higher purpose ;   still he goes.   He will not say one word beyond what he must.   Is there not a sense in which Spinoza was pious and Kant in comparison was not ?   Are there not those in every age who approach religion thus—through an apprehension, vague yet real and not to be denied, of the Infinite and Incommensurable that seems to dawn upon them through the mystery of things, through biology, historical inquiry, the story of man's pathetic search for God in myriad faiths ?   So Otto would defend the master. It is all incomplete, of course.   All the work may have to be done over again in the light of conscience, most of all in the light of Jesus.   Yet for the apologist, in such an age as his, it is no unworthy first step.   The one question

worth asking is not whether we can vindicate the man
who took it, but how far in his later phase he moved
beyond it.

That this general view is not wholly invalid may be
gathered from the effect which Schleiermacher's book had
upon some of his contemporaries. It was mainly through
his study of the *Addresses* that the great Neander was led
from Judaism to a warm Christian faith. Or take the
testimony of Claus Harms, later an evangelical preacher
of great power, who was a student when the *Addresses* were
published and through the instrumentality of a friend had
got hold of the book. He writes thus in his autobiography.

It was Saturday, about midday. In the afternoon I began
to read, having told my attendant to inform everyone who
might call, that I did not wish to be disturbed. I read far
into the night, and finished the book. On Sunday morning
I began again from the beginning . . . Thereafter, I laid by
the book, and walked round little Kiel—a solitary walk ; and
during this walk it was that I suddenly recognized that all
rationalism, and all æsthetics, and all knowledge derived from
ourselves, are utterly worthless and useless as regards the work
of salvation, and the necessity of our salvation coming from
another source, so to say, flashed upon me. If to anyone
this sounds mysterious, or mystical, they may take it as such ;
I cannot describe the matter more distinctly ; but so much
I know, that I may with truth call it the hour in which my
higher life was born. I received from that book the impulse
of a movement that will never cease. More than this Schleiermacher did not do for me ; but so much he did do, and, next
to God, I thank him for it.

§ 5.   RELIGION AND HISTORY

All things in measure are reflections of the Infinite, but
all are not equally so. Schleiermacher therefore draws
what may be styled a series of concentric circles, each
revealing the boundless Whole more completely than the
last. In order they are as follows :

(*a*) *Nature*. Schleiermacher's interest in Nature was surprisingly weak, and he all but dismisses it now as but " the outer court of the Gentiles ". Its laws, rather than the detail of its beauty, impress him as religiously sublime, for they speak to us of the Divine unity and unchangeableness.

(*b*) *The Individual*. To find God truly, man must first find Him within. Each human self is an unique embodiment of the All ; piety intuits the Universe in every single life. In view of the cardinal importance which Schleiermacher always assigned to Individuality, it is strange to note the ambiguity of his language at this period concerning life after death.

The personal immortality you speak of outside time and beyond it [he writes in words often quoted] is in truth no immortality at all. None but he who surrenders his own personality, in its transience, to God in His eternity, none but he is really immortal. In the midst of finitude to be one with the Infinite and in every moment to be eternal is the immortality of religion. Therefore strive after it, strive even here to annihilate your personality and to live in the One and the All ; strive to be more than yourself, so that when you lose yourself you may lose but little.

(*c*) *Humanity*. The individual life is incomplete when taken apart from that of the race. As he puts it : " In order to receive the life of the World-Spirit, and have religion, man must first, in love and through love, have found humanity. The pious feelings are most holy that express for him existence in the whole of mankind." But in this book we nowhere encounter the conviction that faith must view humanity as organized under God for great and spiritual purposes, which form one, though subordinate, aspect of what Scripture calls the Kingdom of God.

(*d*) *History*. " As feeling persons," Schleiermacher declares, " we are ever driven back into the past. The spirit furnishes the chief nourishment for our piety, and history immediately and especially is for religion the richest source." Humanity must be viewed not only as it is, but in its process of becoming. Contemplation of history by the pious mind shows it to be " the greatest and most general revelation of the deepest and holiest ", for in itself it is the redemptive work of Eternal Love.

In all these spheres, with ever increasing adequacy, the Universe portrays itself in the finite, and its presence can be divined by those whose sense and taste for the Infinite has come alive.

This leads on to an eloquent and imaginative survey of the religions which have displayed themselves in the past. They too are individual forms of an impulse or attitude which in itself is endlessly variable. Speaking in the strongest antagonism to the dead uniformity which was the Rationalistic ideal Schleiermacher holds that their very multiplicity is a necessity of the case, for different souls must conceive and react to the Universe in different ways. Not all faiths are of equal value, though each in its place and time is good. A specific or positive religion takes its rise when the individual experiences of men group themselves round some particular intuition or principle. Thus, says Schleiermacher (with curious infelicity, considering the evangelical teaching of the great prophets), Judaism is dominated by the idea of rewards and punishments and cannot be viewed as a true forerunner of the New Testament faith ; Christianity, on the other hand, in its original form stands for the victory of the Infinite over finitude and sin. Its central interest lies in " the universal resistance of all things finite to the unity of the Whole, and the way in which the Deity overcomes this resistance ". Hence its characteristic attitude is that of conflict with the unworthiness of the world ; its permanent mood or feeling is " sacred sorrow ". Jesus was aware of His own Mediatorship. " The truly divine element is the glorious clearness to

which the great idea He came to exhibit attained in His
soul.   This idea was, that all that is finite requires a higher
mediation to be in accord with the Deity."

Thus Christianity, according to Schleiermacher, is both
among the positive religions and above them.   Like them,
it is an individual organization of the omnipresent common
stock of religious feeling, and centres in a particular
intuition of the Infinite.   Unlike them, it has seized upon
the very essence of religion itself to be the constitutive
intuition round which it is built.   But so far as I can
see, it is impossible to derive from the *Addresses* any one
consistent view of the place occupied by Christianity
among the religions of the world.   Christianity is best,
but not absolute, for no historical religion can exhaust all
possible religious feelings.   Jesus, it appears, despite His
unique self-consciousness, makes no claim to be the only
Mediator, and yet on the other hand all positive religions
are destined one day to be transformed into Christianity.
His mind flickers to and fro between differences of degree
and of kind.   Will Christianity always be the highest
religion ?   Two answers are possible, and apparently
Schleiermacher gave both.   And the suggestion that an
intuition of the Infinite higher than the Christian may
yet arise, he takes back at a later point, urging, very
unconvincingly, that it had been meant as an ironical
challenge to his contemporaries.   It is at all events clear
that he was not prepared to take history quite in earnest,
since he inclined to view actually existing religions as if
all were sub-species of a higher genus, not individual and
contingent forms which may well exhibit essential distinctions of quality.   After all, Shintoism, Buddhism, and
apostolic Christianity are not species of one genus ; no
one general conception will cover them all.   We must
conclude, I fear, that Schleiermacher reached his definition
of religion by analysis of his own experience, which he
took confidently to be valid for all religious experience as

such. This he then employed for a logical construction which is just as surely *a priori* and speculative as anything in Hegel.

The fact that in the *Addresses* he brings the historical faiths into his argument at all, is apt to induce confusion. At times, he is thinking in a purely ideal and theoretic way ; at other times, his eye is on concrete facts. Ideally, religion in its completeness is declared to exist in the whole series of actual religions, so that each particular faith has permanent value ; historically, essential religion is present in the Christian faith alone. We feel that as yet he had hardly adjusted his conclusions. It is difficult to hold both views together—first, that Christianity will never be displaced because it made the essence of religion central, and second, that it gladly welcomes new and co-ordinate forms of faith beside it, because to piety the very notion of a final faith is unendurable.

None the less the service rendered by him to that age was of high importance. He had exposed the baseless claims of what was known as " Natural Religion ", the only definite quality in which was its sheer indefiniteness, and which, as he urged, represented at bottom no more than a lifeless and artificial compound manufactured by the scholar out of books. Also he took a significant step towards a better understanding of what the Christian religion is. In his day Supernaturalists and Rationalists were bickering over the question how long Christianity would last, but Schleiermacher pushes all that aside. Our first duty, he said, is not to ascertain how supernatural it is, but what it is. It is the religion, he answers, which sprang out of history to speak of the alienation of the world from the Highest, to satisfy the longing for redemption from above.

On another side, the strength of Schleiermacher's general argument lay in his refutation of the shallow scepticism which dismisses piety as scarcely more than a nervous

complaint. He forced men to consider whether religion
may not be a thing *sui generis*, existing in its own right,
not by the permission of philosophy or science. He compelled them to listen to the plea that it forms an integral
factor in any complete human life, and has its roots in
the abysmal depths of feeling. God is apprehended, not
as a syllogistic conclusion from premises, but so immediately that we cannot shun His presence even if we would.
Yet, so far at least, we are left more than half in doubt
whether by " God " he means a being of specific character,
as well as whether his meaning has any positive relation
to Jesus Christ ; and on matters of that kind ambiguity
consorts with a faith built on the witness of Scripture as
little as pure negation. Deity is active in the world ; and
Schleiermacher, if we may put it so, saw the movement of
God's finger, but His face as yet he had not seen. He
felt for the hem of His garment, as it swept through the
immensities of time and space ; of such things he spoke
movingly ; but regarding the infinite Holiness and Love
disclosed in Christ he had thus far maintained a nearly
complete silence.

III

THE THEOLOGY OF FEELING (B)

SCHLEIERMACHER'S INTERPRETATION OF CHRISTIANITY

§ 1. HIS THEOLOGICAL APPROACH

IN 1821, MORE than twenty years after he had issued the *Addresses*, Schleiermacher published his *Christian Faith*, or *Dogmatic*, a full-sized exposition of doctrinal theology.[1] Next to the *Institutes* of Calvin, it is the most influential dogmatic work to which evangelical Protestantism can point, and it has helped to teach theology to more than three generations. One could no more understand present-day systematic thought without this book—its faults equally with its virtues—than one could understand modern biology without Darwin.

In the interval Schleiermacher had known labour and sorrow. He had been a pastor for years in one of the most neglected parts of Germany. Now an honoured university teacher, he had prepared himself for his task by searching exegetical and philosophical study; he had lectured on every subject in the round of theology except the Old Testament. He was fifty-three years of age, and at the summit of his powers.

There is much to be said for the contention that Schleiermacher stands out amongst the great theologians largely because of his genius for thinking systematically. In

---

[1] A second edition came out in 1830–1, revised in many details, but so far as the author's general attitude to its problems is concerned, not greatly changed. There is an English translation (1928).

striking contrast to Kant's *Critique of Pure Reason*, for example, his *Dogmatic* is all of a piece. He has perfect command over his subject, and a sure-footed habit of making progress. There is a noble width of outlook, an absence of bitter polemic, and a singular richness of detailed exposition and relevant digression. Even if it be held that his basal principles are largely mistaken, we are shown what it might mean to work out the system of Christian belief as an organic whole. After Schleiermacher, it was impossible to go back to the method of *loci communes*. *Loci* were more or less unconnected chapters on particular topics, like beads on a thread, very often loosely strung together without much effort to elicit the generative principle to which their being and their unity were due. It was a method fostered by the dogma of verbal inspiration, since any doctrine covered by tolerably plausible scripture proof might claim a place in the text-book, even if its connexion with the main stem of Christian truth was more than doubtful. Schleiermacher worked on the conviction that a real unity can be discovered, and that each true doctrine acts and re-acts on the others.

He had chosen as his point of departure, in dogmatic thought, the soul's experience of spiritual life within the Christian Church,[1] and went on to inquire what must *be* in order to explain the occurrence of this fact. In his own view, he is taking a purely empirical line ; and in one of his letters to Lücke he speaks roundly of " the analysis of the (Christian) self-consciousness undertaken in my *Dogmatic* ". In contrast to traditional orthodoxy and to Rationalism, both of which set out from objective general principles and used the deductive method, his personal aim is to elucidate the contents of the Christianly

---

[1] For Schleiermacher the consciousness of man, within Christianity as without, includes a communal element. It is a consciousness in which we know ourselves one with others. This emphasis on the corporate nature of the Christian life is one of his best contributions.

pious soul. His method, broadly, is that of introspection, not of listening to God. To quote again his words in the earlier " Soliloquies " : " As often as I turn my gaze inward upon my inmost self, I am at once within the domain of eternity." The believer's experience is something positively given, and the theologian's task is to analyse out whatever of doctrinal import can be found in it. This attitude more or less explains—though it cannot justify—the much-debated contention of Schleiermacher that *Dogmatic* is in essence an historical study. It may be so described, he urges, because *Dogmatic* is called upon to deal with actual Christian life, on the side of belief, as it exists in the Church to-day. It is history, but history of the present. It ought to take account of Creeds and Confessions, by which the Church's mind is rightly or inevitably influenced, and must apply the scientific methods prevailing in the modern world. Hence its task may be defined as that of giving an orderly and articulate view of the doctrines received in a specific Church at a specific time. Later discussion has shown how little this will bear scrutiny. *Dogmatic* is supremely interested not in what has been believed, or even in what is believed now, but in what ought to be believed by those to whom God has spoken in Revelation. As a normative discipline, it brings a certain standard of truth to bear upon the preaching or the confessions of the Church, and, in the light of this standard—the Word of God—it puts past and present alike on trial.

Feeling or " immediate self-consciousness " is still, it might almost seem more uncompromisingly even than in the *Addresses*, fixed upon as the psychological *locus* of the Christian piety Schleiermacher proposes to examine. The specific feeling in question is the feeling of absolute dependence. There religion has its hearth and home ; in such feeling it essentially lives and has its being. Knowing and doing have their own place, but it is that of secondary effects. Such feelings as contrition, joy, or trust in God have and keep their religious character quite apart from any knowledge or action that may come to be attached to them. The feeling of unconditional or absolute dependence is, as he puts it, " the self-identical essence of piety " ; and the consciousness of being absolutely dependent is precisely the same thing as the consciousness of being in relation to God.[1] Let us note how he conceives the origin of this feeling. In every moment of consciousness, he argues, it is possible to distinguish between two elements or factors : a sense of freedom and a sense of constraint, of self-determination and of being determined by things around us. Our human life is an alternating and continuous succession of these two kinds of feeling ; we are never wholly subject to our environment, but also we are never wholly masters of it. Yet a region or zone of experience does exist in which we have the sense of being dependent and nothing else. That zone is religion. There we are face to face, not with this or that finite object, but with the universal causal reality named " God ".[2] By " God " cannot be meant any special reality within the cosmos, or even the cosmos as a whole ; God is the dominant Power behind all phenomena, imparting to them reality, unity and meaning. It is clear that, in this developed stage of Schleiermacher's thought, God and the Universe have come to be slightly more distinguishable. Yet when we ask whether God

---

[1] *The Christian Faith*, § 3 and § 4. Schleiermacher, we may say, discovers God in feeling in so far as he finds there the feeling of sheer dependence. Does not this, abstractedly or logically, imply that every man as such is religious, and may know it if he will only reflect on himself and his feelings ?

[2] Perhaps it is at this point that Schleiermacher probed most deeply and made his nearest approach to a more promising line of thought. He stopped at feeling, but feeling after all is only an accompaniment of something much more profound, something that indeed is the ultimate fact of life, viz., the being in personal relationship. This he failed to see. Cf. Martin Bucer, *Ich und Du*, 95-6.

as now conceived is such that we can have personal relationships with Him, the answer must be pronounced far from
reassuring. He is, we are told, the absolute and undivided
Unity beyond and beneath all things. His nature is such
that in no sense could we react upon Him. Were such
reaction possible, the sense of utter and unreserved
dependence would promptly vanish, and our attitude could
no longer be described as specifically religious in character.
We may call God " Spirituality ", if such a word will serve.

Pious feeling, in other words, can emerge only as we are
face to face with a cause which conditions our freedom
equally with our dependence, and which evokes the consciousness that the whole even of our spontaneous activity
comes from a source beyond ourselves. It is of great
importance to note how Schleiermacher definitely equates
this basal feeling of sheer dependence with being in relation
to God. Implicitly this is an advance on his former view.
In the *Addresses* he had been emphatic that piety may
exist without any idea of God whatsoever ; but in the
Dogmatic, apparently moving on a step, he lays down that
God means " the *Whence* of our receptive and active
existence ". Commenting on the feeling of absolute
dependence, he writes : " In the first instance God signifies
for us simply that which is the co-determinant in this
feeling and to which we trace our being in such a state ;
and any further content of the idea must be evolved out
of this fundamental import." [1] This at least may now
be registered—and the gain, for a reader of Schleiermacher,
is one not to be despised—that the word " God " is a
significant word, such that propositions containing it may
be true or false.

In stressing the fundamental importance of felt dependence, as a factor in religion, Schleiermacher certainly
did not err. The religious man knows himself to be a
receiver only, God the great Doer and Giver. But this

[1] *The Christian Faith*, pp. 16–17.

feeling is not the only one involved ; to mention no more, there is the feeling of shelteredness, of creatureliness, of unworthiness, of obligation. Otto brings up a charge of a somewhat different kind. " According to Schleier-macher," he writes, " I can only come upon the very fact of God as the result of an inference, that is, by reasoning to a cause beyond myself to account for my ' feeling of dependence '." [1] And clearly, if feeling is only an emotion, an awareness of the pulsations of our own inner life, Otto's point must be sustained. I can only say that to me Schleiermacher appears in the majority of passages, especially in his *Dogmatic*, to mean by " feeling " a laying hold by the soul of a trans-subjective Reality, supreme over the world. Feeling is indeed an experience on the part of the Self, yet one in which the Self " apprehends " not itself but God. Schleiermacher thus far is speaking in the rôle not of a psychologist but of a theologian. For him the constitutive element in religion is a certain felt relation of man to a supramundane Fact or Power ; and in virtue of this the general charge that he is proceeding by the methods of simple psychological empiricism must, I think, be rebutted. We are unwilling to believe that as a theologian he could have run into the fallacy that it is only by way of a causal inference from its own immediately apprehended states that the mind becomes aware of an object distinct from itself. This is not to deny that on every other page of his *Dogmatic* phrases or statements may be found which lend a real colour to the accusation. But in fundamental intention he is not arguing from an empirically discovered feeling of absolute dependence to God, its source and cause ; in that feeling itself we grasp God directly as the " Whence " of all things.

At the same time, while Schleiermacher may be acquitted of the charge in the grosser sense that he gives, and designs to give, nothing more than a phenomenology of the religious

[1] *The Idea of the Holy*, p. 10.

consciousness, it must be pointed out that by definition he has made doctrine, including the doctrine of God, something quite secondary and derivative. " Christian doctrines," he writes, " are accounts of the Christian religious affections set forth in speech." [1] This is the old failure, shown earlier in the *Addresses*, to perceive the vital place held by belief in the religious response as such. If words mean anything, doctrine is for him a statement about our feeling, not about God. It does not declare what God is, or what attributes He has, but only what conception of God and what attributes most correctly mirror and symbolize the content of our pious mood. He puts the matter plainly enough at a later point by declaring that " all attributes which we ascribe to God are to be taken as denoting not something specific in God, but only something specific in the manner in which the feeling of absolute dependence is to be related to Him ".[2] In passing, it may perhaps be observed that a general view of this kind is implicitly refuted by its own phrasing. What can be meant by saying that we have to determine which Divine attributes most adequately reflect our subjective feeling ? Either this implies that we merely pore over our own inward state, and excogitate the idea of God which best answers to it ; which is right in the teeth of the essentially objective movement of faith. Or it means that after all we do envisage the Divine object, as presented, and seek for worthy symbols of it. Symbols, that is to say, are aimless except as we have some real notion of what it is they symbolize. As Dr. Edwyn Bevan has pointed out, " We could not detect the merely symbolical character of any representation, unless our thought could in some way reach beyond the symbol and contrast it with the reality ". Happily Schleiermacher's practice is a good deal better than his theory ; in his *Dogmatic* he makes all sorts of definitely objective statements about

[1] § 15.   [2] § 50.

God and Christ, though they may not all of them satisfy Christian standards. His initial error is plainly due to a weak sense of revelation, as the evoking cause of faith and *ipso facto* the criterion by which all doctrine is to be tried. No emphasis on experience can hide from us the fact that only as taught by Christ, the Word of God addressed to us, can we distinguish within experience what is Christian from what is not.

That we are not here protesting too much is proved by a subsequent passage [1] in which, with a curious obstinacy, Schleiermacher persists in arguing that the description of human states of soul is the basal form of doctrinal proposition, other forms or types—that is, those concerned with God or the world—being permissible variations only in so far as they can be consistently developed out of the first. Elsewhere he goes so far as to suggest that the ideal *Dogmatic* could have nothing to say directly about either God or world, but would consist exclusively, to use his fatal phrase, in " descriptions of human states ". Yet he owns, with a certain regret, that the ideal thus indicated is too severe to be followed in practice. The Christian mind is not yet ripe for it ; obedience to it would break all links with the past, and the resulting *Dogmatic* would have lost all churchly character. Thus he is faced by a strange contradiction between that which on technical grounds ought to be, and that which to satisfy the believing mind must be. All doctrines, to be precise, ought to be affirmations regarding what goes on in the Christian soul ; yet incontestably, as he shrewdly suspects, the Church in its doctrines not only intends to make, but actually does make, wholly objective assertions concerning God.

This tenacious vein of psychologism in Schleiermacher is a prejudice and disability that haunts his *Dogmatic* from the first page to the last. He can even declare that " nothing is *given* us except the souls in which we light

[1] See § 30.

upon the pious affections ". At need he can reduce this
or that doctrine—the Trinity, for example—to second rank
on the ground that it is not a description of our inward
experience. Setting out from the believer's states of soul,
he undertakes, by regressive argument, to reach the truth.
Hasty or confused thinkers have at times identified this
with a brave assertion of the spiritual freedom of the
Christian mind, so dear to the Reformers. But the very
reverse is the truth. The Reformers take as their point
of departure, in every chapter of doctrine, not the soul in
its ups and downs, but the Word of God objectively given
by revelation. Faith, they teach on every page, is dependence on the Word. You can only speak of standing where
there is ground to stand upon, and you can only speak of
faith where there is a Word of God on which faith rests.
Schleiermacher's eye—though not always nor exclusively
—was bent on inward facts, as though the soul could feed
on its own vitals. It was because the Reformers looked
unflinchingly to God as self-unveiled in His Word that
they escaped from the deceptive self-absorption and
immanentism of the essential mystic, whose experience
moves only within itself.

§ 2. THE MEANING OF THE CHRISTIAN RELIGION

Schleiermacher's definition of Christianity, given at an
early point in his *Dogmatic*, runs as follows : " Christianity is a monotheistic faith, belonging to the teleological
type of religion, and is essentially distinguished from
other such faiths by the fact that in it everything has
relation to the redemption accomplished by Jesus of
Nazareth." [1] Here the word " teleological ", it should be
noted, broadly means ethical. To us it might seem obvious
that Christianity rests on Christ, yet Schleiermacher feels
he must make the point emphatically in face of the current

[1] § 11.

Rationalism, for which Jesus had become no more than an eminent Teacher who had brought to men some cardinal religious truth and a pure morality, neither of which was distinctively bound up with Himself. Furthermore, Christ is definitely introduced as One who has wrought " redemption ". That is a word of many significations, and even by Schleiermacher himself on occasion it is watered down to mean no more than passing from an evil condition to a better, the escape from " an obstruction or arrest of the vitality of the higher self-consciousness ". None the less by this definition, be the defects of its fuller expansion what they may, " Christ is preached ", and therein like the Apostle we may rejoice. Christ is once more at the centre of His own religion, and He is there as Saviour. The writer is leading his generation back to our Lord.[1]

In Christianity the relation of the Founder to the members of His community is altogether different from that which obtains in other faiths. Those other founders were, so to speak, elevated arbitrarily out of a mass of men very like themselves, and whatever they received in the way of divine doctrine and precept, they received as much for themselves as for other people. But Christ, we read, " is distinguished from all others as Redeemer alone and for all ", nor did He ever need redemption Himself. Thus in opposition to the cosmopolitan enlightenment of the time Schleiermacher insists steadily on the uniqueness of Christ. And as against orthodoxy, he claims that Jesus must be permitted to make His own saving impression ; the way to Him must not be blocked by any antecedently prescribed assent to correct doctrines about His Person, as if He could not best explain Himself. Christ is the heart of Christianity, and He is so because He, and

---

[1] In his second " Open Letter to Lücke ", he declares that *The Christian Faith* was written as the exposition of the Johannine words (I. 14) : " The Word was made flesh and dwelt among us . . . full of grace and truth."

He alone, redeems. In other faiths, redemption is not the main thing. Everywhere else it is overgrown by all manner of dogmas or ceremonies, with the result that the liberation of the sense of God—and this is what " redemption " properly means—is both incomplete and precarious.

A favourite subject of contemporary discussion was " the perfectibility of the Christian religion ", in the sense of its possible evolution into a faith higher and more satisfying than itself. Schleiermacher does not formally reject the idea, but he is clear that Christianity can only be perfected in the sense of " a more perfect exhibition of its inmost nature ". There is no possibility of transcending Jesus. Were it otherwise, He would become no more than a notable point or stage in the development of religion, and eventually, on the appearance of His successor, men would require to be saved *from* Him, no longer by or through Him. We need not labour the point that Schleiermacher has now advanced far beyond the position set forth in the *Addresses*, where, at least in theory, Christ was but one mediator amongst many.

One of the gravest defects in Schleiermacher's approach to Christianity as the religion of the New Testament lies in his failure to understand the Old.[1] He does not scruple to say that, so far as concerns its aim and purpose, the relations of Christianity to the older dispensation and to heathenism are the same. So that for us the Old Testament ranks, say, with Greek philosophy. We do not hear directly in it the Word of God. It is important to observe that what repels Schleiermacher in the Old Testament is not such things as its cosmology or its pictures of history. The reason lies deeper : to him the religion it presents is a form of legalism. He was still more than half blind to the revelation given through the prophets—

[1] This had a pernicious influence on his understanding of Jesus, the Messiah.

their message concerning the Holiness of God or His living and creative Lordship. He failed to see that in the Old Testament God is not, like the Deity in Plato or in mysticism, One who waits to be found by man ; [1] He is One who comes to men personally in the judgment and mercy of events, He strikes into history to establish fellowship with sinning and dying men. And we must not expect justice to be done to the deepest things in Christianity by a thinker who is unable to perceive that the first essential roots of Christian belief go down into the teaching of the Hebrew prophets.

The question whether Schleiermacher did or did not hold to the absoluteness or finality of the Christian religion will have to be answered differently according as we listen to the philosopher in him or to the theologian. So far as the philosophy of religion and of history is concerned, the absoluteness is evidently given up. Here he clings to a purely immanental explanation of the world, and we are given to understand that all through history the same kind of forces have operated uniformly in unbroken sequence. He knows no Divine irruption into a world of sin. Even the Person of Jesus only carries to its issue something which God by the original creation had implanted in the human race as a developmental force. If, as he teaches, Reason and Revelation, Nature and Grace are fundamentally co-extensive each with the other, though possibly different in degree, anything like a unique or supernatural intervention from above must be disallowed. Nowhere is there any action of God which we are justified in calling *special*. The Divine causality is like a vast undiscriminating pressure upon the world, diffused with virtual uniformity over the whole. The underlying assumptions are those of a monistic and evolutionary optimism. Continuity rather than crisis was

[1] To Schleiermacher, on the whole, revelation is only another name for human discovery.

Schleiermacher's guiding thought, alike in his view of
sin and of salvation. All is put in immanent terms, and
a sharp break is out of the question. Everything is
relative, and the question whether anything can then be
absolute is left without reply.

The theologian, when not inhibited by the evolutionary
monist, holds a different language. In the *Dogmatic* he
makes it entirely clear that for him Christianity is *at least*
the highest of all faiths so far known, with " perfect "
redemption at its heart. And when advancing from the
relative perfection of Christianity to its absoluteness, he
is led forward by the guiding-thread of Christology. It
is not too much to say that his discussion of the Person
of Christ is controlled throughout by this interest, and
while he nowhere treats of the question of finality on its
own account, that problem in essence is obviously settled
by the conclusions in which he rests about the relationship
of the Redeemer to the redeemed, and theirs to Him.
Christ confronts us as an absolute Figure. In Him there
exists a conjunction, and a perfect one, of the ideal and
the historical. Jesus' consciousness of God (Schleiermacher, significantly enough, prefers this phrase to " Jesus'
relationship with God ") has boundless power to communicate itself to others as well as to assimilate these
others to itself. Shall we then say that this unique quality
of life—a quality that made Him not only separate from
sinners but distinct from the saints—is of positively supernatural origin, or must it be held that even Jesus was
produced by the resident forces of human nature ? Once
more, apparently, Schleiermacher will have it both ways.
At one time the supernatural reading is given precedence
over the natural ; at another the two views are set side
by side, as simply co-ordinate. No one can doubt that
when he speaks openly as a believer the Person of Christ
takes on absolute dimensions ; there is no analogy for
Jesus, he writes, and there dwelt in Him a spiritual power

such as no human calculus can reckon. Yet, as in a faulty broadcast, the counter-argument of the philosopher can be heard in the background.

This vital point, then, is one on which Schleiermacher speaks with two voices. He is neither for absoluteness nor against it. And indeed when we consider two matters, his cultural evolutionism and his more than half mystical conception of what religion is, it is plain that intellectual reservations forbade him to assert without equivocation the final and decisive significance of Christ. Not even His God-consciousness marks Him off in absolute fashion from other pious souls, for their consciousness of God reveals a steady approximation to His. Apart from Christ, indeed, the normal human God-consciousness can boast a relative strength of its own, which in essence is similar to that which He has and imparts.

On no aspect of Christianity does Schleiermacher lay more wholesome stress than on this, that not by accident but in virtue of its very nature it creates a corporate life. To Kant and his generation, it has often been observed, religion was all but exclusively an individual affair. So far as his relation to God is concerned, each man stands or falls for himself irrespectively of his fellows. " The Church is simply an aggregation, larger or smaller, of a number of such independent units." Schleiermacher struck the note firmly that to be a Christian is to be a member of a living organism, whose life derives from Christ. The mutual giving and receiving of the brethren makes religion, as lived at the Christian level, what it is. So too of Theology ; its essential nature in great part is constituted by its relation to the Church. It exists to serve the believing society, though not in any sectarian or trivial sense. Schleiermacher would have found pleasure in Coleridge's aphorism : " He who begins by loving Christianity better than Truth, will proceed by loving his own sect or church better than Christianity, and end

in loving himself better than all." This emphasis on the
Church, as the scene of constant vital action and reaction
between those who believe, whereby a concrete fellowship
is maintained, is one means whereby Schleiermacher in
part escapes from the perils of his own subjectivism. The
individual thinker is conditioned by the larger life in
which he shares. Unlike most German Protestant theologians of his time, however, he steadily refused to permit
the difference between Lutheran and Reformed to exert
any influence on the handling of the theological system.
His *Dogmatic*, as he explained, proceeded on the assumption that no adequate ground could be given for the continued separation of these two branches of the Evangelical
Church ; for, as he held, the different types of doctrine
they represent in no sense flow from different types of
Christian feeling, nor are they accompanied by really
divergent forms of moral teaching or practice.

§ 3. SOME CARDINAL CHRISTIAN DOCTRINES

Passing from these generalities, let us mark how Schleiermacher applied to some central doctrines the principles
and methods by which he had chosen to be guided.

(*a*) As we have seen, in his stricter moods a doctrine
is a transcript of, or report upon, the Christian consciousness. The development and the characteristic facts of the
Christian mind are his theme ; he is speaking throughout
of the believer's religious states or affections, as they
testify of this or that beyond themselves. Not the creative
self-revelation of God is the object of his study, but the
modifications of the feeling of absolute dependence, as
that feeling takes shape and colour within the Christian
Church. Thus doctrine looks rather in than out. At this
point it is important to recollect that Schleiermacher
divides his treatise into three main parts. First, he

explains what can be affirmed regarding God and man apart from the felt contrast of sin and grace, secondly what in the way of doctrine is implied in the consciousness of sin (this section is brief), lastly what truths are implied in the consciousness of grace.   This explains the odd fact that in *The Christian Faith* the attributes of God are discussed in three distinct sections widely removed from each other.

To take an analogy from another field, knowledge is undoubtedly a representation of things, in the sense that we cannot know things without having ideas.   None the less it is not our ideas that we know, but the extra-mental reality they grasp ; and things go wrong from the beginning except as we assume that in cognition the mind is turned outward on facts, not inward upon itself.   In words, though not presumably in intention, Schleiermacher reversed this.   To him doctrines about God are no more than descriptions of our own feeling.   They indicate something specific, not in God but in us.   The undivided unity of God may appear as if it were differentiated in various attributes, just as white light passed through a prism seems to be broken up in distinct colours ; but it is only seeming.   Deity admits of no distinction.[1]   Holiness, wisdom, love are but distinguishable shades or modifications in our God-consciousness or awareness of God.   It is difficult to recognize this as having any sort of contact with the real attitude of faith.   After all, both faith and theology are concerned primarily with what God is ; their first interest is in Him, not in our own minds.   To say that it is merely because of certain peculiarities of our eyesight that we behold God as almighty, omniscient, righteous, or loving—as if we looked at Him through a series of tinted glasses—but that these words are no index

[1] At one point he roundly declares that " it is not in conformity with the demands of speculative reason to allow difference in God ".

of His real nature, is wholly out of keeping with the Christian thought of revelation. God as disclosed in Christ is God as He truly is. What is more, blankly to identify His knowledge with His will, on the ground that in God ultimately there are no distinctions because His being is the featureless converging-point of all contrasts, runs. directly counter to the Christian certainty that the world contains many things known to God, which yet He has not willed or caused. This at all events is one distinction we must make, if we are not to deny Him a moral character.

We have seen at an earlier point that God, for Schleiermacher, is the Reality that corresponds objectively to the feeling of unqualified dependence, the Irresistible One, the Source from which we and all things derive existence.[1] God is best thought of as the absolute Causality, in which all antitheses melt and are lost. As the correlate of basal religious feeling He is perceived as Supreme Power, and all other attributes (with the possible exception of Love) are but the separate articulations of such Power. The Divine eternity, omnipresence and omniscience are gathered from the general relation of Deity to the world, irrespectively of the Christian experience ; holiness, righteousness and mercy report themselves through our sense of sin ; love and wisdom, finally, come to be known through our sense of redeeming grace. Yet to ascribe personality to this universal Source—this eternal omnipotent Causality —would be to reduce Him or It to the level of finitude. It may be asked how a thinker to whom the Divine Love was so absorbingly real, and who, as his contemporary sermons prove, preached the redemption that is in Christ most movingly, could speak with so much hesitation regarding the Divine personality. All we can reply is

[1] It may be that Schleiermacher's view of God's relation to the world owes a good deal to Plato's teaching about the relation of the Ideas to the visible world.

that Schleiermacher belonged to the by no means negligible
group of Christian theologians who have been acutely,
and perhaps even morbidly, sensitive to the limiting and,
so far, unfitting character of that symbol. There is
something to be learnt from his protest that the notion
of " person " cannot be transferred simply, and without
more ado, from the conditioned life of man to the absolute
and unconditioned being of the Eternal. Schleiermacher
was groping for the idea of God super-personal, in persistent rebellion against all views which incline to represent
Him, in Matthew Arnold's phrase, as a " magnified non-
natural man ". What he failed to see is that no other
term is at our disposal to bring out the cardinal truth
that in His Word God addresses men as a spiritual Will,
as a " Thou " creating personal fellowship between Him
and them. " Personality " is by no means a claim to
describe scientifically how God's life is formed ; it is a
symbol, and an indispensable one, of the fact that the
Infinite and Holy One meets with us in personal relationships and speaks to us as our Father. Schleiermacher's
excessive distaste for the concept is at least an exaggerated
reminder that a certain insoluble tension remains, and
will ever remain, between the thought of God's living
transcendence and that of His personal being. It must
be left to the reader to judge how far Schleiermacher's
objections to conceiving God as personal are refuted by
his own unreserved language about the Divine Love. Towards the close of the *Dogmatic* he sums up the debate
in true Christian style with these words : " We have the
sense of Divine love directly in the consciousness of redemption, and as this is the basis on which all the rest
of our God-consciousness is built up, it of course represents
to us the essence of God." Love stands supreme over
wisdom, which flows from it. " Love," as he puts it
finely, " would not be implied in so absolute a degree if
we thought God as wisdom, as wisdom would be if we

thought Him as love. For where almighty love is, there must also absolute wisdom be." [1]

As he turns to consider the doctrine of the Trinity, Schleiermacher makes the remark—suggestive as regards his all-controlling point of view—that here we must sit loose to ecclesiastical definitions, because the doctrine of the Trinity is not in fact " an immediate utterance concerning the Christian self-consciousness ", but only a combination between several utterances of the kind. Here, be it noted, is the old assumption that in Christian doctrine we are trying to make statements about our own souls and their contents. After some acute observations as to conciliar decisions on the subject, he comes to the provisional result that this doctrine, as stated in Protestant creeds, has not as yet received its definitive form. At the Reformation, the Protestant leaders simply took it over without raising the question whether it ought to be revised. To him the traditional formulation seems to verge too closely on tritheism. But he is very far from wishing to cast the doctrine aside. Indeed, though perhaps with no resounding success, he makes a genuine effort to reach a Trinitarianism which in essence shall be *religious* and nothing else. The intention of the doctrine, he urges, is to affirm that " nothing less than the Divine being was in Christ, and dwells in the Christian Church as its unifying Spirit ". I need not pause here to inquire whether Schleiermacher's description of the Holy Spirit as " the common Spirit of the Christian society ", interpreted as analogous to the spirit of a race or people, is the same Being as the New Testament calls the Spirit of God; though obviously this would be a point of large importance in a general criticism of his argument. Suffice it that the revision of the doctrine to which he looks forward is in tendency Sabellian—static, that is to say, rather than dynamic, and for that reason only loosely related to the

[1] *The Christian Faith*, p. 732.

events of historical Revelation.   This reading of the dogma, only hinted at in the closing paragraphs of the *Dogmatic* itself, was more fully expanded later in a special essay.

Is Schleiermacher a pantheist ?   There have always been many who felt that his peculiar type of theology forces us to use the term.   The reproach was promptly flung at him that he was only a " clever Spinozist " ; and Strauss, in a bitter gibe, said that he had pulverized Christianity and Spinozism so fine, for mixing, that it would take a sharp eye to distinguish the two.   But Schleiermacher, with obvious candour, replied that the characteristic ideas of Spinoza—the idea, e.g., that the lover of God must not expect that God should love him —were quite alien to his theology.   " Since I first read him," he protests, " I have sincerely admired and loved Spinoza, but I have never been his follower for one moment."   Yet the older philosopher's mode of thinking was unusually congenial to his own.   Also there are evident similarities between his general view of things and that of Schelling, who was apt to interpret spirit by nature rather than nature by spirit.

No fair-minded reader can doubt, however, that a pantheist reading of Christianity was no part of Schleiermacher's purpose.   He makes it clear that for him the feeling of absolute dependence points beyond the sum-total of finite being.   " This ' Whence '," he writes, concerning the Source of all, " is not the world ; " and again, " a lifeless and blind necessity would not really be something with which we could stand in relation ".   It has indeed been urged that his determinism wears a pantheist hue.   But as regards determinism, his real interest lay in the rejection of a totally unmotived freedom, which in the last resort is freedom only in name.   Where true religion exists, freedom has become a second nature, and the man feels he must be what he is, whether he wills it or not.   Similarly, his version of the doctrine of Election

may be Calvinist, but it is not pantheist; and indeed, if
his views are culpable, Calvin must stand in the dock
beside him. Even his assertion of the identity of all
Divine attributes can be paralleled by something extremely
like it in Augustine, Hilary, and Anselm. And once more,
it has been contended that his early, and semi-pantheistic,
distaste for the idea that immortal life is anything more
than an eternal present, lasted on into the era of the
Dogmatic. But in reply we may point out that his whole
teaching on Election loses all meaning unless we presuppose
the existence and developing life of the elect after death.
" From the resurrection of the dead onwards," he writes
at a later point, " those who have died in fellowship with
Christ will find themselves, through the vision of God, in
a state of unchangeable and unclouded blessedness." He
would have argued that from the first he had been chiefly
concerned to give full value to the great Johannine declaration : " He that believeth *hath* eternal life."

There are, however, other contexts in which the reader
of the *Dogmatic* is confronted, not with pantheism as
such, but with a type of thought controlled by certain
pantheist prepossessions. This is antecedently made probable by the fact that in the *Dialectic* he had taught that
while God and world are not identical, yet they are correlates, like " right " and " left ". His view of Creation
is a good instance. Brunner observes, not unjustly, that
Schleiermacher introduces this doctrine with a formula
which may almost be said to be habitual with him when
he is going to perpetrate a more than usually serious
departure from Christian teaching ; he announces that
the idea of Creation " is not the outcome of any purely
religious interest ", and " did not originally arise on purely
dogmatic grounds ". A predominantly mystical concept
of God has of course no living interest in the question
whether God and world are eternal correlates, or stand
in the very different relation of Creator and creature. As

the argument proceeds, we discover that by degrees he
is replacing the Biblical thought of Creation by an idea
drawn from the philosophy of Identity, viz., the equivalence of creation and preservation. The immanentist
assumptions, which direct his mind at this point, made
it hard for him to find even a modicum of value in such
ideas as " creation out of nothing ", or the absolute freedom
of God in calling the universe into being. The reason of
course is that the doctrine of Creation, understood as the
Bible understands it, stresses that very difference and
distance between God and man which it is the aim of
mystical or speculative pantheism to abolish. It is in the
same interest that Schleiermacher bluntly denies that the
contrast between " can " and " will " applies to God. All
that is possible for God is real ; there are in Him no reserves
of power. He could not have made the world other than
it is. The whole of God is fact—precisely what Spinoza
taught, but scarcely a legitimate view for one who takes
his religion from the Old and New Testaments. In his
later years even Schelling laid down the canon that
pantheism in the bad sense is present wherever people
decline to distinguish, in God's relation to the world,
between possibility and reality. Measured by this standard, Schleiermacher's position lies under the strongest
suspicion. His words could hardly be more emphatic :
" What does not become actual, is also, so far as God is
concerned, not potential." He does not wish to be a
pantheist, nor is he one in his personal faith ; yet as a
theologian he never surmounts the difficulty of distinguishing the whole and its parts.

But the gravest example of his leaning to a pantheist
reading of God and world is found in his practice, already
noted, of asserting the material identity of Divine " action "
with the nexus of natural causation. It is a subject to
which he devotes many pages of the *Dogmatic*,[1] as though

[1] §§ 46 and 47.

conscious of its essential importance for his whole point
of view, perhaps also with the feeling that he certainly
had his work cut out for him if at this point his conclusions were to be made even plausibly harmonious with
Christian conviction. His argument yields two results.
First : to be conditioned by the system of Nature is
precisely the same thing as to be conditioned by God ;
the two interpretations are co-terminous, and neither
means any less or more than the other. Secondly : our
knowledge of both (perception in the former case, feeling
in the other) is also the same. It is all one whether we
take everything from the Father's hand as His appoint-
ment, or merely recognize the cosmic regularity present
in all events. Human life is to be construed in similar
fashion. " The invisible hand of Providence and the
action of men," he writes in a private letter, " are one
and the same thing." The pattern of the world is unchangeable, for in God its Source no change is possible.
Any other view moves on a lower plane of insight. Thus
the causality of God is presented as operating in the
world as an infinite, uniform and quite undeviating pressure, like that of a hydraulic apparatus, with its allotted
equal weight on each square inch. Does then the reality
of God make any difference in the particular case ?
Scarcely, if new creative preferential action on God's
part is unnecessary, and therefore unreal. This, in plain
words, is Christian naturalism, and has lost all touch
with Jesus' thought of an omnipotent Father freely wield-
ing all that we mean by Nature for the realization of
unspeakably gracious ends.

Thus even in the " Christian Faith " a strong tinge of
Pantheism gives colour to the whole. To Schleiermacher
it appeared not only more philosophical but more pious
to discard the Biblical idea of the " Living God ", and to
speak of the Divine Being rather as unqualified Unity,
the indifference-point of all antitheses, and the like. In

the end, we must conclude, it is not merely the concept of Personality that he judged unfitted to the Divine Nature, but *any* objective determination claiming to be valid of God as He really is, or setting up to be more than an imaginative symbol. Schleiermacher was fully aware of his own pantheist bias, and defended it.

If [he said] the ordinary treatment of the doctrine of God during the past hundred years is to be styled "Church doctrine", I cannot in the story of my own theological development find any approach thereto, but only an ever more definite divergence . . . If the older treatment is "the doctrine of the Church", why then mine certainly is heterodox. But I am firmly convinced, it is the kind of heterodoxy that will soon enough be orthodox.

No prophecy could have gone wider of the truth. The later thought of Evangelical Protestantism has turned more and more resolutely in the direction of a new emphasis on the personal character of God.

(*b*) We turn now to other fundamental elements in the Christian faith. On the doctrine of sin Schleiermacher has something to contribute which is good though not excellent. The theologian, he declares, is bound to say the worst he can of sin—short of Manichaeism. He begins with the experiential fact that our sense of God is weakened and defiled by our lower nature. The secret of sin lies in the conflict of spirit with flesh ; and the course of human development, whether racial or individual, makes it inevitable that the spirit should start under a heavy handicap. The existence of conflict is to be explained, he argues suggestively, by the fact that we can recognize the good long before we attain the will-power to realize it ; flesh has the lead, and spirit never succeeds in overhauling it. Along with this "evolutionary" view, which seems on the brink of defining sin as the relic of the brute in man, and therefore no more than something "not yet" spiritualized, goes a deeper version, which denies that sin is either

an accident or a surface fault, and avers with emphasis that
sin is a profound disturbance of " human nature ", a
complete incapacity for doing good which can only be
cured by redemption, an abnormality and deformation
on which all evil follows as its penalty.

It can be seen that Schleiermacher will find it hard to
reconcile belief in the grim reality of sin with his initial
assertion of an all-embracing Divine causality. In point
of fact, he vacillates between the positions that sin is
non-existent for God and that it is caused by Him. It
is caused by Him in so far as it arises inevitably from the
conditions of human life, which are themselves ordained
by God. The charge of inconsistency often made against
Schleiermacher at this point on the ground that he regards
sin as both necessary (in itself) and avoidable (for our
minds) might seem to have less weight for this reason,
that a kindred antinomy is to be found in the teaching of
St. Paul and the Reformers, for whom sin plainly exhibits
two aspects which our thought is unable transparently to
combine : as springing from original sin it is unavoidably
present in the individual life, yet no less unavoidably we
judge ourselves responsible for it. But what Schleiermacher totally ignores is the fact that sin is rebellion
against the Divine will. On the other hand it can be
viewed as non-existent for God. As his theory has been
admirably summarized, " in order to spur us on to the
pursuit of the good, God works the sense of sin or guilt in
us, although for Him there is really no such thing as sin
or guilt ".[1] The internal strife of which we are perpetually
conscious, and which is necessitated by our history, we
interpret strictly as sin and therefore as if it were of infinite
gravity in God's sight ; from the Divine point of view,
however, it is nothing of that kind, but only the transient
imperfection of something which as yet has not fully
attained its goal. And God cannot be the author of that

[1] Dickie, *The Organism of Christian Truth*, p. 157.

which for Him is devoid of ultimate reality. This tiresome and perverse habit of recurring at irregular intervals to a merely subjective standpoint ; this tendency to represent faith as affirming this or that " as if " it were so, whereas in fact it is not so at all, is specially objectionable in a writer who claims to be reading the truth straight off the Christian mind. If there be anything of which believing men are more certain than another it is that sin *is* sin, with all its damning guilt upon it, precisely as it appears to the eyes of God. Indeed, the meaning of sin cannot be fully known until, led by Jesus, we are brought to see it, as He sees it, with God's mind, and to feel concerning it with God's heart. " Against Thee, Thee only, have I sinned " is the last and deepest word of confession.

But Schleiermacher served theology well in calling attention freshly to the significance of sin in its corporate or social character. He is unquestionably wrong in his endeavour to substitute this for the older doctrine of Original Sin, yet the force with which he insists on the joint sin of the whole race, as a guilty context in which we all come, is most impressive. Sin is at once individual and organic ; it is, as he puts it in a memorable dictum, " in each the work of all, and in all the work of each ". The generations are linked up together by sinful solidarity ; sin is stored or funded in humanity, and kept in circulation by social influence. It is an idea which later told strongly on Ritschl's thought, and its importance for Christian Ethics is obvious.

(*c*) In his Christology more clearly perhaps than elsewhere we see how persistently Schleiermacher strove to escape from the region of abstract ideas into that of verifiable fact. His view of Christ was in opposition both to the purely rational (and often pedestrian) constructions offered by thinkers of the Enlightenment, and to the timeless universal notions out of which Idealism wove the meaning of the world. Speculation had come to hide the actual

Jesus from men ; but now Schleiermacher led the Church
to consider afresh what our Lord was and is to His people.
He made it plain that Christ is the integrating factor in
Christianity. " The God-consciousness, already present
in human nature, though feeble and repressed, becomes
stimulated and made dominant by the entrance of the
living influence of Christ." [1] Thus, though it may be
haltingly, he took the first steps towards a more devout and
religious interpretation of the older dogma. If his conception of God lacked the Biblical notes of holiness and
majesty, and in particular those aspects which form the
background of Divine personal relationships with men, he
indemnified himself, so to say, for this by the special
warmth and intimacy of what he taught concerning Christ.
The Moravian heritage was still unspent. [2] It is hardly
too much to say that, so far as piety is concerned, Christ
for him took the place of God.

He follows what may be called an inductive method.
Within the Church is found, he argues, a specific modification of our human self-consciousness—the experience of
redemption which consists in a gradual liberation of the
sense of God from oppressions of the fleshly mind. That
experience is due to Christ. He is its source because in
Him personally the God-consciousness was present in
triumphant power, and by conveying to us the same
victorious predominance of the God-consciousness, by
taking us up into a share of that which He Himself thus
enjoys, He constitutes Himself our Saviour. In Him there
dwelt the powers of the Divine life with an elemental force
and purity which place Him on the Divine side of reality.
He is the Second Adam, of whom we have no option but
to say that the absolute potency of His God-consciousness

---

[1] *The Christian Faith*, p. 476.

[2] In his warm love for Jesus, Schleiermacher never ceased to be
a Moravian. But, as may be seen from his Life of Jesus, his
conceptions of our Lord are often more imaginative than historical.

is " a veritable existence of God in Him ".   As he puts
it in a sermon, the believer comes to perceive that the
effect produced by the Lord in his soul could not flow from
any less exalted power than that of the fulness of Godhead
present within His life.   There has been a creative inrush
from the fount of being.   Much is made of Jesus' unique
originality.   In one set of passages (there are others of
a different tenor) it is contended that to derive Christ
from the resident forces of humanity is impossible, because
in Him the energies of a new type of Life have broken
through in perfect form.   In His sinless perfection He is
not merely the *Vorbild* but the *Urbild* or Archetype ; and
by this last, the most significant of all Schleiermacher's
terms, is meant that Christ is a Pattern, but in addition
a Pattern charged with assimilative power ; not merely
the model on which the redeemed life is to be formed, but
the Person who can and will so form it.   In the corporate
life which derives from Him, He effects redemption by
communicating to man His own sinless perfection.   His life
was human, but that which made it personal was divine.
He comes by creative act of God, even though (to placate
the idealist within him) it is immediately added that this
involves no real breach in the continuous and uniform
historical development.   All that was ideal in Him was
historical too, all the historical was ideal.   Schleiermacher
was perhaps the first definitely to argue that even so
Christ's Resurrection, Ascension and Return have no vital
connexion with the doctrine of His Person.   He gives up
the idea of pre-existence as though unconscious of its
religious value ;   in a sense he gives up the continued
activity of the exalted Lord, though indeed this last point
can only be made with careful reservations.   Thus he
strongly affirms what can only be described as a " mystical
union " between Christ and believers.   By this he at least
implies that the Image or Picture of Jesus (very obscurely
related, it must be said, to Himself) lives on in the Church,

to pervade and redeem individual souls. Now and then it looks as if his denial of our Lord's living and ruling presence cannot have been meant quite seriously, though at other times he appears to conceive Him as having merely given the first impulse to a religious movement. In that case, Christ can only be present now as a memory. Yet the idea of vital fellowship with Christ is the very pivot round which his thought of redemption turns. However we may question details, he is ordinarily doing his utmost to give Jesus Christ a decisive place in the relations of man with God.

Heim has pointed out that Schleiermacher's attempt to use the contrasted terms " active " and " passive ", in a psychological reference, to express the relation between the Deity in Christ and His empirical finitude, is no more successful than other efforts of approximately the same type. The being of God in Christ—i.e. the absolute and unbroken plenitude of His God-consciousness—is represented as the element which is exclusively active or self-communicating, the human nature being wholly passive. He reminds us that, on Schleiermacher's own assumptions, passivity always involves some faint degree of resistance ; indeed, to *be* passive consists in having this resistance overcome. Yet the *absolute* strength of the God-consciousness, it is plain, could not co-exist with any measure of such inward antagonism, however small.

It might have been supposed that Schleiermacher's view of sin, as an inevitable factor in man's development, racial or individual, would have endangered belief in the sinlessness of Jesus. So far from that, the doctrine is one which he selects for exceptionally cordial treatment. Jesus' moral spotlessness is the certainty or postulate of faith on which his Christology is built up. If we ask : How must Jesus Christ be conceived in order to explain the Christian life ? His sinless perfection stands out as the first and basal part of the answer. That perfection is a miracle,

certainly, in the sense that no other similar fact has
occurred in history ; it is not, however, an absolute breach
of man's normal development, for sin is no part of essential
humanity.   Rather it must be considered the crown and
completion of the Divine purpose in creation.   " Christ
must have entered into the corporate life of sinfulness,
but He cannot have come out of it, but must be recognized
in it as a miraculous fact."   His perfection had its sufficient
ground, not in any outward circumstance, but within His
personality itself.   " From the beginning," Schleiermacher
writes, " He must have been free from every influence
derived from earlier generations which disseminated sin
and disturbed the God-consciousness."   As sinlessly perfect, He was also inerrant.   " Christ can neither have
originated real error Himself, nor even have accepted the
error of others with real conviction ; " nor are we necessarily led to confine this inerrancy to the sphere of His
special vocation as Saviour.   " No possible advance within
the Christian Church can ever bring us to the point of
perceiving anything imperfect in the teaching of Christ,
for which we could substitute something better."   The
higher culture of His nation and His age left no trace on
Him.   Moving thus steadily on the lines of the Fourth
Gospel, Schleiermacher dwells not so much on the development of Jesus as on His power at every stage to communicate to others the Life made manifest in Him.   It is by
passing into us His own sinless perfection that He redeems
us, we renouncing all self-activity and yielding ourselves
utterly to the impression and influence of His Person.

The warmth and unreserved adoration of this witness
to Christ is deeply moving.   Yet at one point Schleiermacher comes very near to Docetism, and casts a shadow
on Christ's true humanity.   Not merely does he depict
Jesus as superior to emotion ; he expressly denies the
reality of His temptations and holds with decision that
His moral experience was totally devoid of the element of

struggle. As God stands above the differences of the
world, untouched by any, so Jesus stood unmoved above
the conflicts of the human soul. It is no accident that
the word " temptation " occurs but once in the *Dogmatic*,
and that Schleiermacher professes himself unable to find
either historical or psychological verisimilitude in the
story of the Temptation in the Wilderness. This is to
make an imaginary Christ, in a vain effort to be wiser
than the New Testament. We are left with a Figure in
whom we can recognize no more than " the natural predominance of a higher principle " ; for a Christ from whose
experience even the minimum of moral struggle has been
excluded ceases to be our Brother and Comrade in temptation, our Surety and Captain in triumph.

The impression is all but unavoidable that eventually
Schleiermacher puts " archetypal humanity " rather than
the personal Incarnation of God at the centre of his view
of Christ. We shall search his *Dogmatic* in vain for the
truth that in the coming of Christ, in the simple fact of
His being here, God Himself stooped down to save us.[1]
For him Christ is a fact that, as it were, wells up inevitably
from the fountain or reservoir of being, and, once the
earthly years are past, retains contact with His Church
only as an " Image " or " Picture " that sustains and
propagates the common spirit of the Church. What the
New Testament reveals, in its thought of our Lord, is a
vast movement from God to God, like the arm of a parabola
sweeping in from incomprehensible distances, then, after
its point of proximity, travelling off once more into
infinitude—but an infinitude which, like that of God
Himself, is both ineffably distant and ineffably close at
hand.

[1] Herrmann of Marburg once said to me : " I regard myself as
infinitely nearer to Nicaea than either Schleiermacher or Ritschl.
They put Christ alongside of God, and argued from one to the
other ; in Christ I find God *personally present*."

Schleiermacher's teaching on the Work of Christ is opaque at many points, though by making an effort we can seize its central principles. The traditional doctrine, according to which our Lord bore the punishment of sinners as their substitute, is rejected, but in its place is set something entirely positive. It might be said of him, as of F. D. Maurice, that he has a bias against all existing forms of opinion ; but let him construct the doctrine for himself, and it will not be so very unlike the original one. So, when he comes to speak of Christ's special relation to us, he insists urgently on its two-sided uniqueness : " As the perfect man, as it were the representative and recapitulation of the race, He suffered with us and for us the consequences of our sins." Yet this suffering, forming as it does an essential part of obedience, must not be called a propitiating of God ; it rather was a means by which the human conscience makes atonement, by dying to sin and attaining in Christ a new life. As Saviour, our Lord has on men two kinds of effect. In the first place, He takes up the sinful into the power of His God-consciousness, sharing with them its triumphant energies ; this is His redeeming work. Thereby, secondly, He takes them up into the fellowship of His blessedness, so freeing them from the unblest load of estrangement and guilt : this is His work of reconciliation. Let us note, as more than an odd feature in terminology, that here the word Reconciliation is used not (as in the New Testament) for something done by God, but for a process in the human soul.

One evidence of Schleiermacher's desire to keep in as close contact with Biblical thought as possible, is the fact that in the event his view of atonement recurs to, and rests upon, the great Pauline conception of Union with Christ. " To be assumed," are his words, " into living fellowship with Christ, when regarded as a changed relation of the man to God, is justification." It was sympathy that moved Christ to take our part and make Himself one

with us. As he elaborates this point, his argument takes
on an ever more deeply positive tone.

Christ, as High Priest, draws us into His fellowship by His
sympathy with us—that sympathy by which He feels our sin
and its wretchedness, while allowing its power to break upon
Himself. This high-priestly love of His, endowed with such
attractive power, is matter of delight to God ; and since God
now beholds us in this union with Christ, a union established
by faith on our part, Christ's person renders us objects of the
divine delight, and presents us pure before God. God has
determined to let all salvation flow to us through Christ's
mediation, and looks upon us in Christ, who therefore is our
substitute.[1]

The point at which his doctrine falls short is its failure to
relate the atonement worthily to the great Biblical ideas
of Divine righteousness and human guilt. He has nothing
to say about the perfect sacrifice which Christ both made
to God and made for men on God's behalf. " Christ, who
through eternal Spirit offered Himself without spot to
God "—not even this perfectly filial oblation of self, a
sacrifice in which by faith we can partake, is admissible in
a system like that of Schleiermacher. His depersonalized
concept of God forbids it ; for, as Denney has said, " there
is as much of Spinoza in his intellectual atmosphere as of
Paul or John, and in his moral atmosphere there is more ".

(d) Nothing betrays a man's genuine standpoint in
theology more unerringly than his view of Prayer. Here
the pantheistic flavour which had always clung to Schleiermacher's idea of God is strongly in evidence and gives its
predominant character to the whole. The definition from
which he starts is meagre and unpromising. Prayer is
the sense of need put in relation to our consciousness of
God and directed towards the future. Not merely is the

---

[1] This is from Dorner, whose three pages on Schleiermacher's
teaching as to Reconciliation (*System of Christian Doctrine*, Vol. IV,
pp. 51–4) have a lucidity and grasp rarely to be found in discussions of the subject.

notion of our influencing God rejected firmly, on the familiar ground that there can be no interaction between creature and Creator; the writer keeps silence even on the cardinal subject of communion with the Father. Our only permissible attitude before the Most High is either gratitude or resignation. Gratitude for past bestowals there may be, and simple acceptance of all that is appointed us; but the Church must put no petitions in her prayers. We cannot say that things took place because we prayed about them. To God our prayer can never be a condition of His own Divine action. He would be a bold man who maintained that the total impression we gain from this account of things is in harmony with the teaching of the New Testament. When petitionary prayer dies out of the Christian mind, its place taken by meditation, men shut their eyes to the fact that the believer is called to hold converse with the Father, and that this converse is a reality not for man merely but for God Himself. The background of prayer has now become a conception which submerges the spirit of man in the eternal and unmoving World-Spirit.

Schleiermacher is perfectly aware that the Church disagrees with him; but, with what we may perhaps call a certain lack of humour, he rejoins that for him to grant that God may be acted upon by prayer in any conceivable sense would be treachery to his first principles of thought. Such an admission, however, actually intensifies our feeling of grievance, for we had understood him to be reporting on the Christian mind, not refuting one of its convictions. It hardly needs saying that Schleiermacher's view of prayer has no foundation in the teaching of Christ. Our Lord offered prayers which cannot be described as prayers of either pure gratitude or pure resignation; if language has a meaning, they were petitions in which definite things were asked from God. The apostles, taught by Him, did the same; faith indeed always does so by instinct when it is childlike and has not been put off by sophistication. It will not sin by dictating to the Father ; to every prayer it will add, " Thy will, not mine, be done " ; none the less it will utter all that is in its heart, of wish as of thankfulness, leaving the issue to God alone.   This is a point in personal religion at which the modern mind, only too faithful to Schleiermacher's lead, has been scared into dumb and sad acquiescence by a purely gratuitous dogma about " the inflexible laws of nature ".   It will only breathe freely once more when it has regained contact with Jesus' thought of the living God.

§ 4. SCHLEIERMACHER'S THEOLOGY IN ITS STRENGTH AND WEAKNESS

It remains to ask how far the great thinker [1] has built his system of doctrine on truly Christian lines.   The question has of late been raised in a specially urgent form. And most fair judges, I think, will own it is a question which Schleiermacher's fatal turn for ambiguity makes it difficult to answer.

We have seen how Schleiermacher's failure to take Revelation seriously creates all kinds of perplexity for the student of his system, and gives rise to the natural accusation that for him theology is less concerned with God than with man's consciousness of God.   The shadow of what is known as " psychologism " lies over all his work, in spite of his frequent efforts to escape from it.   Had he been told that by declared intention his *Dogmatic* was no more than a systematic exploration of the contents of the Christian soul, followed at each point by an inferential

---

[1] More perhaps than any eminent theologian in his century he stood alone.   He cannot be said to have founded a school—if the term " school " is interpreted in its usual sense to denote a number of independent thinkers who, nevertheless, maintain in common a set of important and distinctive conclusions.

advance from these contents to their correlative divine object, he could have pointed, I dare say, with some indignation to numerous passages of an opposite tenor. And beyond all doubt, by " feeling " he does often mean that the Divine Presence is an immediately known reality— a constraining Fact given directly to emotional intuition. So far as conscious purpose goes, accordingly, we must acquit him of any wish to proclaim a religion without an object. The trouble is that critics are in a position to quote no less freely on the other side. On page after page of his main work, his regular method is to proceed by introspection rather than listen to the voice of God speaking in His Word. And thus the crucial question : Is feeling for him merely a subjective state, or is it the emotionally coloured apprehension normally called faith, grasping a self-revealed God ? cannot be answered with any real degree of assurance. To the end his language is equivocal.

It is of course true that in his later work he staked everything on the Person of Jesus, and that at this stage it would be unjust to say that he had placed the foundation for the believing knowledge of God *in* man rather than above and beyond man. Jesus, in his view, is the Divine centre or reservoir of power which can rouse and vivify the God-consciousness already present. This, possessing as it does definite points of contact with the Fourth Gospel, is a view which cannot be denied offhand the right to call itself Christian. The historical Jesus, as the believer knows, is the Bearer of redeeming energies, conveyed to us by influences which are more than purely human and historical. It has been urged that Schleiermacher drives the idea of continuous development so hard as to leave no place for the redemption of the single life through its personal relation to God ; or again, that on his proposed terms the saving influence of Christ is bound to diminish as the centuries pass ; or yet once more, that in the mediating function he ascribes to the Church, his thought betrays more than a touch of Romanism. And doubtless to all these criticisms he would have returned the compendious reply that, as he puts it at the outset of his interpretation of Christ, " every increase in the activity of the God-consciousness within the Christian fellowship proceeds, not from any newly added power, but always and only from an ever-active susceptibility to His influence ". [1]

To other charges, however, it would have been greatly more difficult to find an answer. He has not much to say about the forgiveness of sins. For him the problem of guilt is virtually non-existent. He knew little or nothing of the religious struggle of St. Paul, St. Augustine, or Luther. The felt wrath of God seems in his view to have been an obscure illusion, cherished only at a stage when " the Deity is still thought of as susceptible to irritation, and as not above feeling an injury ".[2] Broadly, he ignores the " law " in its profound New Testament sense. Justification in his eyes becomes a name merely for the subjective echo within us of the beginnings of redemption ; it is the regenerative change we can detect in ourselves as due to the impartation of Christ's own God-consciousness. The apostles could find no words by which to describe the joy unspeakable and full of glory evoked by the Gospel of Divine mercy to sinners ; everything for them rested on, and revolved round, a message of free grace from which, guilty though they were, they derived a new and vital confidence before God. This central Biblical truth Schleiermacher for the most part passes by in silence, or mentions only in a perfunctory fashion that shows how little he understands it ; and in a Christian thinker this may well be thought the unpardonable sin.

[1] *The Christian Faith*, p. 377.
[2] Dr. Flew has said of Schleiermacher with point that " when he treats of human nature, the contrast between God and man is that of power and weakness, wisdom and ignorance, rather than that of holiness and impurity " (*Idea of Perfection in Christian Theology*, p. 369).

With some care we may unearth the secret of his failure
at this point. When all is said, it lies in his governing
view of the God-consciousness in man, which for him
forms the vital core of all religion and therefore of Christianity as the redemptive religion *par excellence*. His argument comes to this, that within the Christian fellowship
this universal God-consciousness is liberated in a unique
degree by Jesus, who Himself possessed it absolutely ; and
His liberating power lasts on in the Church, the vehicle of
His Spirit. Under these conditions, the human sense of
God evolves in an endless movement, alike in individual
and in corporate life, advancing to ever larger measures
of stability and clearness. But are we not to have
explained more lucidly what this " God-consciousness "
really is ? Why does he put it in place of the Biblical
thought of man's relation to God ? Or again, accepting
the term for the moment, is not the believer's God-consciousness characterized, in virtue of his God-given faith,
by a quality of its own ? No, we must reply, it is not and
cannot be ; for, as we have seen, in the light of Schleiermacher's general argument the pressure of God upon the
human spirit must be regarded as wholly uniform and, in
strictness, undistinguishing. No other inference can be
drawn from his fundamental idea of the Divine nature.
It is true that in his dispersed treatment of the attributes
of God, the writer has much that is important to say concerning the grace and goodness, the holiness and justice,
the love and wisdom we must predicate of the Most High.
Near the close, indeed, he goes so far as to say that Love
alone can be considered the essential Divine attribute.
But on looking closer we find that by " God " he means
simply the living Source or Fountain of all things whatsoever—of the world and its multifarious contents, of all
spiritual realities and activities, and, *inter alia*, of religious
or believing life. Hence, while in comprehensive phrase
he insists that Love is the attribute in virtue of which

Divine Life or Being flows out upon the world, this cannot be taken as meaning anything more than that Love is our selected symbolic name for the impact of the Divine Cause on our lives at its highest intensity. Not only so ; we are at the same time obliged to recognize that, just like the other attributes, even Love indicates nothing distinctive or specific in God. This is meagre fare for men who have to live in a world of sin and grief, and whose minds by presentiment cry out for something like the New Testament message of the sacrificial love of God in Christ. Further, the account Schleiermacher gives of man's love to God partakes of the same inadequacy. In the last resort, we can render to the great source of all no more than the speculative love of the essential mystic.

And thus we come upon the gravest defect in Schleiermacher's theology as a whole. *Childlike trust in God the Father*—this is a note he seems curiously unwilling or unable to strike. One may read him from end to end without encountering words that strongly recall the Lord's Prayer or the eighth chapter of Romans—words full, I mean, of the unreserved filial confidence towards the Father animated in the one case by Jesus' sense of His own unique relationship to God, in the other by the apostolic exultation in the Saviour's cross and resurrection. " Faith," Schleiermacher writes in a sentence which owes more to psychology than to the New Testament, " is nothing but the incipient experience of the satisfaction of our spiritual need by Christ." The saving faith which meant everything to the Reformers is barely mentioned. What we are shown, with the utmost technical skill and the most delicate mystical sympathy, is not the believer's personal confidence towards the God of our life and our salvation, but merely how man's eyes open to the uniform presence of the Infinite.

Schleiermacher, it has been said in words already quoted, " takes both sides on every question ". In his pages, side

by side, there are both riches and poverty. It cannot be
denied that at various points throughout his *Dogmatic*
the adumbrations are discoverable of an immensely more
Biblical and evangelical thought of God than that we have
just scrutinized. After all, it is to God we owe the unfolding of our spiritual life ; and in that context Schleiermacher
has much to say that is worth saying about His eternal
purpose to create, and to finish His creative work by
redemption. But to the end we ask ourselves in puzzled
fashion how the God set forth in *The Christian Faith*, with
its warmly coloured pictures of life in Christ, can at the
same time be defined as a merely universal and undiscriminating source of all. If life in Christ be His specific
gift, He from whom such a gift has come must surely,
somehow, resemble the Father of whom Jesus spoke His
eternal words and Who wills to be in fellowship with His
children. He must, in a real sense, not to be cancelled
and lost all over again by semi-pantheistic qualifications,
be intelligence and will—above all love in the profound
significance given to that word by the Bible. He must
be such that both joy and pain are predicable of Him
infinitely more truly than they can be denied of Him. But
all this would be a different religion from Schleiermacher's.
It would be a religion of deeper gladness because of deeper
fear and sorrow. It would not hesitate to utter the greatest
words of the New Testament, and it would look on through
the Son to the Father. In the Son, suffering for man's
sin and bearing the load of human sorrow, it would hear
God speaking to men His word of forgiveness and eternal
life, and calling them to repentance and faith. We should
then see Christ not merely as the Liberator of a God-
consciousness which remains qualitatively the same in man
at every stage, though exhibiting many different degrees
of clarity and scope. To put all in a word, Christ would
then be the Revealer of the Father, addressing to us the
word of Divine reconciliation through His life and teaching,

His bitter cross and passion, His creative and victorious resurrection from the dead.

It is only in a relative sense, therefore, that we can speak of the *Dogmatic* of Schleiermacher as an authentically Christian book. It prepares the way for something better than itself, something inspired by the New Testament, in so far as it attaches faith to the fruitful soil of history, makes the Person of Christ central and all-determining, and places the whole concept of salvation under the rubric of sin and grace. By this alone the author rises far above his contemporaries into the atmosphere of living piety. On the other hand, it would be roughly true to say that he has put discovery in place of revelation, the religious consciousness in the place of the Word of God, and the mere " not yet " of imperfection in the place of sin. Thus the gulf set between him and the Reformers is wide and deep. It is painful to watch this extraordinarily gifted man, who lacked nothing but a touch of childlike and unreserved trust in the Father, expound as the Christian view of salvation what too often is but the attenuated creed of idealistic Monism. We are passing out of his era, but for long his work will remain to bewilder and instruct the theologian. Generations will learn from it the technique of systematic thought. But more and more it will impress rather by its contrast than by its likeness to the faith of Prophets and Apostles.

IV

THE THEOLOGY OF SPECULATIVE RATIONALISM

HEGEL AND THE HEGELIANS

§ 1. HOW HEGEL THOUGHT OF CHRISTIANITY

THE GROUP or series of thinkers now to be studied forms, in certain ways, a strong contrast to Schleiermacher. He took position in experimental feeling, and at times went near to interpreting piety as no more than an emotional state of mind. They are members of the school of thought which in a broad sense may be described as speculative or metaphysical, and which owed its inspiration principally to Hegel. The contrast holds in some respects, yet by no means in all. There is indeed a large fragment of truth in the contention that, in their ultimate views of what religion is, Schleiermacher and Hegel were not far apart. Both represent a view of the world and of human life—briefly, the humanist and æsthetic—which Goethe had made exceptionally impressive ; and it is significant that in one of the best recent studies of their epoch, H. Groos's *Idealismus und Christentum*, Schleiermacher and Hegel are classed together. Goethe had clothed in poetic form what they elaborated more technically, Schleiermacher in terms of feeling, Hegel in those of pure thought. The idea of the totality of the conditions of experience, the *ens realissimum*, to which logic leads, took for both the form of a monistic principle, found by Hegel in the Infinite Spirit rising to consciousness in the finite, by Schleiermacher in the indifference-point of feeling, in which the antitheses of reason and nature are sublimated and overcome. For both the personality of God is wrapped in an uncertain mist and, in consequence, both exhibit a strong inclination or resolve to admit nothing that could properly be styled " supernatural ". We have seen that attachment to the person of Jesus came gradually to modify Schleiermacher's attitude to this problem, at least now and then; but the change is made reluctantly, with a backward longing glance at the logical symmetry of monism.

The two thinkers, contemporaries on the staff of the new Berlin University, looked upon each other with more than a little antipathy. Seldom have distinguished thinkers found it harder to appreciate each other's work. Hegel was the more apt of the two to give vent to his frank detestation of his colleague's intellectual principles, as when he declared that if the feeling of absolute dependence be the core of religion, then of all creatures the most religious is the dog, whose sense of dependence on his master is unqualified. Feeling, to Hegel, constituted the lowest stage or form of consciousness, not to be compared with the nobler power of reason. Above feeling, with its semi-animal confusion, he placed the spheres of imagination, understanding and reason, in that order; and, although each of these has a function of its own in religion, the proper seat of piety, where it is definitely to be localized, is the imagination. To think religiously is to think in pictures, and we may broadly define religion as, in essence, man's imaginative response to the Universe.

No one has ever been quite sure what Hegel believed about God, but we shall not be far out if we describe his general system as a form of pantheistic Monism or logical Evolutionism. When he speaks of the " unity " or " identity " of two things (" thing " being taken in the broadest sense), it is his characteristic way of asserting that between the two there obtains an essential relation, and that this would hold true even if in point of fact they were not actually in harmony with each other. And this must be allowed for in our exposition. Man, for him, is finite spirit ; as such, however, he is ultimately identical with infinite Spirit ; and perhaps from the standpoint of Christian faith the most sinister feature in the entire construction is the emphasis laid on this further point, that it is in the development of the finite mind that the Infinite and Absolute, or God, first rises to consciousness of self. "God," Hegel writes in words as plain as any, " is God only in so far as He knows Himself ; His self-knowledge is His self-consciousness in man, is the knowledge man has *of* God, which advances to man's self-knowledge *in* God." [1] Thus, it would appear, the Absolute has reality only in the thought of those who believe in Him. And history is now seen to be God's realization of Himself through, or in, the process of human experience. [2]

This of course is meant to be construed as the crowning example of the profoundly suggestive Hegelian principle of identity as mediated through difference. Thought, and being no less, is a dialectic process which moves forward by the development and reconciliation of opposites. There is a single principle, manifested in a succession of various and contrasted forms, each organic with its predecessor, and all contributing to the expression of the principle which gives unity to the whole series. If reality be a process of the sort designated " organic ", the process can only be adequately conceived as implying that at every point there emerges the opposite of the antecedent stage, followed by a higher union of the opposites in the next development. Thesis, antithesis, synthesis—these, Hegel argues, are the stages by which thought and being alike

---

[1] *Encyclopädie*, § 565.

[2] The idealism of Hegel being rigorously immanental, the Absolute mind is not *another* mind, but the essence of all finite minds, and they are constituents of it.

take their way onward or upward by a spiral progress, by
the alternate production and removal of contradictions.
The secret of the world is in the relations of Yes to No, and
then of both to Nevertheless. At each point reality makes
headway by evoking antagonism to its own imperfection,
then capturing this antagonism for a richer combination
inclusive of, and completing, both terms in the former
contrast. Each stage of the evolution, that is to say, is
accomplished in three successive moments which are
nothing but the three necessary operations of the thinking
mind ; the triple formula just indicated constitutes the
structure not of thought only, but of all life and history.
In this sense the famous aphorism holds true : " The
rational is the real, and the real is the rational."

The idea that opposites are really moments or constituents in a living process of thought, that negation,
followed by deeper affirmation, sounds the keynote of all
development, is the outcome of a profound analysis of the
mind's logical advance to the possession of truth. " We
are unwilling," writes Croce, " to recognize that opposition
or contradiction is not a defect, or a stain, or an evil in
things, which could be eliminated from them, far less
a subjective error of ours, but that it is indeed the true
being of things." But the principle surely is misused
when, as later by Hegel, it is applied not merely to human
attitudes or partial apprehensions, but to distinct orders
of reality, and even to the being of God Himself. Not
even the Absolute, on his showing, is a finished or irreducible fact complete from the beginning : He, or It,
likewise is the outcome of the unending forward movement
which has been mediated by the tension of contradictories ;
and Hegel claims to be able to detect even in the becoming
of God the presence of one-sided stages which await their
integration in the higher, unique truth. The world is
required to make God not less than God to make the world.
In this light religion itself shows as one logically essential

moment in the unfolding of the Absolute Spirit, for there
we see God returning to Himself after the self-externaliza-
tion in virtue of which the world came into being. Or, to
put it from the objective side and in terms of Trinitarian
dogma, as pure abstract idea God is Father; as going
forth eternally into finite being, the element of change
and variety, God is Son; as once more sublating or
cancelling this distinction, and turning again home enriched
by this outgoing in so-called self-manifestation or incarnation, God is Holy Spirit. Such a Trinity, clearly,
represents that which is in no sense eternal but only coming
to be; it has no meaning, or even existence, apart from
the finite world. It is a dialectical triad, not Father, Son
and Spirit in any sense in which Christian faith has ever
pronounced the three-fold Name.

Hegel finds no cause to deny that religion does make
a useful start with the work of reflection upon this mediated
unity of Infinite and finite. But the work is done most
imperfectly, for this reason, if no other, that the religious
mind invariably thinks in symbols, and, what is worse,
on principle, as it were, mixes up symbol and reality.
Hence when the understanding—which, as we have seen,
is the next higher stage of thought—begins its task of
corrosive analysis and criticism, exposing without fear or
favour the manifest inadequacy of the symbols faith has
called in aid, faith can make no convincing answer. At
this unhappy juncture, when religion is about to be dismissed as an illusion once for all discredited in the forum
of rational scrutiny, Hegel comes forward as its apologist.
But he insists that effectual help can be given only if
religion will consent to have its beliefs transposed, so to
say, into the key of metaphysics. Give the symbols of
the religious man a philosophical form, render them into
speculative terms which will bear the tests of the higher
reason, and all that has value may yet be saved from the
wreck. Philosophy alone, not religion, can pierce to the

truth concerning God, and of man's relation to Him, by which is meant their unity in the Idea grasped by speculation.   It comes then to this, that the believer must take up the rôle of metaphysician, if, in the court of philosophy, he is to make out a rightful claim to his faith.   And with some goodwill the thing can be done.   Once he has left the world of symbols behind and has learnt to breathe the ampler air of speculative thought, he will have cleared his mind of those inevitable contradictions in which faith becomes entangled by its hard-and-fast distinction between God and man.   Philosophy moves at a height where that difference, not inconsiderable in itself, is lost in identity. After removing the crudities of naïve religion, it is able to utilize all that is worth its place, to construct a satisfying metaphysical view of the world.

At first glance it is perhaps surprising that this Hegelian programme for an *entente cordiale* between faith and philosophy should have excited so much resentment in Christian quarters.   Nothing can be more certain than that Hegel meant to be friendly ;   indeed he appears to have been quite sincerely persuaded that for the first time he was giving the Christian religion an opportunity to understand itself.[1]   Reconciliation was to be the watchword of the new era.   The truth formulated by speculation is actually none other than that preached by religion in more childlike tones.   The difference, which of course does not wholly vanish, between the philosopher and the simple Christian has nothing to do with the essential content of the truth they are both concerned with.   The part played by the philosopher is after all that of a translator ;   he does little more than replace the language of the chapel and the heart by that of the lecture-room.   To

---

[1] Church scholars, deeply influenced by Hegel, tended to regard the history of Dogma as representing the necessary, immanent and ideal self-unfolding of the content of faith.   This general view was shown to be untenable, first by Ritschl, and then on a larger scale by Harnack, his famous disciple.

sensitive faith it might seem as if this process of philosophical restatement must jeopardize the Gospel. But
that is to misapprehend. There is quite as much truth
at the end of the operation as at the beginning. Could
there be a greater service to faith than to exhibit its
essential rationality, to prove it something that *must* be
and must be what it is ? In the closing words of his
Philosophy of Religion Hegel declares : " These lectures
have had as their aim to reconcile reason with religion,
and to interpret religion in its manifold forms as necessary."
Faith possesses the right content ; it has still to be given
the right form of thought.

On these terms, Hegel proposed to maintain relations
of the most amicable kind with the Christian creed. The
orthodoxies of tradition—themselves the product of an
immanent unfolding of the content of faith—were all of
them amenable to treatment. The path of accommodation,
long sought in vain, had now been found ; and following
it, Hegel saw his way to put such an interpretation on
doctrines like the Divinity of Christ. or the Atonement,
as would guarantee their truth by giving them a significant
place in the speculative system. A modern thinker like
Karl Heim employs philosophy to serve the interests of
faith indirectly ; he undertakes to bring the philosophical
discussion to such a point that the philosopher has no
option but to confess that the severest tests of thought
leave the door open to the revelation announced in the
Gospel. The enigmas of the metaphysician are insoluble
except as solved by the fact of Christ. Faith has its path
cleared for it by philosophy, then moves forward guided
by its own impulse. But to Hegel philosophy is the
supreme court of appeal,[1] and faith, to be justified in its

[1] On this Feuerbach appositely remarks that according to
Hegel's argument " speculation only lets religion say what speculation itself has thought and said much better ; it determines
religion without itself being determined by religion ".

claims to real truth, must obtain a certificate of competence from the speculative examiner, whose verdict is final.

It is true, Christian doctrine has a price to pay for any such philosophical certificate. Thus no more must be heard regarding the uniqueness of the historical Christ, or the once-for-all character of His mediation ; that too is a symbol or earthen vessel enshrining a grand metaphysical idea.[1] The doctrine of the God-man is a picture, and a sublime one, by means of which human thought has in the past been enabled to rise to, and grasp, the ultimate truth that Divinity and Humanity are one in essence, that the life of man is the life of God in temporal form, and that the two natures, the Divine and human, can only realize themselves through vital unity with each other. In like manner, the death, resurrection and exaltation of Christ are noble imaginative presentations of ideas to which philosophy must ever attach a high importance. They are, so to speak, parabolic statements of the fact that finite man, construed merely as finite, is inevitably the prey of negation and decay ; yet view him in the light of his unity with the Infinite, and straightway he rises and mounts to a lofty and positive participation in the pantheistic world-process. Thus the story of man is the history of God's becoming, the self-evolution of Absolute Reason spelling itself out in the medium of space and time. In this sense, but no other, the Word took flesh and dwelt among us.

It might be thought that Hegel was showing a real willingness to meet Christian faith half-way when he conceded even so much importance as he does to actual history. By taking history as the *locus* of Divine self-manifestation, and refusing to interpret the Eternal in purely conceptual and *a priori* modes, does he not point to concrete events as the medium wherein the traces of Divine Spirit may

[1] See Künneth, *Antwort auf den Mythus*, pp. 30 f.

be read ?   So it might appear ; yet the truth still remains
unaffected that no one event of history is of more value
than any other.   Take the cross-section of past happenings
where you please, and it will be found by the perceptive
mind to reveal the universal meaning or pattern of rational
being.   Each part of history tells the same story, as each
uniform leaf betrays the nature of the tree.   Hence no
event may claim unique significance, nor can faith rightly
profess to see one majestic Divine purpose guiding all
to a sovereign consummation.[1]   All historical facts are
but transient individualizations of an eternal and unchanging content ; it follows that as the humorous poet explains,
" Where everyone is somebody, there no one's anybody ".
Dogma is to be replaced by myth, the personification of
a universal idea.

It would be unfair to say that in this scheme Jesus
Christ is deprived of all reality or meaning.   He would at
all events find a place in Hegel's theory of the " great men "
who represent critical turning-points in the world's progress
and by their mysterious originality inaugurate new epochs.
Jesus was the first to catch sight of a vast speculative
truth.   Though not the God-man, He perceived that God
and man are one.   Yet the general trend of Hegel's argument is sufficiently indicated by the fact that the name
of Christ is not mentioned until the speculative treatment
of reconciliation between God and man has been given
in full, while the name of Jesus is never used at all.   Hegel
is convinced that by the higher logic in its pure form it
can be proved that in the course of history a point exists
at which the idea of the God-man necessarily arises in the
human mind, and that this point corresponds exactly with
the appearance of Christianity.   Yet while urging that

[1] Cf. Brunner, *The Mediator*, p. 36 : " To him history is merely
a picture-book, whose text he knows without the aid of the pictures ; to him it means the Idea made concrete, hence there is
nothing decisive about it.   In its absolute and serious sense, there
is no room here for the category of uniqueness."

everything affirmed in the Church catechism about Christ
fits perfectly into the system of autocratic and creative
reason, with its æsthetic powers of unification, Hegel
silently treats Jesus as, in the last resort, irrelevant.
Christianity obtains rank as the absolute faith, but at
the cost of its bond with history.[1] To quote his own
unequivocal words : " Christology affirms simply that God
comes to be Spirit, and this can take place only in finite
spirit, in man ; in whom there arises the consciousness of
the Absolute, and who then is likewise the Absolute's
consciousness of itself." He is interested in the God-man
solely as a logical construction, not as a living Person.

It is fatally clear that Hegel's mind was completely out
of touch with Old Testament religion. In the age-long
controversy between the Hebrew spirit and the Greek, his
sympathies lay wholly on the side of Hellenism. Time,
for him, had nothing in common with that which it signified
for the Hebrew prophets, to whom God was not " Pure
Being " but free and creative Personality. He could not
away with the idea that events may occur which have it
in them to change and reshape the future of a people or
even of all mankind. Time for the Greek intelligence and
for Hegel is circular in movement, and therefore subject
to logical prediction ; for prophets and apostles, time
receives its direction and content ever anew from the
living God. It is natural that Gnostics of every kind
should have felt the Old Testament to be an incubus.
The speculative conviction of the ultimate non-reality of
time goes to destroy the ethical worth of life, since change
from evil to good is only in appearance. And where
religion is conceived in terms of knowledge as a logical
function, not of faith, the gates of hope have been shut
against the generality of mankind. How thin and external

---

[1] This is in line with Fichte's well-known dictum, in which a
type of theology is concentrated : " The metaphysical only, and
not the historical, can give us blessedness."

many of Hegel's religious interpretations appear on a second reading ! This prescribed and rigid Monism has no place for the sense of God's " otherness ", the ineffably intimate relationship of children to a Father, the consciousness of guilt, or the need for humility and discipline. Why, on its terms, should the words ever have been spoken : " I thank Thee, O Father, Lord of heaven and earth, because Thou hast hid these things from the wise and prudent, and hast revealed them unto babes " ?

Great expectations were sincerely cherished by many of its adherents concerning the work of rehabilitation which Hegelianism was about to do for theology and the Church. Some of the master's leading disciples took it as their life-work to develop and fortify his philosophical system. Intellectually they were content to be lost in him. In their judgment he could have no real successor, and his philosophical empire would shortly be recognized as universal and permanent.

It was small marvel [writes Fairbairn] that the theologians were grateful for ideas which so vivified theology. They were delighted to discover that doctrines translated into the language of the notion became high philosophical truths. . . . God became the essence of man, man the actuality of God. Theology was happy at the supreme good fortune that had come to her, her ability to speak in her own tongue the very identical thoughts of her old enemy. A beautiful and hopeful day of peace had dawned on the field of ancient strife.

The event proved to be far otherwise. Not that Hegel had not won for himself a niche in the temple of philosophic fame : men could not forget how, with noble passion, he had gone, in Marlowe's words, " still climbing after knowledge infinite ". But truth can never become the monopoly of a single intelligence, however profound ; and a system may be all too perfect for our mortal span. The rise of exact science proved fatal to many of Hegel's *a priori* constructions, and forty years after his death to be known in Germany as a Hegelian counted as a professional reproach. But the tide, which had ebbed so rapidly, was certain to flow again. There could be nothing surprising in a renascence of Hegelianism of which the first signs were visible even before the War. Theology has an interest here, in two respects.

In the first place, the Hegelian defence of a spiritual interpretation of the world contains some elements which, at least indirectly, will always possess a high value. The idealistic argument which in a large degree he inspired has gone to supply the critics of materialism with some of their most effective weapons, and in every age the refutation of materialism is a task to which the philosophical theologian will continue to be called. Idealists have stressed the decisive fact that thought is the *prius* of all experience, even of those aspects of it which materialism has isolated artificially and then used with short-sighted triumph to explain the mind. They have been foremost in pointing out that far from being, as has often been supposed, a peculiarly simple and satisfactory account of things, materialism is in fact an elaborate fallacy. It carefully misses the point. What it does is to take the emptiest and least familiar concept we possess—that of bare unqualified matter, or, in the language of the latest or nearly the latest physical science, " specks of electrified ether ", than which nothing could be more unlike real experience—and make this not merely the basis but the staple of a universal metaphysical theory, professing thereby to explain *inter alia* history, science, morality, religion. Everything comes out of next to nothing. This effort to make matter not only independent of mind, but mind's creator, seems unlikely to commend itself to distinguished modern workers in the scientific field. Sir Arthur Eddington, to take an eminent example, declared the other day that " the external world of physics is in the first place approached by way of con-

sciousness, it derives actuality and value from consciousness, and it relates itself only to certain aspects of the
common basis of material and spiritual things ".   What is
of most importance philosophically in a statement of this
character—the insight, namely, that mind and matter
cannot be expressed in terms of each other—goes back to
the idealistic argument concerning knowledge, and was
given classic expression by Hegel himself.

Secondly, the Christological thought of the Church has
found a real stimulus to new activity in Hegel's insistence
on the truth that God and man are not wholly disparate
natures, each definable only by a series of attributes which
contradict each other point for point.   The great Biblical
dictum that man was made " in the image of God " signifies
at least that in the thought and purpose of God for him
man has affinity with his Creator in a sense and degree
that marks him off, decisively, from the animal creation.
The fact that God can *speak* to man means a kinship
between the Speaker and the spoken to.   God is a God
of order, not of confusion, and without putting other
than its own intrinsic limits to the divine omnipotence we
may ask whether certain dispositions or qualities must
not (in the Divine order) be presupposed in a creature who
is destined for fellowship with God.   As Professor A. E.
Taylor has put it :   " Is ' eternal life ', ' fruition of the
Godhead ', even a possible gift to a creature who has been
made in his own nature simply perishable ?   Might it
not, for example, transcend the power of Omnipotence to
bestow *that* gift on a cat or a magpie ? " [1]   Hegel raised
questions about Divinity and humanity, and their relation
to each other, which the Church felt bound to study afresh
in its efforts to construe the Person of Christ.   The union
of the two natures, it came to be felt, as by Dorner, involves
no ultimate contradiction.   " Rather," he writes, " have
they a direct reference to one another, even by virtue of

[1] *Hibbert Journal* for April, 1924, p. 662.

that which is distinctive in them, and an internal relation
to one another, the human because of its receptiveness and
need, the Divine because of the Divine love." [1] If this
be so, there is wonder, but no mere absurdity, in the fact
that God's perfect revelation of Himself should have been
vouchsafed through human personality.

Yet acknowledgment of the service done by Hegel in
canvassing certain problems in the relations of God and
man, compels us all the more to recoil from his ever-
recurring habit of identifying them.[2] Here we may choose
between two paths. We may seek God in man, as the
Reason within his reason, the Conscience within his conscience ; and by this road doubtless we shall reach some
truth. On the other hand, though mindful of the Divine
image in man, we may above all conceive God as the
eternal One over all, Whose being is totally other than
human. To use language which Otto has made familiar,
we face in true religion the *mysterium tremendum* of infinite
and transcendent Deity, in whose presence we go on our
knees. We become conscious of the unapproachable
holiness of God (on which Hegel has nothing to say), of
that unconditioned aversion on His part to sin which the
Bible calls His " wrath ", of that sovereign grace which
in pardon does not recognize but create the goodness of
its objects. This second aspect of the Divine being is for
faith the supreme one, and it is to this aspect, as it seems

---

[1] *System of Christian Doctrine*, Vol. III, p. 313.

[2] " It is the belief of Idealism that knowledge concerning God's
being and God's will is a part of my self-consciousness. I need
only plunge into the depths of my Self, and I am in God . . . But
this ardent longing cannot be fulfilled. Idealism awakens in us
the memory of a lost Paradise, within which, as we feel, we ought
to be had our original destiny been realized, but from which we
are now shut out. Idealism resembles the song of home sung by
Blondel outside the dungeon of Richard the Lion-hearted, to draw
the King to the window of his cell. But the only result is to
make the captive feel all the more bitterly how he is languishing
in prison far from home " (Karl Heim, *Jesus der Herr*, p. 82).

to me, that Hegel and his followers are blind.   Even in the
interest of philosophy they do wrong to overlook the fact
that God's thought is creative, man's only reflective ; and
eventually they turn human reason into part-creator of
the world.   What the Hegelian type of mind lacks in its
more characteristic moods is "the fear of the Lord".
Intellectually, it is on much too easy terms with the Divine.
This idealistic habit of identifying God with man, in
virtue of the creative Reason that constitutes the essence
of both, is opposed to Christian faith in this further respect,
that it bars the way to a true conception of " self " and
" neighbour " in their relations to each other.   If I am
merged ultimately in God, I am also merged in the mass
of those who to me are " others ".   As Brunner has pointed
out, " in Idealism, the ' Thou ' is in deepest essence the
same as the ' I ' ; therefore in the last resort responsibility
falls away ".[1]   We—my neighbour and I—do not confront
each other as individuals, but as " cases " or instances
of humanity.   Hegel has little that is rewarding to say
about fellowship, hence for him " love " can never possess
its full Christian meaning.

From this point of view also we can most convincingly
explain that tendency to minimize the fact of sin which
Hegelian thinkers never quite succeed in throwing off.
In a panlogical system there can be no confrontation of
the Holy God with the guilty creature.   While God and
world are not *simply* equated, and Spirit must first as it
were work itself through an element of obstruction, yet
the obstruction too partakes of logical necessity.   Spirit,
in order to find itself, must be alienated from itself.   In
consequence, Hegel can " place " sin so exactly that in
losing its irrationality it loses much more than half its evil.
He is clear that a continuous dialectical process can be
traced, leading from innocence to sin and from sin to virtue.
Sin is the necessary midway point between the two.

[1] *Das Gebot und die Ordnungen*, p. 665.

More precisely still, sin forms an essential ingredient in
virtue, for all virtue is built on transcended sin ; and what
has been transcended is in some sense retained. It is
not merely that sin *may* lead to increase of virtue, or that
virtue *may* be based on sin. Hegel's teaching is definitely
to the effect that sin *must* lead to virtue, and that there
is no virtue which is not based on sin.[1] Evil is that which
is on the way to good, raw material which is not yet Spirit.
But this deduction of sin, however dialectically entertain-
ing, is one more proof that moral evil forms the hard
pebble-stone on which, sooner or later, a purely speculative
system is obliged to break its teeth. What we start with
as evil, our own and utterly damning, finally emerges from
the process as good, with its own æsthetically justified place
in the scheme of things. Logic is used like a conjuror's
handkerchief, under cover of which, at a certain stage,
there is substituted for one object another that is totally
different in kind. I do not suppose that any expounder
of Absolute Idealism would claim that such a train of
sophisticated reflection has ever actually given comfort
to sinful man in the hour of penitence, or persuaded him
that his guilt had thereby been disposed of ; and indeed,
if Hegel is right, penitence would in any case be little
better than a waste of time. Yet, as we know with perfect
clarity when we face ourselves, sin is a grim and dreadful
fact. Explicable or not, it is there—ruinous, haunting,
accusing. And what Christianity takes as its task is not
to make sin luminous to our intelligence, but to bring us
to repent of it, owning it and then disowning it before God,
trusting Him to make an end of it and, through forgiveness,
mediated by Christ and specifically by His death, to
replace it by His own righteousness.

The Hegelian interpretation of the Christian religion
leaves us with a deeper conviction than ever of the impotence
of man to force his way through to the presence of God by

---

[1] See McTaggart's *Studies in the Hegelian Cosmology*, pp. 151 ff.

the power of speculative reason. No more than by the
ecstasy of mystic feeling, or the moralistic striving after
a self-engendered goodness, can we thus lift ourselves to
Him. If we are to approach, He must stretch forth His
hand and draw us near. If we are to know Him, with the
knowledge which is life eternal, He must speak His free
and gracious Word, and we must hear in faith.

§ 2. THE NEGATIVE DEVELOPMENT IN STRAUSS AND FEUERBACH

As happens in other movements, Hegelianism in theology
before long came to be represented by a left wing, a right
wing, and a mediating centre. The earliest thinkers of this
last type, such as Daub and Marheineke, were eager like
Hegel himself to raise faith to the higher plane of speculative comprehension, for to grasp reality is to master it—
even its contradictions and its evil—by logical insight. But
after they had proved it a necessity of reason that God
and man should unite somewhere within the process of
history, they found it oddly difficult to say why they
should have fixed upon Jesus Christ as the precise point
of union. It seems to be a pure accident, without relation
to what is known of Jesus personally. Nothing in the
Gospel portrait or story is exhibited as laden with the
Father's grace and truth. This means that the motives
which prompt faith spontaneously to assert the Divinity
of Christ have disappeared. There are points in Marheineke's argument where we can see that, at the end of
his metaphysical *détour*, he is trembling on the verge of a
rationalism as flat and unhistorical as that of the eighteenth
century. Thus he writes : " In the Ascension of the
Lord we are taught the truth that religion, which takes
its origin from God, has no abiding place on earth, but
necessarily and eternally returns whence it took its rise."
It could only be a question of time until some member

of the Hegelian group, more discerning than the rest, should speak out boldly and declare that this pretence of harmony between logical pantheism and the New Testament message must end. The decisive word came from Strauss.

David Friedrich Strauss (1808–74) is beyond all question a great writer ; no more effective German prose than his had appeared since Lessing. The problem round which his work principally circled is the significance of the historical Person of Jesus for the believer of to-day, in the last resort for the Christian Church. His famous *Life of Jesus*, issued in 1835 and translated into English by George Eliot, the novelist, marked an epoch in theology in the sense that for a generation theologians took sides about it. It disposed for good and all of the hallucination that Christian belief and consistent Hegelianism are two forms of the same thing. Strauss now made it his business to prove that the Gospel narratives are a collection of myths gradually formed in the earliest Christian communities, a wreath of adoration woven round the Master's head by worshipping fancy. Hegel, as we have seen, held that the believer operates with figurative conceptions, the philosopher with exact notions, supposing that thereby he had brought the two into perfect harmony ; Strauss for pictorial thinking put mythology, and so dug " the ugly ditch " between the two deeper than ever. Though claiming in all this to be devoid of prepossessions, he was in fact merely applying the principles of pantheistic monism to a problem which, at least in part, is historical. This made it easy for him to find the origins of Christianity not so much in a Person as in an Idea, or a group of ideas. As he puts it : " Every unhistorical narrative, whatever its origin, in which a religious body recognizes an element of its own sacred basis because an absolute expression of its constitutive feelings and ideas, is a myth." But myths take a considerable time to develop. Hence the

Gospels cannot in any appreciable degree rest on the testimony of eye-witnesses.

Strauss roundly declares that he is more sure of Hegelianism than of anything else, and that Hegel forbids him to give Jesus Christ the unique place He occupies for faith. It is an elementary historical principle that the initial figure in any development cannot, by the nature of the case, be the greatest in the series. " The Idea loves not to pour all its fulness in one example, in jealousy towards all the rest ; its way rather is to scatter its riches over a multiplicity of instances, supplementary to each other, in a succession of individuals that appear and pass away." What special value can attach to a single fact ? The true God-man is no one person, but humanity as a whole. The attributes supposed to belong to Christ are really those of the race.

Mankind [he goes on] is the unity of the two natures, the Infinite Spirit depotentiated in finitude, and the finite spirit mindful of its infinity ; it is the child of the visible mother and the invisible father, of spirit and nature ; it is the miracle-worker, for in the course of human history the spirit ever more fully takes control of nature ; it is the Sinless One, for its progressive growth is blameless, and impurity clings only to the single life but disappears in the race ; it is the Dying, Rising and Ascending One, for from the negation of its merely natural qualities there springs an ever higher spiritual life, and through the abrogation of its finitude as personal, national and secular spirit it is exalted into unity with the Infinite Spirit of heaven.

It may be observed, at this turn in his argument, that if the concept of God is to be authentically pantheistic, as Strauss would have it, the Absolute cannot justly be illustrated or represented even by humanity as a whole, but only by the total universe of things. You cannot have it both ways : you cannot toss the individual overboard in order to secure pantheism, and then bring him back selectively in order to give the Absolute a recognizable character.[1]

Yet Strauss has no wish to deny that Jesus existed; what place then is assigned to Him ? The answer is given in a statement which in Hegelian Christology tends to become an excessively tiresome refrain : Jesus, we are told, was the first to perceive that God and man are one. Later this was perverted by the Church into the dogma that God and man are one—in Jesus Christ. At first, the critic had been disposed to reject the possibility even of identifying Jesus. " My critical negations," he said, " are directed against the tradition ; I do not deny all factual basis, but have only wished to show that we can really know nothing about it." At a later point, he felt obliged to put a larger emphasis on Jesus' creative power. If at first He had figured only as the vehicle of a conception, it now became clear that in fact He was the Founder of Christianity. This was tantamount to the admission, important for the historian, that not an idea but a Person is the initiating source of our faith. But Strauss hastens to add a disclaimer even to this concession.

To grant so much [he protests] is by no means to give Christ His place once more in the Christian Holy of Holies ; it merely is to assign Him a niche in the chapel of Alexander Severus (i.e. beside Socrates and others). . . . As for the future, we have no real assurance that someone may not appear equal to Him or even superior.

There is no injustice in saying that Strauss had gained his results not by exact study of the data, but under the pressure of speculative postulates. The great realities for him, it has been remarked with point, are neither the

---

[1] Strauss's contention, that while each individual is impure yet mankind as a whole is perfect, in a measure recalls the arithmetic of the old woman who made pies at a cost of twopence-half-penny each, and retailed them at twopence, explaining that it was only because she sold such enormous quantities that she was able to make a living at all.

narratives nor the facts, but his antagonists. Yet his
work was enough to pass sentence of death on the rationalistic criticism of the Synoptics which had been current in
the eighteenth century, while at the same time it forced
the Church to undertake such a careful study of the
Gospels as should no longer rest upon the strained and
improbable conjectures of the harmonists. If his tone in
the *Life of Jesus* had been hostile it became even sharper
in his *Glaubenslehre*, or *Dogmatic*, published five years
later. Here he may be said to approach Christianity with
the purpose of burying what had long been dead. The
doctrines of faith are taken up one by one, with the aim
of showing that, once the Scriptural and supposedly
experiential factors have been drained out, nothing is left
but the faded residuum of pantheistic monism. The
author has no feeling for the sinner's exceeding bitter cry
for deliverance, and can even say that for his philosophy
the ideas of " good " and " evil " have lost all meaning.
What is now stressed is no longer, as with Hegel, the
relative affinity of faith and idealism, but the impassable
gulf between them. In particular, there can be no such
thing as Eschatology. The last enemy to be destroyed,
we are told, is belief in victory over death. It is but a
step from this to the dismal repudiation of higher conviction in every form which we find in his latest book,
The Old Faith and the New. By this time he had become
a whole-hearted adherent of materialism (still clinging in
a pathetic way to some fragments of his earlier idealistic
creed), a view to which he had been guided by a wholly
erroneous interpretation of Darwin. Nothing is now left
for reverence but the law-determined order of the universe.
We may well say of Strauss, as we contemplate his brave,
sad, clear-eyed agnosticism, *Utinam noster esses*.

If Strauss had sought to destroy Christianity, Ludwig
Feuerbach, his contemporary, was bent on uprooting

religion in every form. Feuerbach is the classical sceptic in theology, as Hume is in philosophy. He has given to the theory of Illusionism in religion its most formidable expression, and it is impossible to read him without feeling that his attack on faith is the gravest of all and, in the intellectual domain, represents the ultimate antagonism. A stirring book [1] published in 1912 is curious proof of his importance, for it argues in detail that none of the greater theologians of the nineteenth century had stood up to Feuerbach or given a serious refutation of his argument. They all think so anthropocentrically, the author contends, that as against the famous sceptic they are wholly without defence. Much the same line is taken by Karl Barth, more briefly but with immensely more vigour and penetration, in a lecture published in 1928.[2] A writer of this calibre must be considered with some care.

Feuerbach, a former student of Hegel's in Berlin, began in 1828 to teach philosophy in Erlangen. His academic career having proved a failure, he presently withdrew into the seclusion and what seems, in his case, to have been the penury of a private scholar. He died in 1872. For us his chief works are *The Essence of Christianity* (1841), *The Philosophy of the Future* (1843), and *The Essence of Religion* (1853), this last a series of public lectures delivered in 1848, the year of revolution.

Feuerbach remained a theologian all his life, in the sense that from beginning to end his writing dealt with theology. If we are to believe himself, his chief interest lay in unmasking Hegelianism. "My philosophy of religion," he writes, "so far from being an explication of the Hegelian, sprang from sheer opposition to it, and it is only in the light of this opposition that it can be understood or judged." But this is to misinterpret his own

---

[1] Leese, *Die Prinzipienlehre der systematischen Theologie im Lichte der Kritik Ludwig Feuerbachs.*

[2] It will be found in his *Die Theologie und die Kirche*, pp. 212–39.

tendencies. What he opposed was not the fundamental assumptions of Hegelian thinking on religion, but merely their application : that which Hegel took (on his own terms) as a defence of Christianity, Feuerbach read as its death-warrant. Like the great Berlin philosopher, he strove to deduce religion from immanent principles of cognition, with the result that whatever religion turns out to be, in its last essence, it will be something man is bound to have and cannot be without. It will be as inseparable from his nature as his five senses. But this initial position is one which for Christian judgment is simply wrong. On the one hand, it conflicts with the assurance that true religion in the Christian sense is not something a man possesses already, in virtue of his man-hood, but something freely bestowed on him by the sovereign grace of God. On the other, it is something he can only have by personal decision. Alike from the Divine point of view and from the human, it cannot be anything so obvious as a personal endowment or natural gift.

It is worth while to understand how Feuerbach's theory of religion first sprang out of Hegel, then turned against him. Hegel, particularly in his earlier phase, had insisted that man does stand in a real relationship to the Tran-scendent ; but what this really means is that the human mind objectifies its own infinite life and, having thus endowed it with a *quasi* trans-subjective character, takes up towards it the atittude specifically known as religious. God, so understood, is the reflection of our own deepest being, our real self hypostatized. Thus Hegel's statements, without any forcing of their terms, could be read as asserting that God is the human self in a certain infinite aspect. Feuerbach read them so ; and, accepting their general tenor, forthwith proceeded to argue indignantly that in that case the Hegelian pretence of substantial or constructive agreement with the faith of the Christian

Church must be abandoned for good and all. God is to be conceived as a helpful personification of the infinitude of man's nature ; there is no other God but man, who is the measure of all things.

Man, then, is religious in so far as he projects his own nature into transcendent dimensions. Religion claims to base itself upon the " otherness " of God, upon the fact of a differentiating gulf between God and man ; but in truth, when we look more closely, the gulf or distinction lies within the man himself. All the time the soul is moving exclusively within its own limits. Knowledge of " God " is not false, if it be interpreted accurately, for it is a genuine knowledge possessed by the Ego of its own being. If we may put it so, the transcendence of the individual's life which all religion implies is a transcendence that measures not vertically but horizontally—not above and beyond us, but around us on our own level. Whether consistently or not, Feuerbach shrinks from laying down that in piety the single self envisages itself adoringly ; the infinitude necessary to the religious object he finds in the whole race. The race bounds and overarches my puny personal existence, evoking thereby a specifically religious feeling. But since the race is only myself multiplied indefinitely, the argument can quite as well be carried on in terms of self as a single entity. And this means that transcendence, eventually, is an empty word. Faith in a God other than myself is a fruitless effort to escape from the circle of my own being. We have to translate God into terms of man, never forgetting in the process that the translation, to be correct, must rest on the insight that human terms will cover the whole ground ; they can be so stated as to exhaust the whole meaning of the Divine original, leaving nothing unexpressed. Theology when analysed is anthropology, nothing more. " God," writes Feuerbach, " was my first, reason my second, man my last and final thought." The Absolute Spirit of the

Hegelian system has now shrunk into *homo sapiens*, reverently contemplating the human race as a totality.

Furthermore, once Feuerbach has expunged Deity and therefore also the God-ward aspect of human life, it follows for him that man, the *ens realissimum* beyond which by the nature of the case our minds cannot travel, is a being purely of sense. As he puts it, " The body in its totality is my Ego, my very essence ". Thus we may prolong his aphoristic conclusion and say that if theology is anthropology, anthropology no less clearly is physiology. The real, strictly taken, is the sensibly perceptible. This important circumstance, that in theory of knowledge Feuerbach is a thoroughgoing sensationalist, has often been overlooked. Man can do no more than project his own self into reality, by imagination lending objective existence to the hypothetical irresistible causes of sensation. Thus proofs of the being of God are unconsciously aimed at the externalization of what is inward, positing it as somehow other than man. But, argues Feuerbach, these proofs are in fact only varied and highly interesting forms of thought in which man affirms his own being. We turn our wishes into realities, then take refuge under their imaginary greatness. " What thou needest—needest on inward grounds—that, and that only, is thy God."

In the essay referred to above Barth has two striking pages, on which we may draw for a moment, where he traverses the whole round of Christian doctrines, and shows by quotations from Feuerbach what they become once he has submitted them to his special illusionistic treatment. Thus God is the self-feeling of man freed from all the limitations of reality. In the personality of God man celebrates the supernatural and immortal character of his own personal nature. The absoluteness of God represents the effort of our mind to reach by abstraction an absolute datum for reflective thought. We differentiate the direct and non-discursive knowledge of God from the lower piece-by-piece knowledge possible for man, but this in fact is only the distinction necessary to our own thinking between knowledge *a priori* and *a posteriori*. We call God " love " because we wish for, and have formed a picture of, a Being that will satisfy all our desires and dreams. God is the sigh of the human soul personified. Faith in providence is a conviction of our own worth as immeasurably superior to that of the world. Miracle is the magic power of fancy to mitigate the cruel predicaments of life. The Holy Spirit is the soul of man in its urgent or enthusiastic character, objectified by itself. The Trinity is a hypostatized form of the social impulse. Manifestly the pattern of all these formulations is the same. Feuerbach stands ready with an idealistic apparatus into which any given doctrine may be inserted, and which may be trusted to stamp upon all the same mark of ultimate futility. To the believer's protest that God took the initiative and revealed Himself, it is answered that revelation could in any case be no more than man's speaking to his own heart ; the devout mind has started from itself, made a *détour* by an imaginary object it calls God, and returned to itself again. " Man is the beginning, the centre, and the end of religion."

It is significant that Feuerbach displays no interest in the question who or what Jesus Christ may actually have been. Christ, the real God of Christians, is to him but an idealized conglomerate of all the excellences admired by man. Not that the existence of some such person as Jesus need be denied ; imagination always has something to work upon. But it is lost labour to endeavour to distinguish between the facts of history and the fanciful embellishments of faith. Beyond the certainty that the Figure pictured in the New Testament is a creation of desire, a wish-fulfilment, we need not and we cannot go. And when men had become possessed of this supposedly perfect Saviour, it became habitual for them to exhibit

a culpable indifference, even blindness, to the prospects
and challenge of cultural progress, and with craven other-
worldliness to escape from the hard toil of civilization to
the hopes of immortal bliss. As Feuerbach puts it, in
ringing tones :

My aim has been to change my readers from friends of God
to friends of man, from believers to thinkers, from devotees
to workers, from candidates for the next world to students of
this one, from Christians whose creed makes them half animal,
half angel, to men who are complete men.[1]

There is no reason why we should not readily acknowledge that Feuerbach's illusionistic theory of religion cannot
be refuted, if we add that in itself this is not a fact of any
particular importance. That a statement should be incapable of refutation is no evidence of its truth. Solipsism,
for example—the doctrine that nothing exists outside
my own mind and its contents—cannot be put down by
any coercive theoretical logic ; though no doubt it is
permissible to point out that by discussing the subject
with other people the solipsist, in effect, gives away his
whole case. The belief that others exist is a fundamental
belief essential to specifically human life ; but if its truth
be denied, I am unable to refute the denial. The circumstance, then, that Feuerbach in one sense is irrefutable
need not greatly disturb us.

In another sense, he can be refuted easily enough.
Defects in his reasoning can be exposed, and it can be
shown that he is left with much more serious difficulties
on his hands than are his opponents. Very briefly one
or two points may be made.

(1) Eduard von Hartmann, the philosopher of pessimism,
who was certainly not concerned to defend religion, has
called attention to the fact that the argument of Feuerbach

[1] See a striking chapter (pp. 27–48) in a too little known volume,
C. A. Bennett's *The Dilemma of Religious Knowledge* (1931).

—who took a special pride in the cogency of his logic—rests
at bottom on a simple fallacy. His one original idea is
that God is only a projected desire. Now it is plain that
things do not exist because we desire them ; but from
this it does not in the least follow that, because we desire
them, things do not exist. My longing for dawn, after a
night of pain, is no proof that the dawn will not arrive.
To call God a wish-fulfilment is in one sense a statement
which has no bearing of any kind on the question of His
reality or unreality. It simply admonishes us to use
special care in scrutinizing the evidence for and against.

(2) Feuerbach, like the colour-blind, is apt to conclude
that what he does not see is not there. That one man
does not have a certain experience, and finds it non-
significant when described to him, affords no justification
at all for supposing that another, precisely through an
experience of the kind in question, may not be brought
into contact with a supramundane Reality, a transcendent
Person Who, in mere grace, has spoken to him com-
mandingly and irresistibly laid hands upon his life.

(3) It is in the name of theory of knowledge that Feuerbach has pronounced sentence of death upon religion.
But his own epistemology may be described without
injustice as a rather crass and flimsy form of sensational-
ism, for which knowledge is a product of the mere rain of
sense-impressions.[1] But if my sense-impressions be all,
Feuerbach is entitled to say no more than " I know only
those occurrences which I myself experience sensibly ".
And this is solipsism. That clearly is a theory which does
much more than condemn belief in God, it equally condemns all science. On Feuerbach's assumptions, *all*
knowledge is illusion. For the utmost you can now say

---

[1] To Feuerbach, man is a mere creature of sense, who for that
reason naïvely projects his own sense-impressions, in heightened
and intensified form, on to the absolute World-Spirit. For that
reason theology is anthropology pure and simple.

is that knowledge, or what is called such, emerges accidentally out of the strictly determined sequence of sense-impressions in the mind ; but, and this is usually forgotten, the working of this mechanical sequence produces error no less than true belief. All our beliefs, in short, must now be taken as inevitable, and the difference between veridical beliefs and those which are erroneous has vanished. Thus the epistemology which Feuerbach employs to discredit faith proves fatal also to that exact scientific reflection in whose name he speaks. And there can be no more serious flaw in a philosophical argument than to prove too much.

(4) Finally, as has been pointed out, Feuerbach's mind has two blind spots which disqualify his theory of religion from the start. He ignores death and he disregards sin. Let it be remembered how his argument comes to this, that in religious thinking man deifies himself. But man is the prey of death and is sinful throughout his whole being ; is it a convincing theory, or even a plausible one, that the materials out of which we build our conception of the Absolute Lord of heaven and earth, the Holy and Eternal One, are to be found in our own nature, our life of pathetic guilt and decay ? Is it not a vital mark of religion that, notwithstanding the relative truth of anthropomorphism, an object is felt to be worthy of reverence not when it is simply like us, but only when it is also, and predominantly, unlike ? We can only worship what in some sense is " wholly other ". Nothing which is merely homogeneous with, or an extension of, the self, and which therefore cannot fail to be infected with the partialities and imperfections of the self, can evoke the specifically religious response. Thus, whatever view may be right, the view that theology in essence is anthropology must be wrong. Theorists may if they please derive religion from the glories of nature or the sublimities of the moral order, or from any other source where the

transcendent powers of Destiny are believed to have their
seat. But reason forbids that they should propose the
essentially incredible theory that the content of the name
" God "—the Lord, the Creator of the ends of the earth,
Who is of purer eyes than to behold iniquity—is in fact
drawn from human life, the sphere of death and sin.

Fas est ab hoste doceri. Feuerbach's interpretation of
religion is a grave indictment of any theology which, for
reasons however commendable, fails to give the majesty
of God a fundamental and determinative place. His
work, taken along with that of Strauss, destroyed irrevocably the impression that Christian faith and speculative
philosophy are somehow identical in nature. He was the
great precursor of views often supposed to be the discovery
of the New Psychology, and these views he set forth with
a vigour and interest to which later advocates have added
little. The case for Illusionism is never likely to be
stated more powerfully, and it is for this reason that his
argument has been somewhat fully analysed. On the
surface negation could hardly go further than with him.
Yet even in reading Feuerbach we may well recall the
saying of Renan, that you ought never to believe a
German when he tells you he is an atheist.

§ 3. POSITIVE CONSTRUCTION IN BIEDERMANN

We now turn to consider briefly the dogmatic thinker
in whom theological Hegelianism true to type is seen,
probably, at its best. This is Alois Emanuel Biedermann
(1819–85), professor in Zürich, who stands up amid the
divines of the nineteenth century like the austere summit
of one of his own Swiss mountains. In his chief work, a
Christian Dogmatic, he set himself the task of passing the
figurative images of faith through the processes of dialectic
and thus rendering them into the pure speech of the
notion. The very structure of his book is indicative of

much. First comes a philosophical introduction, defining
religion as a reciprocal relationship between God as
Infinite Spirit and man as finite spirit ; while revelation,
instead of determining all, becomes only a subordinate
factor set in this framework. On this follows the main
body of the work, divided on a threefold plan. To begin
with, an impartial account is given under each doctrine
of the Biblical data and the historical developments of
Church dogma—this is often exact and skilful work. A
critical section comes next, not inferior to Strauss in
relentless vigour, and meant to bring out the sheer ontological inadequacy of traditional modes of statement.
Lastly, what Biedermann felt to be his chief task is
grappled with, that of reducing the affirmations of faith
to terms which, because strictly philosophical, are also of
permanent value.

The idea of God, Biedermann teaches, is formed in the
human mind by necessity ; it is neither childish and
arbitrary as for Strauss, nor illusory as for Feuerbach.
But for the idea of the Divine personality he has an
insuperable distaste. God may be personal, or, on the
other hand, absolute and infinite ; He cannot be both.
" The pure and only adequate concept of Absolute Spirit "
can be reached, he argues, in no other way than by
scrapping all imaginative thought-forms without exception—even " consciousness " is discarded as unduly human
—and confining ourselves strictly to ideas of the most
abstract and least pictorial type. But of course, since he
can only think with a human mind, Biedermann's sub-
stitutions for the symbols of the ordinary man turn out
to be merely symbols of a more attenuated sort. With
all its defects, " consciousness " is a spiritual or mental
word, its meaning in some degree known to us ; but
Insichsein, or " being-in-self ", which Biedermann prefers,
is really no more than a spatial term once the suggestions
of " consciousness " have been cast aside. None the less

Biedermann denies with obvious sincerity that to conceive God as " personal " is pure illusion ; in moments of prayer, he declared, he too conceived God thus and felt altogether free to do so. The category may be a defective one, yet it is both right and inevitable at the religious plane of thought. Is this a possible way out ? Can we as thinkers hold that God is definitely *not* personal, yet as believers convince ourselves that He *is* ? Must not clear speculative insight win the day ? There appears to be no escape from the rigour of Biedermann's dictum : " The assertion of the personality of God is only the shibboleth of an imaginative Theism." If this be so, sin can no longer be taken as the violation of a personal relationship. Biedermann accepts the inference, and sin then becomes for him that which is contrary to the self-determination of the finite spirit. " Redemption from sin otherwise than by the intrinsic powers of man's own nature," he insists, " is neither necessary nor possible." When the Church ascribed redemptive might to the God-man, rather than to man's absolute religious self-consciousness, it had lapsed into mythology.

In Christology his main interest lay in distinguishing sharply, if not irrevocably, between what is called the principle of redemption and the Person of Jesus. By an optical illusion the Church has seen these two as one. Theology must separate them. The incarnation of God, traditionally misconstrued as a once-for-all event, is an eternal fact present for ever in the being of God as the self-externalizing Absolute One. To some extent, I feel, Biedermann is misled here by his peculiar misconception of the task set for the theologian. That task he assumes to be to interpret, not revelation apprehended by faith, but rather the elaborated forms which the several doctrines have received in orthodox tradition. Not merely does this pass easily into the view that to refute dogma we only need to know its history : it is accompanied, in Biedermann's mind, by failure to see that dogma is not necessarily so pure an expression of truth that it may not need to be corrected by the New Testament.

The principle of redemption, we are told, means the idea of God-manhood, which in the sphere of human life takes reality in the form of Divine Sonship. But if Christianity is to remain the absolute religion, this principle must not be identified with Jesus. For the Person of Christ we must learn to put the Christological dogma with its literally unbounded speculative value. Yet as a believer, who somehow had found God in Jesus, Biedermann could not merely stop at this point. In spite of all, the principle and the Person come later to be bound up together. We must not suppose, he tells us, that " the principle would *eo ipso*, prior to and apart from the fact (i.e. the historical appearance of Jesus), have realized itself in the development of man ". Thus for all time Jesus Christ remains the Person in whom the principle took flesh ; nay more, it is specifically through Him that the principle has touched and changed human life. Far from being merely the first to exemplify Divine Sonship, Jesus, it is laid down before the end, is One Who by the efficacy of the redeeming principle in Himself guarantees its triumph in all who are united to Him. Inconsequent as this may be (for it is wholly at variance with the initial severance of principle and Person) it at least pays one more tribute to the transcendent religious power of Jesus, Who insists on being our Saviour.

After Strauss and Feuerbach, in whom Hegelianism took its most radically negative form, and Biedermann, who meant to be as Hegelian as possible, but always found Christianity breaking in, a few words may be given to Dorner, chief of the dogmatic theologians who took up the challenge Strauss had flung down. His massive *System of Christian Doctrine* had a wide influence in English-speaking lands in the generation before our own.

Idealism and Christian faith, he urged, are or ought to be allies. Robust faith must seek to become knowledge, objective insight. What lifted Dorner's work high above mere speculative rationalism is his absorbing interest in the moral revelation of God in Christ. His doctrine of God, unduly metaphysical in aspect as it may seem, brought some valuable ideas into Trinitarian discussion, especially by way of safeguarding the doctrine of the Godhead against the perils of tritheism. He sought above all an ethical construction of the Trinity through the distinction of the elements of necessity and freedom, and their unity in love. Yet even behind an argument so Christian in purpose we too often discern rather the abstract form of the Absolute than the concrete facts of historical revelation.

But in his Christology Dorner was constrained to break with the idealistic habit of operating with an abstract idea of Divine-humanity rather than with the picture of Christ held forth in the New Testament. We have to learn from the fact of Christ what Divine-humanity signifies, not to impose upon Christ the limits of an *a priori* concept. Human nature is both things—distinct from God yet receptive of God ; and in Christ is seen the great confluence between the universal self-communicativeness of God and the infinite receptivity of man for the Divine. Such a realization of perfect God-manhood, which is an essential part of God's plan, would have been vouchsafed to men even apart from sin. In Jesus, " the adequate personal organ of Deity ", faith beholds One in whom the advancing coalescence of Divine and human life is made complete at the Resurrection.

§ 4.   CONCLUSION

What value can be assigned to the sustained effort, made from different angles of approach, to state the

Gospel in the intellectual terms of Hegelian Gnosticism ?
It may be useful as we close to note three major points
of difficulty.

(1) We have no cause to doubt that the genius of
Christian faith is hostile to the implicit claim to possess
speculative omniscience, or something like it, which the
Hegelian thinker is apt to make. The philosopher invites
us to share his vision of the reason-pervaded organism of
things. There is a marked tendency to find in a general
principle of reason, the necessary issues of which can be
continuously unfolded, the universal instrument of explanation. But this, at least in design, is to assume the
standpoint of God Himself. To Him all secrets are naked
and open ; mystery by the nature of the case there cannot be ; and the convinced Hegelian is intent on directly
thinking God's thoughts after Him and sharing His divine
intuition of the world. But can this be done ? Is it not
at once franker and more profound to confess that it
cannot ? The data of our reasoning are not transparently
luminous for us as for the Divine Thinker ; and on this
account alone Bacon must be right in saying that " in
divinity many things must be left abrupt ". Of these
" abrupt " things one certainly is the problem of sin,
which vanishes in the dialectician's grasp just when his
efforts to " explain " it seem on the point of succeeding.
No logical rationale of sin ever gave comfort to the guilty,
or armed him against temptation ; and human life is far
too closely interlaced a unity for us to suppose that it
would not in some degree have done these things had it
possessed real value of an intellectual kind. The Christian
intelligence has no option but to suspect a system, or a
point of view, which makes the impression of attempting
to ignore the element of mystery in our moral and religious
experience. Even in our sinning " we feel that we are
greater than we know ".

(2) Human thought operates under the relations of

time; but the status and importance of time and its contents are discounted, more rather than less, by Hegelianism as a method of interpretation. This for Christianity is an unpardonable sin. Neither morality nor religion can look for justice on such terms. Thus self-sacrifice, to take morality first, cannot be completely real unless time and what fills it are also real; but to speculative rationalism time as such is no more than an illusory vesture of unchanging metaphysical relations. "Nothing real ever moves." But if time lapses into mere appearance, with all the thinness and second-rateness which that word connotes, sacrifice has parted with all meaning. In the words of Professor A. E. Taylor, "Moral victory and moral defeat would be alike impossible in a timeless world, and in a world in which time-order was reversible the one would be indistinguishable from the other".

So likewise the truth of religion is confined within limits that destroy its special character. As our study of Biedermann has shown, the same fastidious or nerveless horror of time prevents a convinced Hegelian from acknowledging that a full and saving revelation of God can have been given in Christ Who lived, died, and overcame the grave. The Gospel shrinks to the dimensions of a general truth of philosophy, discoverable by the efforts of the higher logic. Absolutism has no love for unique persons. In its secret heart it feels that history essentially is gross and carnal. To believe in the Logos presents no insurmountable difficulty, but to believe in One Who died for our sins and to Whom we owe everything for our relation to God—this is a burden too heavy to be borne. But the point is one on which the New Testament has said the last word : "Who is he that overcometh the world, but he that believeth that Jesus is the Son of God ? This is He that came by water and blood, even Jesus Christ." The Gospel is as real as the life-blood of the Redeemer. So far from being superior to history, or ideally detachable from it, its secret lies in One Who at a certain date lived the human life and tasted death for every man.

(3) These faults of interpretation are traceable, in the last resort, to the specifically Hegelian conception of God. The pantheistic monism which he brought with him to the consideration of Christianity hid from Strauss the face of the living God, and Biedermann, under a like disability, was driven to think of God alternately as personal and as impersonal. But an Identity in which differences vanish, or a Unity conceived merely as the aggregation of differences it includes, is not what Christian faith means by God.

By God [said Lord Balfour, rightly interpreting the mind of the Church in every age] I mean a God whom men can love, a God to whom men pray, who takes sides, who has purposes and preferences, whose attributes, howsoever conceived, leave unimpaired the possibility of a personal relation between Himself and those whom He has created.

This is the living God of prophets and apostles—One who invades history, who forgives sin, who receives the dying. But to Hegel and his disciples in theology God is Mind in general without being a Mind, so that when we pronounce the Divine Name we are thinking of a logical " Universal " inherent in all things, the abstract rationality of the world. This depersonalized Absolute will no doubt to the end of time present itself as the fitting shadowy correlate of a metaphysical temper that finds it natural either to overlook or to misapprehend the sorest troubles of sinful men. Hence the matter is one on which, ultimately, we have to give a vote for or against. We have to decide whether we deem it truer to our profoundest certainties to think of God, with Absolutism, as the all-inclusive logical Unity—the universal needle-eye, to put it so, through which pass all the threads of cosmic relation—or, with Jesus Christ, as the Father Who is Holy Love, a Spirit for spirits, and the transcendent object of faith and worship.

V

THE THEOLOGY OF MORAL VALUES

ALBRECHT RITSCHL

§ 1. BIOGRAPHICAL AND LITERARY DETAILS

IN THE last quarter of the nineteenth century no influence in the field of theology could compare, for breadth and vigour, with that of Albrecht Ritschl of Göttingen. He died in 1889, yet even to-day his thought is a living factor in the dogmatic constructions of the Church. Theological fashions change quickly, in Germany most of all; but some of his most unrelenting critics are unconscious debtors to Ritschl for ideas they would be extremely unwilling to part with. Harnack was not far out in calling him the latest of the Church Fathers.

Ritschl was born in Berlin in 1822. His father, a preacher of some repute, became in 1827 General Superintendent of the Lutheran Church of Pomerania, and the boy grew up in Stettin. By 1839 he had gone up to the University, taking lectures at Bonn and afterwards at Halle, and hearing at both places the leaders of what was then known as the mediating school—Nitzsch, Tholuck, and Julius Müller. Later, in Heidelberg, he came into personal contact with Rothe, an eccentric genius. Finally he studied in Tübingen under Baur, head of the famous school of radical New Testament criticism, and under his influence became for a time a whole-hearted champion of that movement. From its standpoint he wrote his first book—a spirited attempt to show that Marcion's apocryphal Gospel formed the basis of the canonical Luke.

Eleven years later, in the second edition of his *Die alt-katholische Kirche*, he himself delivered what proved to be a shattering blow to the Tübingen hypothesis as a whole. The book presents a new view of early Church history. It is shown that no such sharp division existed between St. Paul and the other apostles as Baur had argued for.

The original apostles and Paul [writes the author] are certainly different in the individual expression they give to their Christian thought, but they agree in recognizing unconditionally the newness of the covenant inaugurated by Christ, and the newness of religious and moral life within it, as contrasted with the old covenant.

In 1846, at Bonn, Ritschl began his career as a University lecturer. He started with New Testament work, teaching in subsequent years the history of doctrine, and, from 1852 onwards, Dogmatic. In 1859 he became a full professor. He accepted a chair at Göttingen in 1864 and continued to teach there until his death. It was during these final twenty-five years that his powers as a thinker and a writer came to their height. To the end he lectured on New Testament Theology, and did some exegesis, but his main work lay in the department of Systematic Theology. It is of some importance to note that Ritschl had been a practised historian before he took to dogmatic theology, and that his lifelong aim was to re-interpret the Reformation understanding of the Gospel in opposition to the different versions made current by Romanism and Mysticism, Pietism and Romanticism. Back to the New Testament, by way of the Reformation—this is the motto that guides him steadily.

In 1870 his best-known work, the great monograph on *The Christian Doctrine of Justification and Reconciliation*, which had been prepared for by a number of shorter studies, began to appear. There were three volumes, respectively historical, Biblical and systematic in character. It is significant that in this order the Biblical

volume stands next to the systematic, as though to mark
the point that, if he has to choose, Ritschl prefers to
agree with the New Testament rather than with tradition.
Three editions of the work appeared during the author's
lifetime, and the occasionally important changes they
exhibit have been carefully set out in a special book by
Fabricius. The practical religious ideas involved in his
argument Ritschl put more concisely in a short treatise
on *Christian Perfection* (1874), one of his most characteristic pieces. In the same year he reviewed the dominant
tendencies of nineteenth-century Christian thought in a
pamphlet on Schleiermacher's *Addresses*. Twelve months
later he issued a compendium of his theology in a small
volume entitled *Instruction in the Christian Religion*, meant
as a text-book for schools, but one which proved to be
much too difficult for its declared purpose, and dropped
out of use.

Two other publications ought to be named. The first
is *Theology and Metaphysics* (1881), a somewhat acrid
onslaught upon orthodox thinkers of the type of Frank,
contemporary leader of the Erlangen school, which contains among other things a good deal of half-confused
and highly unconvincing epistemology. In the second
place, after 1876 Ritschl had again taken up historical
study, with an interest mainly theological ; and the chief
outcome (1880–6) was a three-volume *History of Pietism*,
full of force and solid erudition, though its authority has
considerably fallen off in recent years. Pietism was
Ritschl's *bête noire* ; and his more bitter opponents were
in the habit of saying that if you wished to know how little
real religion there was in the man, this above all was the
book to read. He regarded Pietism as a false revival,
within evangelical Protestantism, of Catholic ideals of the
Christian life.

Even in the Bonn period some few adherents had been
gained for his special theology ; but after 1874, on the

completion of his *Justification and Reconciliation,* accessions
were numerous. Among the first to join the new movement were Harnack and Herrmann. The best-known
members of the " school "—if we may use the word—
were not so much personal hearers as students of his
books. By 1890 they had come to exert a preponderating
influence in the theological world of Germany.

Ritschl was a man of energetic character, masterful,
cool, swift and sharp in judgment, much too fond of
controversy, but honest and solid, with a strong dislike
for sentimentality. Never was there a life more completely absorbed in scientific theology.[1] He could not
rival Schleiermacher for wealth and variety of gifts, yet
in his century he comes nearest to him in the deep impression he was able to make by the disciplined concentration of his work. His books were not written for the
populace ; the style was heavy and shapeless ; and for
long, students found it hard to make headway. But if
they read on, they increasingly felt themselves in the
presence of one who for many was opening a new stage
in interpretation. It proved difficult to classify a spirit
so independent under any of the familiar rubrics ; and
not infrequently the attacks delivered by liberal and con-
fessional critics alike were seen to be bitter with the
bitterness of the puzzled. Criticism at first was apt to
touch little but the surface of his argument. He himself
felt that he stood outside all parties. As early as 1857
his letters reveal a consciousness that the new theological
method on which he had fixed, and which he was to

[1] Barth (*Kirchliche Dogmatik*, p. 293) thinks that Ritschl helped
to give modern Dogmatic a journalistic tone, and describes his
theology as simply going back, behind Idealism and Romanticism,
to the essential tenets of the *Aufklärung*. In spite of a certain
Deistic flavour, e.g., in Ritschl's view of the living Christ, this
is much too strong. Ritschl at the moment belongs, like Tennyson,
to the " middle distance ", too far for gratitude, too near for
reverence. He is behind a passing cloud to-day.

apply with unusual rigour and confidence, was one for
which his predecessors had been groping in vain.

§ 2.   NEGATIVE AND POLEMICAL FEATURES

Our study of this method may suitably begin with an
allusion to two pernicious influences which, at every stage
of his development except the first, Ritschl sought to
drive from the field. One is Speculative Rationalism,
with its claim that the true basis of theology is to be
found in theoretical metaphysics. No doubt in a broad
sense most of us are speculative rationalists in so far as
we try to think out and think through the implications
of Christian faith, in an effort to correlate each belief
with all the rest. And in calling for the expulsion of
metaphysics from theology, as I think we shall see, Ritschl
in form asked for more than could be conceded, and as
it were drove the nail in so hard as to split the wood.
Faith must always be metaphysical, for it rests upon
convictions which, if true, must profoundly affect our
whole view of the universe and the conduct befitting us
within it. In this important sense, a metaphysical import
belongs to every judgment concerning Ultimate Reality.
Yet the belief or judgment in question need not have
been reached by way of metaphysical argument, and in
point of fact no essential Christian belief has ever been
so reached, although metaphysical argument may later
have been employed to defend it. And this, in the last
resort, is the point Ritschl is bent on making. There is
a Speculative Rationalism which comes to meet the Gospel
with a ready-made framework of philosophical conceptions,
insisting that faith is bound to use these conceptions, and
no other, when it proceeds to formulate its own living
content, and this in spite of the fact that its fundamental
categories may have taken shape quite irrespectively of
the experiences that make a man Christian. Philosophy

as such is, even for the believer, the final court of appeal.
This type of thought, of which Hegelianism is the classic
instance, Ritschl strove not without success to dislodge
from the seat of power.   Anyone who knows more than
the rudiments of his thought will acknowledge that his
view of the living God, of revelation in Christ, of miracle,
of the Church, is such as to lift the mind beyond the
range of any metaphysic operating with general ideas.   It
becomes plain that, in spite of its great intellectual value,
technical philosophy leaves on one side just those problems
which possess a life-and-death interest for believing men.
No books on metaphysics can be named which contain
a serious handling of such matters as fellowship with God,
the guilt of sin, the hearing of prayer, above all the
redeeming Person of Jesus.   By insisting that the Christian
mind must at every point of religious belief be guided
solely by the revelation of God in Christ, Ritschl did his
utmost to expel any and every presumptuous form of
Speculative Rationalism ;   and it may well be that the
future historian will reckon this to have been his best
service to theology.

A somewhat false importance has been ascribed, alike by
friend and foe, to Ritschl's professed desire to exclude metaphysic from theology.   But the truth is that we inevitably
go wrong when we approach his system from the side of
philosophy.   For one thing, his idea of what metaphysic
is—a study, on his showing, in its very essence indifferent
to the distinction between nature and spirit—is much too
narrow for the facts, and was apparently derived from his
reading of Lotze.   Furthermore, as Barth has pointed
out, the legitimacy or the reverse of using in theology
an idea which has metaphysical significance wholly depends
on the context in which it occurs.   And in the last place,
to be quite exact, Ritschl's aim was not so much to expel
metaphysic as to keep it firmly in its right place.   He
resents the intrusion of metaphysical principles and modes

of inference into the constitutive meaning of that which faith asserts, or ought to assert ; yet he is far from denying a regulative value to metaphysic in so far as it determines, e.g., the meaning of the concepts of cause or final end. Has not the plausible term " regulative " carried him too far ? He may be justified in rejecting as merely theoretic ontology some later developments of the doctrine of the Two Natures in Christ ; but the really important question is whether by wrongly labelling them " metaphysical " he has not been misled into discarding certain vital elements of truth in this field, as, for example, the essential deity of Christ.

In any case, Ritschl does not press the distinction between religious and philosophical thought to the very limit. His final suggestion is to the effect that philosophy, which constantly though vainly strives for a unified view of things, should in its own interest and in order to attain the ultimate aim of cognition, take over the Christian idea of God. As may be seen from his vacillating treatment of the theistic proofs, he had never really made up his mind on the question whether, in whatever degree, the philosopher is or is not competent to furnish a true idea of God.

The other pernicious influence of which Ritschl desired to be rid was Subjectivism, with the no less objectionable phenomenon that so often follows in its train, Mysticism. Schleiermacher had been the great subjectivist ; broadly speaking, he had found the starting-point of theology in what happens within the believing soul, not in historic fact. As we have seen, he had declared in so many words that doctrines, so far from being statements about what is objectively given and apprehended by faith, are descriptions of our own pious mental affections. To a pragmatic mind like Ritschl's this was intolerable. In his view it amounted to romantic sentimentalism ; and the one way to escape from it is to have a firm foothold in history.

Enough on this subject has been said at an earlier point, and the matter need not delay us now. The needed foothold Ritschl found in the Person of Jesus Christ, the revealer of the Father, as set forth in the New Testament. Living faith springs from the soil of past events.

Subjectivism, then, is indifferent to history and in consequence leaves us in the lurch ; so, for the same reason, do Natural Theology and Mysticism. The weakness of Natural Theology is that it builds on general ideas unconnected either with revelation or with vital Christian faith. The famous proofs of God's being—cosmological, teleological, and ontological—start from outside personal Christianity and hence can never bring you inside. They may perhaps render a Supreme Being more probable than not ; but a Supreme Being, even if proved, is so far devoid of all moral character and can never satisfy those who above all are seeking the forgiveness of sins. God in Christ—this is a sinner's only religion. We can only know God in the measure in which He makes Himself known to us. " Every claim," as Ritschl puts it roundly, " to teach something concerning God in Himself apart from some real revelation on His part, felt and perceived on ours, is baseless." [1]

Mysticism too is essentially unhistorical in basis and character, perhaps also uninterested in morality ; and Ritschl showed himself peculiarly sensitive to its religious shortcomings as a Christian thinker must judge them. Not, at all events superficially, without very good reason. In one of Miss Evelyn Underhill's authoritative books this revealing sentence is found : " We cannot honestly say that there is any wide difference between the Brahman, Sufi, or Christian Mystic at their best." [2] Ritschl could not wish to have his point put more exactly. The Christian mystic, *qua* mystic, is virtually indistinguishable from his

---

[1] *Theologie und Metaphysik*, p. 34.
[2] *Essentials of Mysticism*, p. 4.

Brahman counterpart, which (Ritschl would add) is tantamount to saying that he is not distinctively Christian at
all.   He does not take the authentically Christian attitude
to Jesus.   In rising up to God, and communing with
Him, he affects to transcend and dispense with the Mediator.   Once the lamp has been lit, the taper may be cast
aside ;   and Ritschl finds that all thoroughgoing mystics
treat Christ as a merely temporary aid in mounting to
the really supreme experience.   They make light of the
Gospel of the New Testament as well as of the means of
grace ;   they tend to cut loose from Church fellowship ;
they teach the deification of man ;   they give little place
or none to the forgiveness of sins ;   they indulge in an
irreverent familiarity with the Saviour which may well
have deplorable moral consequences.   On three central
points Ritschl meets the mystical view with a direct and
unqualified repudiation.   He repels the suggestions that
the true relationship of the soul to God can be fully realized
only in isolation from the Church and the world ;   that
the highest type of communion with God is not necessarily mediated by acceptance of the New Testament
message ;   and that love rather than faith is our proper
attitude to Christ.

It is now widely felt that Ritschl failed to distinguish
fitly between different types of mysticism, less and more
evangelical in character ;   and that while in the main his
censure of pantheistic mysticism is just, he has certainly
not proved his case against that personalistic type of mystical thought which is to be found at its profoundest in
the pages of St. Paul and the Fourth Evangelist, and is
indeed very much equivalent to the deepest and most
intimate kind of personal religion.   To this no doubt
Ritschl would answer that no writer of the New Testament
is a mystic in the sense which the word properly bears in
general religious history, as when we speak of Indian,
Persian or Greek " mysticism " ;   for the sufficient reason

that no New Testament writer ever employs or recommends a mystical technique, or is tempted to rise superior to historical revelation or to the distinction between good and evil.   We cannot now debate the meaning of a word. But at all events it may be laid down that, as against both Natural Theology and Mysticism, Ritschl was wholly in the right when he insisted that we can only know God in the measure that He puts Himself sovereignly within reach of our knowledge.   This does not imply that apart from His self-disclosure in history God is totally unknowable ; we cannot but ascribe to Him the power to reveal Himself through Nature if He should will this, and in so far as He wills it.   There is a certain divine significance in the two qualities of Nature, that it can be construed by intelligence and that it culminates in man.   Yet Ritschl did not err in holding that apart from Christ we cannot know or grasp God as a redeeming Father ; and on our own account we may add the point that even what God has written of Himself into Nature can only be truly read by those whose eyes have been opened by the great revelation in Jesus.   If our relationship to God is to be that of accepted children, it must be mediated by apprehension of His decisive Word, spoken in Christ, of judgment and mercy.   With all the fathers of the Reformed Church, Ritschl taught that this Word of God is to be found in Scripture only.   The New Testament in particular, he added, is our supreme source of truth because its writings spring from a living connexion with the primitive age of the Church and reveal a unity of vital tissue with the faith of the Old Testament.   Once we have understood this, we need no special doctrine concerning the inspiration of the Bible.

The chief and most fruitful distinction between Ritschl's theological method and that of the majority of his immediate predecessors—liberal or mediating—is that he starts not from the " Christian consciousness ", but from

the " Gospel " given in Jesus Christ. What Dogmatic is
called to do is not to describe or elucidate the existing
state of the Christian mind ; its proper task, rather, is to
bring out and expound with all possible completeness the
norm to which Christian piety must conform ; for in
revelation God makes insistent *claims* on man.   There is
such a thing as the obedience of faith ; and theology is
summoned to set forth the revealed truth apprehension of
which is thus incumbent on the believing mind.   In that
sense theology has a definitely authoritative character.
What man is to believe concerning God, what duty God
requires of man—these things are to be gathered not, as
by Schleiermacher and some later thinkers, from an analysis
of this or that in man, even Christian man, but from the
presentation of God in Christ set forth in the New Testament.   When we try to " place " Ritschl in the historical
succession, then, it is this newness of approach, of persistently applied method, that we have to fix upon.   As
Kattenbusch has rightly insisted, Ritschl was a great
teacher because without robbing men of theological independence he called them to a certain *task*—" the task
of shaping the system of Christian doctrine by reference
to the controlling principle that God is to be thought of
ὡς περὶ Χριστοῦ. God's self-attestation in history being
the starting-point, not the conclusion, of dogmatic reflexion
—to have brought *this* out is the importance of Ritschl,
and it will remain even when much in the detail of his
work has lost value ".   " A Ritschlian," he adds, " is
spared the agony of self-analysis ; he will not seek to
discover ' scientifically ' how rich his heart is, or how
poor ; nor is it for him by taking stock of himself to fix
the factors by which he can best make clear, to himself
or others, wherein the content of Christianity lies."   His
business is to spell out the infinite meaning of Jesus Christ
for our conception of God.   Whether Ritschl's actual performance was equal to his intention is quite another story ;

but at all events his deliberate and announced purpose so far merits grateful recognition, and, amid the successive developments of nineteenth-century theology, stands out arrestingly by its originality and power.

§ 3.   SOME ASPECTS OF HIS CONSTRUCTIVE EFFORT

It scarcely need be said that in this brief sketch no attempt will be made to furnish a complete or all-round exposition of the Ritschlian system. Ritschl himself left various doctrines all but untouched ; on the Trinity, the Christian sacraments, and eschatology he wrote no more than a few sentences. I only wish to illustrate by some special examples how his newly found method for treating the dogmatic problem led him to think and write.

(a) *His practical conception of religion.* In Ritschl's view, religion is a practical, not a speculative affair ; in it knowledge is subordinated to will, and by it moral personality is vindicated over against the challenge of the world. Schleiermacher was wholly right in claiming that religion has an independence of its own, and that it is to the religious man himself we must go, not to the philosopher weaving theories about him, if his believing life is to be understood. The idea that the truth of religion can be made evident to any man of ordinary intelligence, apart from his possession of a specifically religious experience of his own, is to be rejected once for all. He cannot, that is, be compelled to acknowledge the being of God if he is not already conscious of standing before One to be reverenced and adored. The object of religious feeling is definitely not capable of being demonstrated on grounds which ignore the feeling itself.

One of Ritschl's best-known passages may serve as text.

The distinction of worth or value [he writes] is of no importance whatever for the metaphysical theory of the universe, whereas the religious view of things rests on the fact that man distinguishes himself in worth from the phenomena around him.[1]

And again :

In every religion what is sought, with the help of the super-human spiritual power reverenced by man, is a solution of the contradiction in which man finds himself as both a part of nature and a spiritual personality claiming to dominate nature.[2]

Religion comes, that is, to solve a practical tension. As we confront the world helplessly, faith rises up to affirm the existence of transcendent spiritual powers by whose aid we are enabled to cope with the ordeal and thrust back the otherwise annihilating forces of Nature.[3] Here we see the champion of personality and moral values at odds, on the one hand, with contemporary naturalistic pessimism and, on the other, with the idealist submergence of the individual in the mass.

Now it cannot be said that Ritschl's views of the specific character and tendency of religion are altogether to his credit. Not only, as Brunner points out forcibly, does he eventually apply this general idea of religion to Christianity, and in doing so wipe out the absolute distinction between universal religion without a Mediator and a definite rev-elation *with* a Mediator. This certainly is serious, but there is more than this. His view of religion as such is utili-tarian and intramundane. Broadly speaking, he argues that religion has emerged as a product of the struggle for existence. As he puts it roundly, and in a fashion that seems more than half unjust to his own deepest convictions, " religion is the instrument man possesses to free himself from the natural conditions of life ". God is the needed prop of ethical aspiration, the trustee of

[1] Cf. *Theologie und Metaphysik*, pp. 9 and 34.

[2] *Justification and Reconciliation*, p. 199.

[3] Here, it should be observed, Nature includes " the natural effects of human society ".

our moral interests. But, we must ask, in a description
of this kind is there anything that radically distinguishes
religion from civilization, which also in its own way is
the conquest of nature, the realization of man's free sway
over the world ?   On Ritschl's terms the attitude of man
to the cosmos is made central and all-determining, not
his attitude to God. The point is one at which the
theologian wholly loses touch with Scripture. At the
supreme level of the Psalms, or in St. Paul, communion
with God, clearly, is sought essentially for its own sake,
and no room is left anywhere for the insinuation that
when turning to God in prayer the believer is animated
by ulterior motives lying outside a desire for such fellowship itself, even if these should actually be motives concerned with the gains of moral self-improvement.   Ritschl,
it will be agreed, was fully justified in stressing the fact
that faith does create a new attitude to Nature in the
widest sense of that word, and to this he gives noble
expression in his doctrine of the Christian's lordship over
the world. He was all the more bound to make clear
that such lordship flows from the gift of a new and
creative relation to God Himself. But to speak, even
incidentally, as if the function of God were to stand
surety for the attainment of human purposes, even though
these purposes at their highest are moral, was to invite
the graver error of *Kulturprotestantismus* in the next
generation. It could only end in " this-worldly " religion.
Closely related to this tendency to make ethical values
the first interest of faith is Ritschl's predominantly moral
view of what the New Testament means by the " Kingdom
of God ". The Kingdom for him becomes pretty much
equivalent to " the moral unification of the human race,
through action prompted by universal love to our neighbour ". Thus religion tends to become only a new aspect
of moral activity. The Kingdom of God, stripped of the
eschatological transcendence that belongs to it in the

Gospels, is now hardly more than (as with Kant) a realm
of moral ends, a purely present and mundane common-
wealth. From this total lapse Ritschl barely saves himself by periodic recurrence to the famous figure in which
he pictures Christianity as like an ellipse with its two
foci—the moral focus being the Kingdom of God, the
religious focus, on the other hand, redemption through
Christ.

(*b*) *The contrast of theoretical and religious knowledge.*
Two principles of general epistemology, which for Ritschl
have almost the status of axioms, ought to be noted here
by way of introduction. One is more nominalistic : it is
to the effect that only particular ideas have any correspondence to reality, whereas general ideas—like that of
space—are pure abstractions, merely subjective notions
formed in our mind when in memory we unite the common
features of different objects. Universals, in other words,
are in no sense *in rebus*. The second axiom is phenomenal-
istic, and teaches that we cannot pretend to know individual
objects in themselves ; all we can know is their appearances, their relations to and connexions with ourselves ;
but *Dinge an sich* escape our perception altogether.
Experience alone, not ratiocination or the methods of
logical deduction, brings us to knowledge. The application of this is to be found in an uncompromising statement
of theological positivism : " we know God only in His
effects upon us ". Unless we confine our apprehension of
God within these limits, we have no guarantee of religious
certainty ; and indeed there is one disconcerting passage
in which, throwing all prudence to the winds, Ritschl
declares that his theological method is a revival of Schleiermacher's analysis of the individual religious consciousness.
A study of Ritschl's disquisitions in this general field
leaves on the reader's mind the impression that he had
not sufficiently clarified his theory of knowledge ; for he
commonly uses language which, as it stands, has to be inter-

preted in a subjectivistic sense, but which he sets aside
without compunction when the need for realistic expression
becomes urgent.

Over against the claims of idealistic rationalism, which
finds the basis for theology in philosophy, Ritschl argued
for the view that specifically Christian knowledge of God
takes shape in value-judgments evoked by revelation.
It was largely because they fixed on this idea, according
to which all vital dogmatic affirmations represent " judgments of value ", that the various members of the Ritschlian group held together for years as a coherent whole
and definitely became the object of criticism.   In sentences often quoted,[1] Ritschl underlines the distinction
between judgments of a theoretical kind, which make
relatively disinterested assertions concerning objects as
they exist in their own nature, and judgments of worth,
in which we apprehend realities that are unconditionally
valuable or precious for us.   The contrast, of course, has
long been familiar in ethics.   There we are accustomed
to distinguish between fact and value, between an existential proposition and a moral estimate.   If the distinction
be carried over to religion, and brought to bear on revealing
data, we then have Ritschl's view in broad outline.   Thus
" Jesus Christ died on Calvary " is a simple judgment of
fact, which the pure historian might make ; but " we
have redemption through His blood " is, in Ritschlian
terms, " an independent value-judgment ", or, in plain
English, a personal conviction.   It announces what we
find in the Cross to appreciate and cling to for our relation
with God.   Ritschl struck a new note by trying to work
out consistently the principle that " we know the nature
of God and Christ only in their worth for us ".   Dogmatic,
he held, ought to contain nothing but just such personal
convictions, kindled in the mind by revelation and leading

[1] See *Justification and Reconciliation*, Engl. transl. of Vol. III,
p. 203 ff.

on to a new obedience ; for a judgment of value may be said to be by itself the sufficient cause of a direct act of will. He exhorts us to put nothing into theology except what it takes faith to apprehend—nothing indeed, as he puts it, perhaps somewhat rashly, which might not be used in preaching or in the private talk of Christians.

" Value-judgments in theology ", as a war-cry, caused a good deal of stir. Some of the criticisms, it must be said frankly, were needlessly perverse or even childish. Thus the doctrine is not, as was suggested at the time, a new way of saying that Christian people may believe what they like, if only they like it very much. And it is wrong-headed to insinuate that the very term " value-judgment " denies the objectivity of that which is valued, or is at best neutral on the point. The judgment that a thing is good presupposes or includes the judgment that the thing is real.[1] In our living experience, fact and value never exist apart ; both are presented together as a complex whole which is indissociable, or dissociable only for thought. What is more, Ritschl proceeded throughout on the fundamental assumption that faith, in making value-judgments, bases itself upon, and responds to, the saving revelation of God in Christ. Our findings in science and our convictions in religion, in short, are reached by different avenues. Once the thing has been pointed out, it is surely plain that the Fatherhood of God, His forgiveness of sins, and the hope of eternal life are not equally real and sure to all minds. To be certain who Christ is we must accept His absolute claim upon our lives, and the man whose heart is not set upon righteousness cannot see what the Gospel is for. Thus in

---

[1] " There is, in fact, no such thing in our experience as a pure and undiluted judgment either of value or existence. All judgments of existence imply some activity of valuing, and all judgments of value imply an existential judgment " (W. R. Matthews, *Purpose of God*, p. 113).

the realities disclosed through Christ, faith has a norm or standard to which it is ever striving to conform; so that, evoked and sustained at every point by revelation, it lives and moves not by sufferance or permission of philosophy or science, but by the meaning of what God has done in Christ. Christian men do not throw out their minds at mere wishes or dreams, defiantly or wistfully projected into reality; they are not postulating anything,[1] or taking the presence of a desire as sufficient proof that the desired object exists. They only seek to let God in Christ tell them what they ought to believe about Himself, or sin, or pardon, or eternal life.

As to the objective intention of religious value-judgments, then, no question ought to have been raised. The vital issue emerges at quite another point. It is whether the standard of value we apply in thus affirming our recognition of God in Christ is merely moral, or also transcendent; or, to put it otherwise, whether in confronting Christ and forming the judgment of faith upon Him and His work we bring with us, as it were read made, the standards by which He is to be estimated,[2] o have them new-created in us, through specific revelation, by the Spirit of God. In the one case, revelation comes through One of whom all we can say is that He is morally indistinguishable from God—One whom man by himself can recognize as such; in the other, the sovereign unanticipated God is revealed through a Person in whom He gives Himself in utterly free grace, declaring His will sovereignly, and creating thereby the very faith by which He can be apprehended.

(c) *The historical revelation of God in Christ.* The criteria

---

[1] Not that there are not passages which teach that faith postulates the being of God as essential to realizing the moral purposes of man, but they are overborne on the whole by his emphasis on revelation.

[2] To Ritschl, Brunner has said, Christ is " the Bearer of a moral religious idea which in itself is valid " (*The Mediator*, p. 97).

he was to make use of in theology Ritschl drew from his scientific interest in history. Solid research, as he felt, would make an end of purely subjective speculation. Religion must feed upon concrete facts and events. When it takes flight from historical realities, it becomes either mysticism or rationalism ; and these temporary aberrations are pardonable only when the weight of tradition is on the point of suffocating vital faith. It was indeed his regard for the facts of history that gave Ritschl his charter of freedom in critical research ; to him nothing mattered but the revelation of God given not alongside of history but within it, given in great religious personalities and their experiences, above all in Christ. Here lies one secret of his power over the contemporary youth. He was felt to be building theology afresh on the bedrock of actual events which could be ascertained, and men were encouraged to investigate all such events with perfect freedom. Life owes to the past all that makes it rich. " If you want a picture of spiritual beggary," says a vivid writer, " contemplate the mind of man stripped of all its historical accumulations and sitting naked among the eternal truths of reason." An age hungry for fact was taught by Ritschl that true Christian religion, no less than literature, science, art or political knowledge, has its roots in bygone events and is nourished by their sap. Hence he took his generation back to the New Testament, read in the light of the Reformation. Earlier movements had sought to take hold of the past, but the past they selected had not always been the right one. Their efforts had too often issued in a mere restoration of outworn orthodoxies, instead of regaining touch with the vital springs of revelation as they rise and flow in Scripture.

Luther was to him the great hero who had freed the Gospel from its chains and presented it to the world more purely than had been done since the days of the apostles. As it has been put, Ritschl did not start from

Lutheranism, then ask whether it agreed with the Bible; he ended with it, because he felt it to be the Biblical theology *par excellence*. No modern German theologian has ever been more eager to have Luther on his side. Here, above all in Luther's primary works, Ritschl finds that religious appreciation of the Gospel for which he himself stands—its practical concern with the ultimate ends of human life, its derivation of repentance from the sight of God's love rather than from fear of His law, the living bond between faith and assurance, the rejection of all cosmology and metaphysics that might interfere with the direct apprehension of God's pardoning mercy in Jesus Christ.

Yet it cannot be said that the bearing of revelation and history on each other is quite so simple as Ritschl takes it to be. Christ, the Revealer of God, is indeed *in* history ; but Ritschl failed to see, or at least failed to insist, that He is not *of* history, and that for this very reason His being in history at all is a Divine marvel. The historian's business is to make each event luminous as the outcome of its antecedents and its *milieu* ; but if the being of Christ is in fact transcendent, if in a sense upon which everything depends He has come " from the other side of reality ", if, as we contemplate Him in the Gospels, we become aware that God is present in Him *incognito*, then to approach the interpretation of His Person with the normal assumptions as to what history is, is inevitably to confuse the issue. We have to think harder and more persistently about the problem, which has no parallel because it is the only one in its class—how the eternal can be present and be recognized in the temporal.[1] It is clear, also, that Ritschl ignores the fact that when in faith we betake ourselves to Scripture, it is not to employ

[1] As Kähler of Halle a generation ago urged the Church to do, and as the Barthians now are doing. See, especially, Brunner's *The Mediator*.

it as a historical source-book, but rather as authentic witness to Christ, in which the voice of God Himself is heard. The insight of faith is something else than historical perception, just as the grace of God is something more than historical affiliation. The same tendency to read everything in terms of the immanental factors of development led him in effect to replace the action of the exalted Lord on the Church by a merely posthumous influence.

Christianity is defined as the absolutely ethical religion, based on the Person and Work of Jesus Christ, who founded the Kingdom of God. It imparts the blessed freedom of God's children. The Kingdom, described as " the organization of humanity through action inspired by love ", is at once the supreme purpose of the Father and man's highest good—a Divine gift and a human task. It is the Kingdom of love because God Himself is love.

Thus Ritschl takes the simple apostolic words, " God is love ", and out of them constructs a definition in the strict sense. It is a thought of the Supreme Being, he declares, to which no other faith offers a parallel ; it is sufficient and all-inclusive, and as such entitled to expel from the Christian mind every other concept, like the philosophical notion of " the Absolute ", which has long struggled with it for supremacy even in Church doctrine. If we take " love " seriously, analysing its implications, it will be seen as involving the Divine personality and all other attributes of God which it is the interest of Christian faith to affirm. Now, that God is love no Christian thinker, I suppose, has ever sought to deny. But Ritschl takes it much too easily for granted that the whole meaning of " love " explains itself as it were by nature, and certainly the conception he expounds betrays nothing of that tension and antinomy which so obviously characterizes the Biblical interpretation of the word. The holiness of God is put aside on amazingly slender grounds, and with its disappearance much else is lost. There is here no idea of divine punishment, of a divine righteousness manifested in punishment, of a divine wrath. But as Herrmann insisted, Ritschl's denial of the wrath of God was a great sin against the Christian soul. To assert unflinchingly that love and holiness are one in God, despite their seeming antagonism, is as much the business of a true theology as to assert that deity and manhood are one in Christ. Brunner has made the point so effectively that his words deserve to be quoted.

When Ritschl deliberately suppresses the idea of the holiness of God alongside of the love of God, this is not merely a special element in his doctrine of the " Divine attributes ", but a fundamental contradiction of the scriptural knowledge of God. It not only renders his idea of God incomplete and in need of correction, but it makes it something fundamentally different from the Christian idea of God altogether ; it is rational and one-sided in contrast to the paradox of the Christian faith.[1]

This rationalism and over-simplification could not but reflect itself in Ritschl's view of sin. After all, there is nothing in God for the sinner to be afraid of, except, oddly enough, in the final consummation of all things. Pursuing his constant aim to remove from theology all such elements of abstract metaphysic as had lost their value, Ritschl turned the Augustinian doctrine of Original Sin out of doors, mainly on two grounds. In the first place, he felt, it implied a false hypostatization of the race as distinct from the individuals composing it ; in the second, it is discordant with the plain fact of experience that men are sinful in varying degrees. He contends that sin can be understood as essentially an individual phenomenon, each of us in turn being led astray by the bad influences emanating from our collective life. But human life as such, the movement of history itself, is not radically

[1] Brunner, *The Mediator*, p. 282.

corrupt. This explains his curious insistence on the real
possibility of sinless lives, which, according to Ritschl, is
not to be denied either on *a priori* grounds or in view of
the actual conditions of experience.

As a further important detail it ought to be noted that,
in Ritschl's view, " sin is judged by God as ignorance ",
since otherwise it would be unpardonable. Not only is
this out of line with Biblical thought and reminiscent
rather of the Greek doctrine that virtue is knowledge,
but it is an idea which it is impossible to hold before our
minds in the hour of penitence.

We cannot enter upon the Christology of Ritschl without remarking that he would not have claimed to teach
any Christology in the older sense of the word, though he
had of course his own view of our Lord's Person. But
he did not start on familiar lines. Thus he contended
that some traditional problems, like that of the " Two
Natures ", or the relation of the Son to the Father within
the Trinity, have no real bearing on experience and ought
to be put aside as lying beyond our range. Similarly,
he preferred to leave undiscussed such questions as the
Virgin Birth, or particular aspects of the Resurrection,
not at all because his findings on these points were
negative, but because the religious valuation of Christ
ought not to be encumbered with problems so superfluous. " Where I find mystery, I say nothing about it."
But it was a sound principle with him that the discussion
of Christ's Person cannot be usefully separated from His
Work. There is no Christological problem at all for
those who lack the Christian experience, whereas tradition
was apt to demand certain orthodox concessions before
that experience could itself be had.

He starts, then, with the historical Christ, not the
dogma of the God-man, still less any principle that can
be conceived in abstraction from His Person. His point
of departure is the recorded manifestation of God in

Christ, apprehended by believing historical perception. It is an axiom with Ritschl that in theology every detail must be Christocentric, though his system is so in avowed method rather than in reality. The uniqueness of Christ for him is grounded not in His being but in the fact that His supreme personal purpose is one with the God-appointed final purpose of all things.

We shall best understand Christ's Person, then, by understanding what He has done for men. As it has been admirably put, " What Ritschl holds is that the only possible way in which we can know that Christ is God is from His having the worth of God for our souls, and that He has this worth for them because He does a work which only God can do." [1] The fount of all redemption is Christ's supreme act in establishing the Church on earth. In perfect fidelity He fulfilled the vocation given Him by the Father, suffering all that hatred and unbelief could inflict and exhibiting utter patience unto death ; and this great act of obedience is the ground on which His followers, as a community, are declared righteous by God and have their sins forgiven. Jesus being its representative, the Church has imputed to it the position relatively to God which He held for Himself inviolably to the end. From first to last by His obedience He kept Himself in the love of God, thereby securing pardon and access to God for all His people. The fact that in the title of his most famous book " Justification " comes before " Reconciliation " shows of itself that, at a vital point, Ritschl had failed to keep touch with the New Testament. To the apostles " reconciliation " is something God has done, in virtue of which the sinful can come to be right with Him. To Ritschl, reconciliation is an experience of man ; it is man's giving up that distrust of God which had been due to a misapprehension of the Divine character and is removed by the sight of Christ's

---

[1] J. Dickie, *Organism of Christian Truth*, p. 297.

faithfulness in His vocation even unto death. Yet, as
we must interject, the distinction between an act of God
and an experience of man constitutes the distinction—
wide as the poles—between " objective " and merely
" subjective " views of Reconciliation.

The New Testament speaks of Jesus' death as a sacrifice
to God ; but in Ritschl's exegesis this is a sacrifice of
obedience, not of penalty. The traditional doctrine,
according to which Christ was punished for our sins, is
sub-Christian.

That Christ, through vicariously enduring the penalty in-
curred by sinful mankind, appeased the righteousness or the
wrath of God and liberated His grace, is a view which cannot
be proved by any clear and direct passage of the New Testament ; it rests on assumptions of Natural Theology obviously
derived from Pharisaic and Hellenic sources.[1]

It is an error to put the righteousness of God in opposition
to His forgiving love. The Divine righteousness, Ritschl
argues with relevance and point, is not shown to us in
Scripture as clothed in a vesture of pitiless rigour ; it is
in reality the faithfulness of God to His people, and thus
an expression or specific form of His grace. Tradition
leads us to say : " A just God and yet a Saviour." The
Bible says : " A just God and *therefore* a Saviour." [2]

Such is the Work of Christ, and the reality of His Person
shines through. Nothing but a confession of His Deity
will do justice to the mission He accomplished in the world.
For the theologian, that estimate or doctrine of Christ is
based primarily in an ethical judgment on His fidelity to
His task. He is the archetype of moral personality.

What in the historically complete life we recognize to be
the real worth of His existence, gains for ourselves, through
the uniqueness of the phenomenon and its normative bearing

[1] *Unterricht,* § 42.
[2] Readers of McLeod Campbell will find themselves here on
familiar ground.

upon our own religious and ethical destiny, the worth of an
abiding rule, since we at the same time discover that, only
through the impulse and direction we receive from Him, is it
possible for us to enter into His relation to God and to the
world.

Along with this ethical judgment goes a religious one, to
the effect that in this person God reveals Himself as love.
Thus Christ becomes the absolute Authority, the Lord of
the Church. " An authority which either excludes all
other standards or subordinates them to itself, and at the
same time bends all human trust, without remainder,
upon God, has the value of Deity." If we take these
two judgments or estimates together, the religious and
the ethical, our path is clear. " The twofold significance
we are compelled to ascribe to Christ as being at once
the perfect revealer of God and the manifested type of
spiritual lordship over the world, finds expression in the
single predicate of His Deity." [1]

This confession of our Lord's Godhead is, in form, a
direct value-judgment based on historical perception.
Now with Ritschl it is an axiom that no assertions ought
to be made about Christ the full meaning of which cannot
be exhibited from His earthly life. But as His pre-
existence is not historically perceptible, it strictly forms
no part of Christology; in Ritschl's phrase, " as pre-
existent, Christ is hidden for us ". On the other hand,
we are led to expect a fuller and more Biblical doctrine
of the exalted Lord by some arresting words found at
the very heart of his discussion. " Our faith in Christ,"
he writes, " is not faith in Him as One Who was, but
faith in Him as One Who continues to work." [2]   None
the less this is followed by the statement that the influence
of the exalted Lord is to be viewed simply as a prolonga-
tion of the effects of His historical existence, and that
there is nothing convincing about the idea of His living

[1] *Justification and Reconciliation*, p. 389.   [2] *Ibid.*, p. 400.

Deity as it is now except as the features of it can be pointed to in His earthly career. Thus the activity of the Exalted One has no new or special content of its own. What Christ is doing for His Church now is the posthumous result of what He did in the first century. The full significance of the words, " All power is given unto Me in heaven and on earth " must be capable of being found, without remainder, in the Gospel story. In consequence that transcendent declaration is translated into the merely ethical judgment that Christ is still Lord of circumstance in the same sense (but no other) as when He triumphed over the world by accepting the Cross.

" As the author of the perfectly spiritual and ethical religion," Ritschl declares, " Jesus is above all other men." He is " the Founder of Christianity " ; for He inaugurated a new relation between God and man, a relation which He fully realized in His own life and which as the Creator of faith He reproduces in believers. He therefore has for us the religious value of God. It is in just these qualities that His Deity appears. It is not explained by or based in a special Divine " nature ", underlying His moral character and action, and distinguishable from them. It is identical with His ethical will itself, which stamps Him as One who belongs to the Divine side of reality. The confession of Christ's Deity by its very nature thus springs out of the experience of His grace.

That this vein of reflection has its own peculiar value is not of course to be denied. To Ritschl as much as to any single thinker it is due that to-day the general Christian mind discerns the Person of our Lord through the medium of His actually redeeming influence, exemplified though not exhaustively disclosed in the treatment of sinners while He lived on earth. So far from being a merely modern idea, this type of interpretation goes back to Luther, who never wearied of insisting that to construe

the Incarnation we must start from the earthly facts of
Jesus' personal history—must, as he puts it, " begin from
below and then come upwards ". Ritschl's argument,
then, so far as it goes, is both religiously wholesome and
indispensable for apologetics. If Christ does for men
what none but God can do, is not the inevitable question
raised how we shall rightly name Him except by calling
Him God ? But does Ritschl let the argument carry
him all the way ?

To answer this is much less easy than might be supposed.
Here, as so often, we are confronted by the possibility of
divergence between a writer's personal convictions and
the logical implications of his actual words. No doubt is
possible on the subject of his personal belief. " Christians,"
he declares roundly, " are called to trust and worship
Christ as they do God the Father." And in a private
letter he dwells upon his special formulation of the old
truth and justifies it :

I am quite clear that I affirm the Deity of Christ, although
I reject the older method of its presentation, for that earlier
view fails alike to show how in the historical person the Deity
and the humanity are identical, and to bring out the close
relation between Christ's Deity and the universal reconciliation
He accomplished.

The sincerity of such an assertion is indubitable.

But in the light of some definite forms of argumentation,
the matter becomes much less clear. Thus it is explicitly
laid down that the Deity of Christ must be capable of
imitation by His people. Moreover, it is a question
whether for Ritschl the predicates which are validly
ascribed to the exalted Lord are not also in consistency
to be affirmed of the Church, since by their living union
with the Church believers enter into the same relationship
to God as that of Christ Himself. Waiving this point,
we cannot easily pass by the assertion that in no sense
is there an impassable gulf between Christ and us. This

plainly is not the believing attitude to Jesus as the New Testament discloses it. That Christ is *also* on the human side of reality leaves unaffected the truth that He is infinitely above us. And it will not do to cancel the unapproachable uniqueness of the Lord by putting Him at a level we can rise to by imitation. Of course all is quite clear if Ritschl means simply that Jesus is the organ of the Divine will, the first representative of all that men ought to be, and the most perfect representative of this ; and that we gather up both these affirmations in the doctrine of His Deity. In that case, Ritschl's Christology manifestly belongs to that familiar type which asserts that our Lord is Divine not as being one in essence with God, but as being perfectly united and harmonious with Him in will. On such terms it is hard to see how, except presumably in degree, He is to be distinguished from prophets or other pious men. Harmony of will, if it be no more, may conceivably lapse into disharmony. And if the Church is right in holding that Christ is as Divine as the Father and as human as ourselves, the differences between Him and us cannot be merely ethical in character.

Similarly, it is urged by Ritschl that the dogma of His pre-existence would give Christ a solitary greatness of which His people could not partake. To be sure, he makes a sound point when he protests that " we must first be able to prove the Godhead that is revealed before we take account of the Godhead that is eternal ". Nor must we bluntly say that he denies pre-existence outright ; his precise contention is that it is real for God only, not for us, though how exactly we can *know* it to be real for God except as it is somehow real for ourselves, may be difficult to understand. In any case, Ritschl displays little sense for the ineffable religious fact of which the idea of Christ's pre-existence is a symbol. In one way or another the vast evangelical truth must be put in words that in the

coming of Christ into human life God gave us nothing
less or lower than Himself. Sacrifice that touches God's
very being is involved in Christ's being here at all. All
the redemptive grace present in the Saviour existed in
God from before all worlds ; and it was out of immeasurable Divine self-bestowal in personal mercy that He came
forth Whom in time we know as Jesus. This, whatever
the shortcomings of human language, is what the idea of
pre-existence stands for ; and it is idle to suppose that
the scope and dimensions of the Gospel can remain
unaffected when it is left out.

(d) *The mediation of the Church.* We have the less need
to dwell on Ritschl's teaching about Forgiveness that, on
the whole, it conforms more closely to familiar Reformation doctrine. To him, as to Luther and Calvin, justification is to be defined as God's effective will to receive into
fellowship with Himself the sinner who accepts Christ
and His work. It is, in short, forgiveness. This Divine
act, imparting as it does blessedness and goodness to its
objects, has as its one precondition simple faith—that is,
a humble confidence in the grace of God, evoked and
sustained by the good news of pardon in Christ. Such
faith is an act of will, and must not be confused with a
mere form of knowledge. It is rather, as Ritschl phrases
it, " a new direction of the will upon God ". The religious
importance of justification cannot, in his view, be over-
estimated. It is, he declares emphatically, the fundamental principle of Christianity as a religion ; it is something which alone makes possible all those " functions "
or specific activities of the believing life that answer to
it. It removes the separation between God and mañ
consequent upon guilt, abolishing the mistrust which guilt
by its very nature engenders. To be called into the
Kingdom of God is an experience which actually deepens
and intensifies the feeling of guilty separation from the
Father, and unless this were taken away by God Himself,

at the first and ever anew, the founding and the main-
tenance of the Kingdom would be impossible.

On two points Ritschl lays a stress that is largely his
own. In the first place, the judgment of God in forgiving
sin is synthetic in character, not analytic ; which, being
interpreted, means that pardoned men possess no claim
to pardon in themselves. Nowhere in them, be it their
faith, their penitence, their love or good works, is there
a human basis of merit which entitles them to be forgiven.
They are pardoned altogether irrespectively of the *moral*
quality of their life, for the believer knows himself to be
the chief of sinners ; forgiveness is a *creative* act of God.
Here Ritschl proves himself a true child of Luther.
Secondly, justification as a gospel is bound up indissociably
with Christ.   The love of God, so far from being a natural
certainty, can be known only by revelation ; in like
manner, it is vain to make forgiveness a logical inference
from some general concept of God.   The validity of forgiveness definitely hangs upon the truth that God is
known as Father only through the specific life-work of
Jesus Christ.

If it be asked how men can make saving contact with
the work of Christ, and how His obedience can become
theirs, Ritschl answers with great decision that this
happens solely through the mediation of the Church as
the community of believers, the living fellowship in
which the Gospel is preached and the work of Christ
perpetuated. Justification, as he puts it, " is related in
the first instance to the whole of the religious community ".
As the Reformers saw, the whole is essentially and con-
ceptually prior to its parts, the Church to its members.
Christ as Priest is the representative of His people as a
corporate body ; to say that He founded the Church and
that He mediates to men the assurance of forgiveness is
one and the same thing. It is in the society of the
faithful that a man enters into personal relations with

Christ, so that to be a member of the Church is identical with being in pardoned fellowship with God. " How," he exclaims, " shall we regard the community as the original subject of the Gospel, unless we consider it at the same time as the original object of the justifying grace which continues to operate in the Gospel ! " [1]

It is perhaps not difficult to understand why at this point the accusation should have gained currency that Ritschl had lapsed into Romanist modes of thought and given a new lease of life to the old hierarchical maxim : *Extra ecclesiam nulla salus.* Does he not place the Church where Christ ought to be, as the actual depository of salvation ? But this is to misapprehend. It was not in all his thoughts to set up a legally ecclesiastical system of mediation through which alone the individual sinner could find God. He was asking how the Gospel of pardon reaches us, how it is laid down at our door and commended to us by word and life ; and with perfect truth he answers that this comes to pass through the mediation of the Christian society, whose life touches ours. In addition, it must be observed that for Ritschl and for Rome the Church means different things. What is before his mind is not the Church as an institution created and legitimized by its hierarchy, with a regularized priesthood and a legally obligatory creed ; for him the Church is the *communio sanctorum,* the living body of believers, in the midst of which the redeeming Gospel of Christ endures throughout the generations. It is within this Church, truly represented by its members however imperfect, that the individual comes into saving attachment to the Lord. The grace which he meets and enjoys in Christ he could not have discovered, in Luther's phrase, " all by himself in a corner " ; it is invariably put within his reach by those who bear witness to its reality. There is no need to say that Ritschl's exposition of his principle is adequate ;

[1] *Justification and Reconciliation,* p. 550.

it could in fact hardly be altogether adequate if, as we
have seen, he conceived of the living Christ's relation to
His people, in semi-deistic fashion, as more or less equivalent to a posthumous influence. But in itself the principle is sound ; and we owe him something for the fresh
accent he thus laid on the truth that the Christian life, in
origin and continuance, is not accidentally but essentially
corporate.

(e) *The idea of Christian Perfection.* Theology, as
Ritschl saw it, must in the first place be completely
religious and in the second be firmly based on the fact
of historical revelation. But also, reaching out to concrete life, he strove to give it a vitally close relation to
religious practice, and there is no part of his work which
more obviously than the final chapter of his great book
reveals a desire to put aside abstractions and get close to
reality. That chapter deals with the religious " functions "
which spring from reconciliation to God, and with the
religious aspect of moral action.

Perfection, the supreme end presented to all believers
in Christ, has two sides, the religious and the moral. As
an ideal it consists, we are told, " in the two aspects of
striving for the Kingdom of God and His righteousness,
and the exercise of freedom over the world ".[1] At this
point there are questions of detail—such as whether Ritschl
has not construed the Kingdom of God as a purely moral
ideal—in which for the moment we need not entangle
ourselves. Suffice it to pick out the two elements in this
concept of Perfection into which Ritschl as an expositor
of doctrine threw his energies with a special predilection—
the religious idea of lordship over the world, and the
moral idea of " vocation ".

Dominion over the world is a conception by means of
which Ritschl circles round once again to his primary view
of what religion is, and one reason why he expounds it

[1] *Unterricht,* § 47.

with such obvious delight is that here he felt himself to be reviving Luther's great message of " the freedom of a Christian man ". This perfect liberty, which in different modes we enjoy through faith in Providence,[1] humility, patience and prayer, was to him the very purpose of all that God has done for man in Christ. " The lordship over the world possessed by believers is the aim of reconciliation with God in the Christian sense." Such dominion, as Dr. Flew rightly insists, " is religious, through and through. It is given by God, it is the believer's destiny as willed by God, it is only attained by the identification of the end of the individual with the world-end willed by God, which is the Kingdom." [2] Jesus' mastery of all things was in Him one of those qualities which Ritschl felt justified the epithet " Divine " ; and this mastery He shares with His people. In the idea of such dominion there is nothing fantastic, as if the believer could alter the laws of nature ; it is based on the confidence, gained from Christ, that all things serve for the good of those who love God, and is enjoyed in the fellowship of His Kingdom. " The believer," it is explained, " occupies a position of lordship over the world, in the religious sense meant here, because he stands so near to God, and belongs so peculiarly to God as to ensure his independence of all the elements of the world." [3] " All things are yours, for you are Christ's."

To this religious aspect of the Christian life there corresponds the moral aspect—viz., the steadfast fulfilment of our appointed " vocation ". Each of us is called to serve God in his station and its duties. The idea of " vocation ", as Ritschl employs it in dependence on such predecessors as Schleiermacher and Hofmann, has been assailed on

---

[1] One of the best things in Ritschl is his ever-repeated contention that faith in Providence stands rooted in the sense of reconciliation through Christ.

[2] R. Newton Flew, *The Idea of Perfection*, p. 379.

[3] *Justification and Reconciliation*, p. 646.

the ground that in suggestion it is deeply and incurably *bourgeois*. " Nothing more," one critic writes, " is asked of man than that he should take his historical place in the ordinary life of the good citizen." But Ritschl did not mean it so. Our special calling, he lays down, is recognized as *ours* because it forms for us " an integral part of the Kingdom of God ". It is the specific life-work committed to our charge ; and if we are fulfilling it, we may with a clear conscience put aside the thousand and one competing interests which otherwise would bewilder and distract. Ritschl held that these two ideas— lordship over life and fidelity in vocation—are both of them caught and copied from Jesus Christ. Alike in acting and in suffering He was Master of life ; taking the vocation of Redeemership from the Father's hand, He finished the work given Him to do. If in both respects we have learned of Christ, then, Ritschl contends, we are living at the level of what may justly be called Christian Perfection. For " perfection " consists not in quantita-tive sinlessness but in qualitative direction and quality of life.[1]

§ 4.   THE VALUE OF RITSCHL'S THOUGHT

Ritschl was a masculine thinker, with the strength but also with the limitation and impatience of his type. His way, as Herrmann put it, was "to speak sharply and exactly of what moved his heart ". Religion, he perceived, is no mere feeling ; it is a force or power that in Christ makes us masters of the world, the freemen of God. One of his deepest convictions is that we possess authentic faith only as we are living it out in the activities of obedience. He and those who learnt from him gave life, variety and freshness to the dogmatic field for a whole · generation ; and in virtue of their sustained contention that Christian

[1] We may leave undebated at this point the question whether this is an accurate or helpful use of the word.

faith is its own sufficient basis, that theology must rest
entirely on the revelation of God in Christ, and that
systematic doctrine exists to further the practical work of
the Church, they were widely felt to be liberators of the
theological mind. It is now some years since Ritschl's
great successor, Karl Barth, stepped into the arena ; and
that Barth is definitely a more Christian thinker than
Ritschl no one, I should suppose, can doubt who takes
revelation seriously. But in declared intention and programme the two theologians are much nearer to each
other than has often been supposed. The difference may,
perhaps, be shortly put thus : that Ritschl undertakes to
furnish a theology inspired throughout by Scripture, but
too often fails to keep his promise, whereas Barth is set
upon thinking out something that will deserve to be
called a " Theology of the Word of God ", and has so
far proceeded with a consistency and power which is
engaging the attention of the whole Christian Church.
It is in performance, not in chosen aim, that the two men
stand so far apart.

What appear to be the main influences by which Ritschl
was diverted from his course ?

(a) *His rationalistic moralism.* It was in virtue of his
ethical idealism that Ritschl showed himself most eminently
qualified for so stalwart an opposition to the materialistic
tendencies of his age, as well as inspired for the dauntless
if also somewhat inconsiderate optimism with which he
developed his theology of " moral personality ". Life,
for him, revolves round the moral man. The demands,
the outlook, the standards or prepossessions of the moral
man are allowed to lay down the law to the believing
mind, and to forbid it to grasp in their fulness the transcendent new truths and gifts that God is offering in
Christ. What Ritschl teaches is sober in tone, but it is
seldom tinged with the wonderful feeling of the New
Testament ; we do not easily think of it as stimulating

the reader to joy unspeakable and full of glory. Yet if
the Gospel is a theme of wonder, the theology which
ought to catch and absorb something of that glow but
does not, fails even as theology. It has in part lost touch
with the great realities. As we read Herrmann of Marburg, Ritschl's follower, we recall the Psalmist who wrote
how the Lord " brought me up out of the miry clay, and
set my feet upon a rock, and put a new song in my
mouth ", for Herrmann had learned the despair of sin.[1]
Ritschl stands erect in God's presence rather than goes on
his knees in utter contrition. His moralism has left him
slightly insensitive. It cannot be denied that the deliberate limitation of thought to what is capable of being practically experienced and translated into active life, which
Ritschl had learnt from Kant, tended incidentally to
foster an earthly perspective in religion and to suggest a
much reduced version of some of the greatest Biblical
conceptions. Moral values by themselves are never the
primary interest for faith.

Of this tendency three examples may be given. To
the first attention has already been called : Ritschl's
habit of putting a series of historical and ethical judgments
in place of the living Lord. His aversion to metaphysics
and mysticism made him suspicious of all kinds of professed
communion with Christ, and in his legitimate eagerness to
stress mediation through the facts of the Gospel story
he lost sight of the fact that fellowship which is mediated
through knowledge of past events may none the less be
immediate and personal. Not only so, but resolute pre-
occupation with moral values is apt to render a man
blind to the absolute newness and transcendence of God's
self-revelation. God is conceived of as accrediting Himself to our moral canons of what is good rather than as
breaking *creatively* into our life and making all things
new—even our conscience and its standards. Where

[1] See Flew, *The Idea of Perfection*, p. 389.

revelation is, there is miracle; but miracle may be
rejected or overlooked in the ethical sphere as much as
in the physical. Ritschl, in short, shows himself wholly
unaware of the paradox inherent in the believing response
to Christ, viz., that while He does appeal to our sense of
right and wrong—and thus is acknowledged and appraised
in what may be suitably called a judgment of value—yet
His effect is to transform from end to end our very
capacity to judge of what is good. Ritschl saw the first
side of this antinomy, not the second. The value-judgment, as he views it, " is not ", Burger has well said,

sheer submission to One Who overpowers me in living presence ;
it is measuring a historical phenomenon by a final standard
of value which exists prior to the phenomenon, by the morality
which man brings along with him. Jesus is measured by the
ideal of ethical personality ; that which does not fit this ideal
falls away, sacrificed to the destructive prejudice or modifying
tendencies of the theologian.[1]

A preformed system has fixed the dimensions of Christ,
the boundaries of moral being which He must not pass.

In like manner we may account for the meagreness of
Ritschl's teaching on the Holy Spirit. He somewhere
observes that no point in theology has been so steadily
neglected as the conception of the Spirit, and it must
be regretfully confessed that he himself has done all too
little to supply the want. Not that he ought to have
been charged with reducing the Holy Spirit to " a cognitive function of the Christian mind ", or a mere name for
the generalities of religious experience. And beyond
dispute he has the New Testament on his side in putting
the Spirit in exceedingly close relation to the believing
society, as well as in insisting that the Spirit is not an
external addition to the revelation vouchsafed in Christ.
Neither is there anything to object to, but the reverse,
in his dissatisfaction with the thought of the Spirit as

[1] K. Burger, *Der lebendige Christus*, p. 125.

" a resistless natural force which runs athwart the regular
course of knowledge and the normal exercise of the will ".
Yet the reader of *Justification and Reconciliation* is scarcely
confronted with the fact, to which every page of St. Paul
bears witness, that Christian life and life in the Spirit
are the same thing.   Believers, according to Ritschl, are
those who have adopted the purpose of God, not those
in whom the Spirit of God dwells and who receive from
the Spirit all their power to know and do God's will.
The ground of this error, we may reasonably conjecture,
is to be found in Ritschl's comparatively superficial
thought of sin.   Sin judged by the existing ideal of moral
personality, as a failure to realize ethical values, is
much less formidable and grave than sin lighted up by
the awful holiness of God.   It is only as we feel ourselves, each moment, faced by the unconditional demands of the absolute, as we recognize unreservedly that
our nature is antagonistic to God, that our need of the
indwelling powers of the Holy Spirit will be deeply confessed.

Once more, Ritschl's supreme interest in moral autonomy
leads him to sever the vital tie between religion and
morality.   It is with a sense of sheer mystification that
we read his deliberate words : " Good works do not
follow directly from faith in so far as faith experiences
reconciliation with God." [1]   It reads like a confession of
failure to understand the Gospel of the Reformation.
Justification, he declares at another point, has no immediate bearing on right moral action.   On the first page
of his system an impenetrable wall had been erected
between religious and theoretic knowledge ; now, on the
last, a similar barrier is placed between the religious and
the moral life of the Christian.   All he can bring himself
to say is that the two aspects of life are parallel or homogeneous.   As the independence of morality emerges and

[1] *Justification and Reconciliation*, p. 522.

becomes clearer, religion sinks into an influence which
" guarantees the Christian aim of dominion over the
world ". And since the inspiration of moral life does not
on these terms flow from faith, yet must have some real
source, it is on Ritschl's showing derived from the independent resolve of the believer to adopt as his own the
ethical tasks of the Kingdom of God. Moralistic prepossessions have hid from him the New Testament truth
that reconciliation with God *ipso facto* brings power to
do God's will. It is a point in theology—and a central
one—at which he barely gets beyond Pharisaism.

(*b*) *His historical positivism.* At various points in the
preceding survey it has become evident how in the main
Ritschl's type of thought was positivist and pragmatic
in colour. As it has been put, he held that " what works
in religion is true as revelation ". Always constitutionally
averse to transcendent interpretations, he urges that we
should be content to find in given phenomena those values
that satisfy our religious needs and enable us to dominate
the world. The same vein of reflection guides him in his
refusal to give a place to the Biblical idea of Original Sin
(on the ground that experience supplies no direct verifica-
tion of it), or to permit the thought of sin itself to interfere with an optimistic view of progress. Similarly, no
warning is anywhere given that the Christian mind
must not regard the progressive developments of culture
and civilization as being fully justified to faith by the
simple fact that they exist ; and the New Testament
view of " the world " as lying under the judgment of
God, and therefore such that it cannot be accepted by
faith without criticism, because the forward movement
of humanity is itself sinful, has no place in his pages.
To this positivist temper we may also trace his lack of
sense for paradox and antinomy in Christian belief, as
not merely incidental to its temporary form but constitutive of its very essence. Again, his Christology

exhibits this positivist tendency in a high degree. Here too the Christian mind is encouraged to move simply within itself. We can know what God or Christ is *to us*; we cannot grasp what God is in Himself, or what Christ reveals Himself to be in His relation to God.

It is, however, apropos of history as the sphere or realm of Divine revelation that this positivistic temper comes most plainly to the surface. Not, of course, that his intention is to enforce anything of the kind, but the argument as actually unfolded often appears to rest on the assumption that the Person and life-work of Jesus confront us as a homogeneous piece of " profane " history, the divine import of which is accessible to direct historical inspection, or can be made plain by sober rational deduction from obvious facts. The facts simply *qua* history are revelation. As Brunner shows, Ritschl's system as a whole revolves round " the ethico-rational purposive principle of the Kingdom of God "; and in attaching this idea to Christ's life-work in the past he is chiefly guided by the consideration " that the idea only becomes historically effective from a definite point in time, and that it only reaches the individual through this historical medium ".[1] Jesus figures as the Person who first presented this idea in effective power. In addition to possessing this chronological priority, He has also embodied the idea in the historically enduring Christian movement, to have a living share in which is salvation. History brings forth Christ, and, by means of Christ, the life of the Church. To say that He is " the historical Founder of Christianity " is therefore for all practical purposes equivalent to saying that He is the Revelation of God. Jesus is homogeneous with the texture of human events. " There is no rent in the life of history as such, which could not be healed by the historical process itself." [2]

Thus the emphasis on history as the sphere or *locus* of

[1] *The Mediator*, pp. 62–4.   [2] *Ibid.*, p. 138.

revelation, which had been Ritschl's strength in his conflict with Idealism, came eventually to form a source of
the gravest weakness. We can now see him to have
been nearly blind to the difficulties that arise, for a simple
and direct appeal to revelation in history, from the
progress of literary and historical criticism. He over-
looks the fact, though it is plainly crucial, that objectively
given history is not as it were automatically and by its
very nature a Divinely meant disclosure of revealing
significance. The Gospel picture of Jesus, the events of
His career, read simply as a chapter in the record of the
past, are not in themselves an immediate or transparent
disclosure of God. To be that, they must be illumined
from above. For one thing, they must embody the
personal presence and act of God, as events in which God
is approaching and addressing us ; and for another, the
Spirit operating within us must open our eyes to their
transcendent meaning. Thus revelation and the Holy
Spirit are realities which interpret each other, and apart
from the other neither has any significance that we can
apprehend. Hence to study Christ historically and to
believe in Him as the sole and sufficient Word of God are
wholly different things. Only as God is in past facts do
they reveal ; only as His Spirit brings home their import
does the revelation become effectual.

We must therefore conclude that Ritschl had done
hardly more than make a beginning with the uniquely
difficult problem—a problem really peculiar to Christianity
—of Revelation and History in their relations to each
other. It is the problem which most of all preoccupies
theology at the moment, and what is perhaps the leading
part in the discussion is being taken by Karl Barth and
the distinguished thinkers who are, or were, his coadjutors.

The careful student of the subject, it should be added,
will be wise to guard himself against the mistake of hastily

identifying " the theology of Ritschl " with what is known,
more generally, as " the Ritschlian theology ". Comparatively few of the objections raised in the foregoing
pages to the teaching of the master himself could fairly
be urged, at all events as they stand, against the views
set forth by Herrmann, Haering, or Kaftan. In their
pages we find a resolute effort to state the meaning of
revelation, and specifically of Jesus Christ, in terms more
in harmony with the New Testament. Ritschl was a
pioneer ; and in this imperfect world pioneers of thought
are apt to be one-sided, casting round a few large ideas
an intense light. Their disciples have commonly much to
do in correcting exaggerations and supplying still more
numerous omissions. The story of Ritschlianism as eventually worked out by writers of a more positive type
cannot be told here. But, on the other hand, we shall
study in the next chapter one tolerably negative sequel
or development of the original impulse.

VI

THE THEOLOGY OF SCIENTIFIC RELIGIOUS HISTORY

ERNST TROELTSCH

§ 1. THE REACTION AGAINST RITSCHL

THE PROGRESS of thought, at least in theology, is rather apt to proceed by way of what is called the swing of the pendulum. Its movement is of a zigzag kind, sometimes with violent dashes from one extreme to the other. Each new school takes as its guiding interest those elements in the complex problem which its predecessor had tended to overlook ; the left or advanced wing of the older group assumes command of the situation and enters on a fresh campaign. This, clearly, can be seen happening to Ritschlianism. Somewhere about 1900 the more radical members of the party broke off and set up on their own account. They claimed for themselves in a special way the descriptive title " modern " ; they raised new issues of a vital kind. Liberal Protestantism, fully conscious of itself, had assumed the stage.

To begin with, these men felt that Ritschl had unduly neglected apologetic questions springing out of Natural Science. His tendency had been to shut religion off from science by water-tight doors—a thing that can be done in books only, not in living minds. In pressing this point they ran the risk, it can now be seen, of repeating a mistake which Ritschl had spent a lifetime in exposing—that of measuring all facts by a philosophy which made little distinction, or none, between persons and things, in

short by Naturalism. Also they took the field in a new
polemic against miracle, a subject on which the older
thinker had at times made statements of a definitely
positive kind. They had much to say about the cosmos
as a system pervaded by inviolable law, apart from which
no such thing as science can arise ; and frequently they
were content to leave the matter there, oblivious of the
fact that faith too has its own specific view of the cosmos,
and one of a very different complexion. Those who have
learned faith from the New Testament will never let
themselves be persuaded that trust in the living God
can be fully expressed in terms of law, uniformity, evolution. These categories furnish no proper account of such
things as prayer in which real fellowship obtains between
God and man, the experience of forgiveness, or, to take
the supreme instance, the fact of Christ.

Two other features of Ritschl's thought, however, gave
deeper offence still, and are more apposite to our present
theme. In the first place stands his conviction that the
full and final revelation of God has been mediated through
the facts of history. But, it was asked with some heat,
has not history been a sore burden to faith from the
beginning ? If we have God and He has us directly in
and through believing experience, historical facts are
surely no better than an intrusion. However great Jesus
may be, He lived centuries ago and is ever becoming more
distant with the lapse of time. Nothing in history is
quite certain ; by degrees the past is absorbed, then
antiquated, and we pass on to something new. All things
considered, to build on history is to build on sand. The
ground and guarantee of faith must be sought elsewhere—
in rational intuition, perhaps, or in immediate feeling.

The second point is even more important. Ritschl was
charged with ignoring the new facts brought to light by
the scientific History of Religions. He had isolated
Christianity, except for its connexion with Old Testament

religion ; he had dealt with it almost as if there were no
other religion in the world. Indeed, the brilliant scholars
of the time who led the way in elucidating the Hellenistic
background of the New Testament might be said to have
done their work rather in spite of Ritschl than under his
impulse. This was a matter, accordingly, of which much
more was certain to be heard.

§ 2.   THE HISTORY AND PSYCHOLOGY OF RELIGION

The new school which grew up in Germany, in the last
decade of the nineteenth century, to fight under the
banner of the History of Religions, contained an unusually
large number of gifted men. They threw off the reserve
of academic scholarship, and resolved to write for the
man in the street. Under the title of *Religionsgeschichtliche
Volksbücher*, they issued a series of what might in a sense be
called " Tracts for the Times ", some of which, like
Bousset's *Jesus* and Wrede's *Paul*, came to be well known
in English translations. And they collaborated in pro-
ducing, to begin with, a popular but careful Commentary
on the New Testament, edited by Johannes Weiss, perhaps
the ablest of them all ; a book marked by this great merit,
that it renounced the practice, so often fatal to exegesis,
of putting each single word under the microscope, and
made it its aim to understand paragraphs or sections as
wholes. The systematic theologian of the movement, of
whom we must speak presently, was Ernst Troeltsch,
famous as a teacher in Heidelberg and, at a later date, in
Berlin.

The movement may be said to have opened with
Gunkel's book on the operations of the Holy Spirit,
published in 1888. To him Christianity is " a syncretistic
religion ". It is a familiar idea that the doctrine and
practice of the Early Church, say by the fifth century,
betray the influence of pagan worships. But the thesis

now put forward was to the effect that things had gone
wrong within the Apostolic Age itself. Ceasing to regard
the New Testament as a holy island in the sea of history,
we must read it in the light of the religious speculation
and mythology that filled the Græco-Roman world during
the centuries before and after Christ. As Johannes Weiss
put it concisely :

Modern study of religion shows that the whole circle of
ideas and thought-forms—soteriological, Christological, sacra-
mental, eschatological—as they crowd the pages of the New
Testament, were already present in some form in the world
of Jewish, Hellenistic, Oriental or syncretistic thought.

This is perhaps a phase of New Testament scholarship
which might have been anticipated. Nothing could be
more likely than that after a literary and historical
investigation of the primitive Christian documents, an
inquiry would be set up into the pedigree, so to say, of
the religious ideas with which these documents are charged.
It cannot be denied that many valuable results were
gained. Much in the Book of Revelation, for example,
takes on a new meaning by having the ancestry of its
startling and mysterious symbolism revealed. New light
is cast on various features of the Pauline eschatology, or
on certain aspects of the apostolic conception of the Spirit.
True, the new fashion went to some people's heads with
intoxicating power, and even at times led to wild excesses.
In particular, a good deal that could not be proved was
said regarding the contagion passed on from the pagan
cults to the religion of the New Testament, and especially
to its teaching on the sacraments. Much was heard of a
curious amalgam known as " the theology of the mys-
teries ", but closer scrutiny showed that it fell to pieces
when confronted with the original texts. A typical book
is Heitmüller's *In Jesus' Name*. There the analogy of
other worships, in which the name of some deity is uttered
as a charm or spell, is confidently applied, with the sug-

gestion that a like tendency is all we need to explain the
New Testament use of the name of Jesus. We should
never gather that " the name of the Lord " is a familiar
Old Testament phrase, uttered by prophetic men without
any trace of magic because for them the name of God
is just His revealed character. There is a difference
between faith and magic, even when they hold identical
language. Not only so, but to speak of syncretism in
this connexion is inaccurate and misleading. To be strict,
syncretism is only present when elements derived from
various religions are admitted on equal terms ; and anyone who can believe that, in the New Testament, ideas
drawn from Hellenism or from Oriental mythology rank
equally with truth as it is in Jesus, appears to have a
confused mind, and to have abandoned fact for fancy.
But the tide of this extremer prejudice has for some
years been ebbing. As we look back, it is surprising how
peripheral are the features of the New Testament thought-
world it has helped us to understand.

Some ardent champions of the movement, at one stage,
made themselves responsible for the suggestion that the
comparative Science of Religions should take over the
business of Christian theology. The work, it was argued,
could be better done on the larger scale. We might well
expect that the man who studied Christianity, not by
itself, but as one of a group of religions—say, the monotheistic faiths—would take a wiser and more flexible view
of its character and capacities of development than the
man who is a Church theologian and no more. This, of
course, is a thoroughly good argument for a more exact
knowledge of other religions than the Christian, such a
knowledge as will widen the outlook of theologian and
missionary alike, enabling them to understand more clearly
how the appeal of the Gospel may be most hopefully
addressed to adherents of those faiths. In point of fact,
the comparative study of religions has long been pursued

with this precise end in view. But if we are invited to begin the examination of Christianity with the assumption that, from the nature of things, it *cannot* be in a class by itself, and that in consequence the teaching of the New Testament must be interpreted by the light of other worships and within the limits of ideas common to all the higher faiths, the argument appears to bear its false-hood on its face. Not to speak of deeper theological issues, this narrow and doctrinaire aversion from all that is fresh and unprecedented is a temper unworthy of the best scholarship. To take it in earnest and let it dictate our conclusions is to close our eyes to the surprises amid the commonplaces of human life.

The new movement, it soon became clear, attached scarcely less importance to the Psychology of Religion. Here also it cannot be doubted t at theology gains by every new insight into the hopes and fears, the desires and aspirations of men ; thereby a new sense of reality is imparted to our interpretation of the Gospel, as a living Word of God which answers with a final relevance those wistful or despairing questions uttered in all ages by the human heart. But scholars in sympathy with this group were too often apt to lay a special stress on that in religion which is rudimentary, on experiences of a weird or morbid kind. Occasionally they seemed actually to be guided by the principle that the key to religion lies in its origins, and that the elementary is, *ipso facto*, the authentic. The rudest forms display its real being ; elsewhere it is camouflaged and goes under a disguise. The further remark was occasionally thrown in, almost by the way, that in the last resort these primitive unspoiled expe-riences or expressions of piety are the same in every religion. Thus the phenomena of ecstasy, enthusiasm, and tremulous excitement—common to every religious society in which the tide of life is running strongly—came insensibly to rank as the elements by which religion proper is constituted, whereas the *beliefs* which invariably underlie pious feeling and impart to it its characteristic tone, were on the whole relegated to the background. Either that, or, if these beliefs also came into view, they too were apt to be seized in their crudest and most aboriginal form, from which light should be derived for the study of the New Testament faith. Thus the new Romanticism, like the older type with which the nineteenth century had opened, gave its attention largely to beliefs and feelings other than those evoked and purified by the operation of the Spirit of the self-revealing God. It cannot be said too emphatically that this is a mental habit full of delusions. Its effect is to make men the victims of words. To take but one example, " prayer " outside the range of Biblical religion and within it are not the same, though the term " prayer " occurs in both instances. If God has spoken His sovereign Word, He has made all things new. The secret of the higher faith cannot be found in earlier stages.

§ 3. TROELTSCH'S RELATION TO THE PAST

By general consent the leader of the new movement, on its systematic side, was Ernst Troeltsch (1865–1923). His academical work was done for the most part in Heidelberg, where he taught theology and also some philosophy, and in Berlin, where he belonged to the philosophical faculty only. As a student, he came under the influence of Ritschl.

Troeltsch's interest, like that of our own Rashdall, was divided almost equally between theology, philosophy and history. This is faintly indicated even by his first book, a short treatise on reason and revelation in Gerhard and Melanchthon. The problem he had selected lay as it were on the watershed between the Reformation and modern times ; and here, in a particular connexion, he

offered a characteristic study of the history and influence
of ideas. Similarly he sought to inquire how in the early
centuries the great new ideas of the Old and New Testaments had coalesced with ethnic factors to produce that
unprecedented fact—the Christian Church.

Troeltsch's life-work as a whole may fairly be indicated
by the phrase " Christianity and Philosophy ", or the
Philosophy of History in the broadest sense. Windelband
and Rickert told upon him latterly, but in early days he
felt himself perhaps more deeply in sympathy with Eucken
than with any other philosophical contemporary ; they
were united by the conviction that a spiritual life has to
be recognized as existing above and beyond all physical
mechanism, as well as in holding that the problem of
religion can only be understood or clarified by means of
historical study. To his historical interpretation of
Christianity we shall return ; here it may be enough to
say that the comprehensive problem he sought to grapple
with was the relation that must obtain between specifically
Christian thought and the intellectual principles at work
in the higher life of our time—its science, literature,
political and economic thought. His own religious life
was of a mystical cast ; taking religion as the direct
feeling of God's presence, he spent much thought and
pains on the task of distinguishing what is religion from
what is not. His equipment for the discussion of Christianity and the thought of to-day consisted on one side
in a quite exceptionally profound knowledge of what is
called " the modern mind ", and in a keen sympathy
with its ideals. Encyclopædic in learning, he often appears
to know too much. His books now and then leave the
impression that the author has emptied out the contents
of his notebooks into the printed page without too much
regard for form or clarity. A distinguished thinker used
to say that every German philosopher ought to be obliged
by severe penalties to write in French, and the saying

comes often to mind as we read Troeltsch. Especially in his later years, the gain would have been immense had more time been spent on the shaping of his materials, in obedience to Goethe's never-to-be-forgotten maxim : " The artist is known by selection."

In our study of his books, it is essential to watch the two interests—religious faith and intellectual freedom— as they meet and contend with each other on every page. Troeltsch will abandon neither. No man indeed ever had a shrewder sense of the dangers attendant on what is familiarly known as " the reconciliation of science and religion ". As he puts it vigorously : " Religion which has been reconciled to culture is for the most part nothing but bad science and superficial morality ; the saving salt of faith is gone." There is a real sense in which Christianity would cease to be itself were its conflict with modern thought to end. He enjoins believers to turn their back unhesitatingly on the facile proposal that they should take their religion from philosophers.

A religion based upon philosophy [he writes] is an illusion that cannot last once we have seen how the religious elements of philosophies were themselves actually derived from the great historical religions, or if, in addition, we observe how impotent is any religious cult that has a purely individual and intellectual character.

Troeltsch obviously felt himself called to assume the task that Schleiermacher had left half done. He is quoted as having said that Schleiermacher's programme remains the great programme of all scientific theology ; it only needs working out, not the substitution of new methods. In his view the older thinker had given in his *Glaubenslehre* the first sketch of the sort of theology requisite for the modern world, inasmuch as he had con- structed his system on a double basis : that of a general philosophy of religion *plus* a critical survey of Christianity in the light of the general scientific history of religions.

And it is significant that to Troeltsch himself the kernel of philosophy of religion lies in a psychological analysis of the religious consciousness, an analysis which takes the form of a criticism of the successive stages of the religious idea as it has been manifested in history.

It is interesting to compare the two, Schleiermacher and Troeltsch, so long as we do not forget that Schleiermacher initiated a movement that Troeltsch only continued. In both minds there can be seen a remarkable fusion of empiricism and idealism. But Troeltsch came late enough to have behind him the prolonged debate of the greatest century in theology since the fourth ; in particular, he found himself able to adapt to his own use some important general results of the Hegelian interpretation. He could look back to the imposing religious philosophy which Hegel and the Hegelians had derived from a speculative concept of the Divine nature, and in which the whole fact of Christian experience was construed as issuing by a logical necessity, to form the final stage in the self-evolution of the Divine Spirit. From this general view he was in a position to adopt some appreciable elements in forming his own construction.

Thus, in spite of the historical relativism which we shall find to be decisive for Troeltsch's thought, he does not in the least feel himself driven to nihilistic scepticism. He still has norms or standards of value on which he can rely, though the old-fashioned methods of obtaining and verifying these standards—by appeal, say, to special revelation—have become ineffective. The empirical historian may none the less be guided by a philosophy of history. It is this line that Troeltsch takes with confidence. His work as a whole rests on a single great metaphysical assumption—that, as Hegel put it, the real is the rational, the universe a significant, because reason-pervaded, system of things. History, so far from being a chaos, is shot through by the progressively self-revealing

thought of God. Not that with Hegel he believed that
we are capable of construing the Absolute speculatively,
or that antithetical dialectic is the key to all being. But
to him, as to the great idealists, the world-process displayed itself as the effect in time and space of a supersensible Reality. We must see in it the fulfilment of
Infinite Spirit—Spirit that has issued from its transcendent
origin, that is striving on and up through all kinds of
human error and failure, that in uniform and rational
development is conquering by degrees the limitations and
hindrances inseparable from bondage to nature, and is
gradually rising by the native powers of immanent purpose
to its absolute completion. That completion, in fact, is a
return to the origin of all. Even in his *Glaubenslehre*,
published after his death, it transpires with an almost
startling clearness that behind all Troeltsch's views of
God and man stands this commanding heritage from
Absolute Idealism. There he can still speak of " the
self-transformation of God into nature and creature ", and
of these " being re-transformed into Spirit by means of
redemption ", and can refer to the tension in the world
between the necessities of nature and spirit as pointing
back to a tension within the being of God Himself. To
the same source can be traced his reading of history in
general as the conflict of spirit with flesh and his view of
sin as arising from the metaphysical make-up of human
nature, as well as some influential (and fatal) ingredients
in his eschatology.[1]

It is therefore not unfair to speak of Troeltsch as having
made an impressively able and persistent attempt to bring
the Christian idea of God into harmony with, if not under
the control of, the idealistic philosophy of Spirit. It is
in this context that he finds the thought of such writers
as Rothe, Dilthey and Carlyle so congenial, and is naturally

[1] See O. Kübler's excellent study, *Mission und Theologie* (1929),
pp. 190 ff.

led to conceive the philosophy of history, of culture and of religion as forming a single whole. The norms by which progress is to be estimated can themselves only be won by a speculative treatment of history and of the higher types there evolved. By no other avenue can we approach a true comparative understanding, critical yet positive, of the great religions. Such norms emerge within the age-long temporal succession by means of " the free conflict of ideas ". Our acceptance of them, no doubt, is a subjectively conditioned decision, or, as Troeltsch puts it, " an axiomatic act ". But it is not for that reason simply arbitrary. There is such a thing as the *a priori* element in religion, to which our decision can be related and in which it can find a foothold and confirmation.

The idea of the religious *a priori* was formed by Troeltsch in direct dependence on Kant. To Kant the *a priori* element in knowledge is that which does not rise out of experience, but of itself makes experience possible, belonging as it does to the nature of reason or faculty of cognition as such ; though this does not mean that experience is not instrumental in bringing it out directly into conscious realization. What the *a priori* factor does is to give knowledge its necessary and logically universal character, as empirical sense-perception could never do. But when Troeltsch urges that in religion, as in knowledge, morality and aesthetic life, we must recognize an *a priori* factor analogous to that found in the other three spheres, he appears to ignore two considerations of real importance. For one thing, religious faith is a matter not of necessity but of freedom ; a man need not believe in God, but must *choose* to believe, thus making response to the Divine claim imposed upon him. In knowledge, on the other hand, he has no option but to perceive the world in spatial and temporal forms. And again, the expression " religious *a priori* " ascribes to religion a rationally logical character which it is as far as possible from exhibiting. Even from the ethical *a priori*, at its higher level, religious faith is separated by a wide remove; for faith relates itself to the transcendent fact of God Who cannot be likened to, or included within, that material of experience which elsewhere it is the function of the *a priori* factor to shape and organize. For these and other reasons, the idea is better put aside as misleading.

The strongly marked idealistic elements in Troeltsch's thought were, however, in a large degree held in check by influences derived from Ritschl. It was not for nothing that he had sat at Ritschl's feet and learnt from him that religion is not philosophy but something wholly different, because it confronts you independently in its own right, with the consequence that it is impossible to reach what faith designates as " God " by the simple expedient of pushing scientific or metaphysical explanation a little further. He does go with Hegel in holding that religious thinking is essentially symbolic in type, but he diverges from him widely by the conviction that there can never be any question of elevating religious ideas, however transmuted, to the level of the abstract notion. So to transpose faith into the key of philosophy would change its very nature. The process of translation would bleed faith white and drain out the vital element of mystery. Not only so; but speculative constructions as such are hypothetical, whereas the hidden life of faith is certainty.

All this might have been passed as sound by the tests of Ritschlian orthodoxy, yet Troeltsch's found the dualism set up by Ritschl between faith and reason to be unbearably sharp. He rebelled against such " exclusive supernaturalism ", protesting that Hegel and Fichte were right after all in trying for a final unity of view; though it must be added that his own endeavours to prove or state that unity were left regrettably vague. He rarely goes further than to insist that the theoretical idea of God

must of necessity include both these aspects—first, that
He is the ground and basis of the cosmic laws, the world
having a uniform nature because God ever abides the
same ; and secondly that God works creatively, calling
into existence that which is new and unpredictable.   In
like manner, there are definitely metaphysical elements
in the doctrines of creation, providence and miracle.   In
these the believing mind formulates convictions which
imply a specific view of the universe and of the conduct
befitting man within it.   But in turn metaphysic is affected
by religion.   Faith has a part in shaping our philosophical
conclusions about the nature of ultimate reality.

§ 4.   THE LAWS OF DEVELOPMENT AND REVELATION

If we now turn to Troeltsch's distinctively theological
work, it is important to note that he regards the Philosophy of Religion, like the history of Christianity, as a
genuinely scientific discipline, whereas Dogmatics rank as a
branch of practical theology.   He insists that theology
as such has no special method of its own, but simply
applies one common to all forms of mental science.

Dogmatics [he writes] has the task of setting forth the
Christian faith in God, or in other words the ideas involved
in essential Christianity, and this in complete independence,
without the least intermixture of historical elements.   It
expounds our faith in God as something which has reality in
present experience and renews itself with each individual in
the experience of redemption.   It is made up of purely present-
day convictions.

Modern Protestant dogmatic work must base its proof
of the final authority of Christian faith on general considerations drawn from the philosophy and history of religion.   The genuinely Christian character of such theology
is sufficiently vouched for if the essential core of it can
be attached to the Hebrew prophets, the Person of Jesus,

and the Bible. In effect, Dogmatic so construed has ceased to be Dogmatic proper, for it no longer acknowledges any fixed " dogmas ", but regards its task as being to set forth in a general manner the thoughts that arise out of Christian faith, on a scientific and philosophical basis. In other words, it functions no longer as a system of normative doctrine, but as a practical guide to preachers.

There can be little doubt that the idea of a special revelation had disappeared from Troeltsch's mind. When we speak about revelation correctly, in his view, we are really describing how the depths of man's own mind yield wonderful intuitions of unseen reality. Not the act of God is in question, but the upthrusting vigour of man's religious spirit. Revelation is but the objective correlate of that which, on the subjective side, is conceived as " the essence of religion ". Here are three typical sentences. " The whole of the world or God [1] can only manifest itself through itself, through that inner feeling and certainty of the whole and its being, which we call religious feeling or religious sense, and which we clearly feel as the presence of this whole within ourselves." " It is revelation such as everyone can experience and testify to who has a real religious life, were it only for moments of time." " Christianity is not the only revelation or redemption, but the culminating point of the revelations and redemptions which are at work in the elevation of humanity to God." These quotations are drawn from Troeltsch's well-known article on Revelation in the lexicon *Religion in Geschichte und Gegenwart.* Brunner's comment on them is entirely just.

Thus Troeltsch [he writes], the outstanding leader of this whole theological school, has formulated its essential common creed. It is admirable in the frankness with which it expresses the renunciation of all that is specifically Christian,

---

[1] The pantheistic colour of this is obvious.

and in its recognition of general religion and revelation as the
only form of religion.[1]

God's revealing act has been turned into an interior experience of man.   As in Kant, the place of revelation
has been taken by what are really illustrations of a general
truth ; and these illustrations may be many in number.
Besides, what they illustrate is simply the greatness and
resource of the spiritual powers and tendencies immanent
in man's own nature.

It is plain that one thing absent from Troeltsch's general
outlook is a real apprehension of the transcendence of
God.   In spite of candidly meant phrases which echo
Biblical thought, the God he points to is the ground of
the world, its immanent reason, rather than the sovereign
Lord of all things.   No deity or power so constitutively
and reciprocally involved in the world-process can be
clothed with real transcendence.

At an earlier point it was noted that Troeltsch ranks
as the systematic thinker *par excellence* of the " Religious
History " movement, and beyond all question he shares
wholeheartedly in the view taken within that group
of the relation of Christianity to other faiths.   Christian
history for him is no more than a particular vein in history as such, just as Christian theology comes to be dissolved in the general Philosophy of Religion.   *Historism
and its Problems*, the title of one of his last volumes,
might well stand as indicative of his whole approach to
the Christian faith and its interpretation.   It must be
recollected at this point that in his view our historical
conception of the world is the indispensable presupposition
of all our judgments on human norms and ideals.   For
that reason, as he puts it,

historical research is now not merely one side of our way of
interpreting things ; it is not merely a partial satisfaction of

---

[1] *The Mediator*, pp. 68–9.

the cognitive impulse ; it is the basis of all thinking about values or norms, it is the means by which the race takes stock of its own essential being, its origins and its hopes.[1]

A standpoint so rigorous and decisive could hardly fail to suggest the elaboration of a new scientific method ; and in a special essay on historical and dogmatic method in theology [2] Troeltsch took sides on the question. The dogmatic method, he declares, makes what intellectually is an unwholesome distinction between historical research concerned with saving facts and untroubled by the thought of relativity, and on the other hand a form of historical research which is profane or secular, critical and relativistic. But historical method proper puts this patchwork style aside and works on the principle that all history is on one level and of one quality. Moreover, the modern mind is quite clear that no method can be accepted but the second. " Let a man give it his little finger, and presently he must give it his whole hand ; hence from the genuinely orthodox point of view it shows a certain likeness to the devil." Hence cordial adoption of it is the one way to be rid of our worst apologetic troubles. Thus the idea of development is made absolute, for history is the Absolute strung out in the temporal series.

In this field, Troeltsch insists, three laws of inquiry obtain—laws which govern religious phenomena in the past as they do historical phenomena of every kind. They are the laws of criticism, of relativity, and of analogy.[3] One remark of a preliminary kind may not be out of place. It is always depressing to be told in advance how much we are going to be permitted to believe. " Summary and *a priori* decisions," as they have been called, " in which courageous spirits lay down the law beforehand to a world of which we know so little," hardly predispose

[1] *Die Absolutheit des Christentums* (first edition), pp. 3–4.
[2] *Gesammelte Schriften*, Vol. II, pp. 729 ff.
[3] See *Gesammelte Schriften*, Vol. II, pp. 731–4.

us to hope that the real evidence for wonderful things in Christianity will be listened to with an impartial mind.

(*a*) According to the law of *criticism*, no historical judgment can assert more than a probability, or rise higher than a moral certitude. On this point, we may perhaps assume, there will be universal agreement. To take a crucial example, it is not from scientific historical investigation that we derive the conviction, if we have it, that Jesus revealed Himself to the disciples after death as the Living One, or that His so appearing forms an amazing manifestation of the transcendent power of God. A conviction of such magnitude and significance, bearing as it does on the issues of life and death, can only be reached by faith. For the Gospel appeals not merely to the trained historical judgment, but to man's entire personality, flowing in upon us by a variety of channels, and in particular probing conscience to the quick with creative touch ; our motives, too, in responding to it are in no sense the product of merely historical argument, but of something much more diverse and constraining.

(*b*) The law of *relativity*, as its very name conveys, is of a kind to bar out all facts of a unique or " absolute " character. Even facts alleged to be of a supernatural order must, it is declared, be reduced to a scale at which they become amenable to scientific treatment. Past events after all are no more than phenomena, and phenomena without exception have each a strictly calculable place in the uniform sequence of causes and effects. Their setting makes them what they are.

The history of mankind [writes Troeltsch] forms an unspeakably complex, yet altogether coherent, whole of immeasurable duration both in the past and the future. It is as part of this array and system that we must survey and estimate our own existence, and find its rationale and origin. On the analogy of the events known to us we seek by conjecture and sympathetic understanding to explain and reconstruct the past

. . . Since we discern the same process of phenomena in operation in the past as in the present, and see, there as here, the various historical cycles of human life influencing and intersecting each other, we gain at length the idea of *an integral continuity*, balanced in its changes, never at rest, and ever moving towards incalculable issues.[1]

The important single word in this passage is " continuity ", which is to be taken strictly. All events are woven into the same web and are of the same general pattern, all are explicable by immanent forces, all are such that an exhaustive interpretation of their emergence can be undertaken with good hopes of success. The whole conception is applicable to religious facts no less than to political or economic, to the historical bases of Christian faith no less than to the bases of Islam. Anyone can see that a theory of this type, if confronted with Jesus Christ, will be tempted to disparage His uniqueness, and to do so on principle. History, on this view, is a quite specific kind of reality ; it is the sphere of purely relative and correlative events. Nothing absolute can have a place in it, nothing absolute can even touch or enter it. That God has spoken in Christ once, and once for all, is made incredible in advance by definition. Doubtless the personality of Jesus is in a real sense an index of the Power behind cosmic phenomena, but an index which, though in a high degree suggestive, is by no means final or conclusive, and may yet be antiquated or transcended.

(*c*) The law of *analogy*, in turn, is explained to mean that from the nature of the case religious thought in history has everywhere been at work on similar lines, with the result that, as the discerning might have predicted, virtually all the important doctrines of Christianity have a counterpart or *vis-à-vis* in other faiths. If, Troeltsch urges, we take pains to realize this fact clearly, we shall find

[1] Article on " Historiography " in Hastings' *Encyclopædia of Religion and Ethics*, Vol. VI, p. 718 (italics mine).

it easier to make an understanding approach to such transcendent Christian beliefs as those which affirm the Incarnation, the Resurrection, or the miracles of Jesus. Ideas of that sort have no historical or strictly doctrinal truth; on the other hand, they have the beautiful and timeless truth of religious poetry. They belong, in short, to that profound and irreplaceable symbolism in which the soul is wont to clothe its ultimate intuitions concerning the nature of the Unseen.

There is no reason why we should lose our heads over a theory of this kind, concluding, whether sadly or gladly, that it has made an end of the Christian religion. We have not the least cause to deny that from the beginning man's wistful religious mind has been probing reality, so to put it, in certain great ways. It is true, this of itself would apparently imply that the writers of the New Testament had no need to lapse into plagiarism, since the vast mythological ideas they are supposed to have lifted out of Eastern legend would in any case have arisen in their own minds as hopes or dreams. Only, in that case they would have been recognized as hopes or dreams, nothing more. The fact has still to be accounted for that, to take the example of the Resurrection, these hopes of a " Divine mortal " who should overcome death became certainties; and this, it may well be argued, was due to the irresistible force of fact. And speaking generally, if we assume two things, viz., the perpetual pressure of God's seeking love upon the human spirit, and man's incurably religious disposition, we need feel no difficulty in recognising in these alleged analogies—often most inaccurately described as *parallels* [1] to Christian beliefs —instances or dim expressions of the eager questions

---

[1] Parallels they cannot be, for they are found to arise in relation to quite dissimilar conceptions of God. The Christian idea of Incarnation, for example, is only relevant to Ethical Monotheism, and can have no real counterpart in any faith which lacks the Biblical thought of Divine holiness.

which from the earliest times man has been asking himself about God. Incarnation, atonement, sacrifice—these incontestably are ideas which the Gospel found pre-existing in the world, and which it was able to baptize and transform for Christian service. What is more, the hopes, longings, premonitions of which these ideas are the vehicle were given perfect fulfilment in Christ. Our faith becomes loftier, not lower, when it is seen to have a real though not a genetic relationship to these immemorial questions or desires. A great missionary once said that he had never preached the Gospel anywhere without finding that God had been there before him. Yet that antecedent and preparatory presence of the Holy Spirit did not make the Christian message superfluous ; rather it helped to make it welcome when it came.

In the light of these all-determining laws or principles it could not be difficult to forecast the conclusions Troeltsch was bound to reach as to the proper place or status of Christianity. They may be formulated thus : All religions come within a uniform field of development, though not in a single line of evolution. The deepest thing in them all is not primitive animism, or the craving for happiness, or any kind of speculative impulse to explain the world. It is mystical and intuitive contact with the supersensible. Nor, again, is the history of religions to be regarded as but a confused medley of random or opposed tendencies. On the contrary, it exhibits a real forward movement, and makes for a goal whose nature we can elicit and describe after careful study of the facts. One religion amongst the others is Christianity. It took its rise in a syncretistic Judaism, gathering up into itself various elements from other faiths. The whole process is one to be interpreted by the same laws of advancing change as obtain elsewhere. It is vain to argue for the truth of Christianity by claiming for it an isolated position or the dignity of a special or supernatural revelation. All religions claim to rest on revelation; it is, indeed, the consciousness of debt to revelation that forms one of the most salient features by which religion is distinguished, say, from magic. Even prophecy and miracle, taken at their face value, are by no means a monopoly of the Bible. It will not help us to appeal, as the Erlangen School did fifty years before, to the special experience of regeneration, for regeneration in the sense of radical moral change occurs at various other points in the historic development. The plain inference, which Troeltsch does not hesitate to draw, is that the Foreign Mission enterprise of the Church ought not to aim at converting men, but at uplifting them by education.

The idea of a general evolution in religious history, it is obvious, is here being employed in such a manner as to make a peculiar or exceptional self-revelation of God, such as the Bible has been thought to attest, not merely unlikely but wholly inconceivable. The conceptions of revelation and of faith have a way of varying together, and here faith is tending to part with its essentially transcendent reference, and to take on the complexion of an intuitive and semi-æsthetic awareness of cosmic reality. Through contemplation of the world's evolutionary advance there arises man's felt contact with an Absolute that is everywhere active in finite history. God, formerly thought of as One Who perpetually creates faith by His revealing Word and almighty Spirit, is now submerged in the unlimited fact of the universal Divine transparency of the world. Hence, on the vital issue of revelation, Troeltsch would say something like this. Historical science, once it has begun to take the idea of historical evolution seriously, assumes the duty of interpreting by its aid, in strictly immanental fashion, all events in the spiritual world. All things are in flux, all are conditioned reciprocally. Let historical science do its levelling work, accordingly, and it is by the nature of the case impossible to fix on a quite special revelation anywhere in bygone process. But if, thus lowering our flag to scientific history, we perforce disclaim the thought of revelation in any exceptional or unique sense, all the more we are bound to insist on the fact of a universal or general revelation. Nowhere in the past is any spot discoverable where God utters Himself in an incomparable manner, but all is Divine. So that, although Troeltsch finds no difficulty in affirming that " in the historical process there ever emerges the fact of the *new*, which is no mere transformation of existent forces, but an element of essentially fresh content ", such novelty is after all familiar in type or pattern, and born of finitude. In spring the fresh leaves differ minutely in size or conformation ; yet they are all similar buds on a tree whose roots go down into an earthly soil.

To all this two objections, one bearing on method, the other on the intrinsic meaning of New Testament religion, may not unreasonably be made. In the first place, quite evidently Troeltsch and his adherents get out of history, in the way of revelation, just so much as they have resolved beforehand that it can be permitted to contain. The possibilities have been fixed in advance ; the facts are compelled to fit the method by which they are to be treated ; just as, though an automatic machine when opened may disgorge nothing but unbent pennies, this is not because the outer world is made up of unbent pennies and nothing else, but because the selective mechanism at work will accept no other sort. To vary the metaphor, historical research as these writers conceive it may without offence be characterized as a particular kind of game, one rule being that wholly unique events, or miracles, do not happen ; and if you are going to play the game, you must keep the rules. You must never discover in the past anything that is supernatural. There can be no objection to this special view of the science of history, so long as we do not regard it as necessarily giving a true

representation of the real world of events. When in-
spected more closely, indeed, it turns out to be a purely
abstract treatment of its subject-matter, as dogmatic in
temper as the latest papal Bull. The sweeping conclusion,
that no special revelation is possible, has been secured by
turning it into an axiom. When will men understand
that no method of research can ever prescribe a decision
on facts ? And how often in the history of science have
false and hasty assumptions been called axioms, only
because they were simple and could not be proved.

Assuming,[1] as we may, that history is the fruitful mother-
soil in which we mortals stand rooted with all our existence,
inward and outward, one may raise the question whether,
and where, in the whole realm of temporal happenings
there may be found some central stretch of phenomena
which unveils the meaning and secret of the whole. It
is a question we cannot answer by making the most
comprehensive possible survey of the entire process, from
the standpoint of a neutral observer. This could only tell
us what events have impressed men most profoundly, but
could not decide what their influence ought to have been.
Nor could we reach the secret of history inferentially,
by employing some criterion of ultimate value of which
we found ourselves in possession *a priori*, irrespectively of
all experience ; for no such criterion is within our reach.
What Christian faith declares is that the true understanding of history can be had solely from a point of
view supplied by God Himself. The insight of faith is
a product neither of *a priori* thought nor of empirical
observation ; it is the spiritual certainty possessed by
one whose eyes God has opened to the fact of Christ.
But the presuppositions underlying Troeltsch's argument
forbid us by definition to contemplate this as a possibility.
They bar out " uniqueness " in God's method of revealing

[1] On this paragraph see Heim, *Leitfaden der Dogmatik*, II Teil,
pp. 7–8.

Himself. Yet it is the consentient witness of the New Testament writers and of all those who have listened with believing joy to their message that in point of fact the Divine salvation has come as an " unspeakable gift ", in a fashion so amazing as to scout all efforts to define antecedently how it could or could not come. As has been said : " It pleased God to select one nation from the rest as a priestly nation, and for all time to give one Person from its midst the power to speak the liberating word, the word of reconciliation, and to seal this word with His passion and death." We therefore must reply to Troeltsch that not to know how a thing can be is no proof that it has not been.

In the second place, it must be pointed out that this proposal to treat the whole domain of human religion as a single field, in which throughout Biblical and non-Biblical experience alike the analogous phenomena of prophetism, inspiration, miracle, etc., occur in indistinguishable and equally justified forms, runs clean contrary to the New Testament view of the revelation mediated through Christ. As has recently been contended with great force, the movement of human religion in general is regarded in Scripture as a movement from man to God, whereas the Christian gospel testifies rather of the movement of God to man. It is, by its very nature, such a judgment on all human religion as is, in ultimate meaning, the judgment of grace. To quote the searching words of Dr. Camfield :

Its consciousness of a universal mission and a universal validity does not arise from a sense of mere superiority to other religions, but of a fundamental and decisive otherness in relation to them. It arises from the sense that God has come, that something final and all-decisive has happened . . . not on a conviction of the superiority of its thought-content to anything that can be discovered elsewhere, but purely on the nature of the divine event to which it witnesses . . . a great divine event which is essentially " once for all " and nonrepeatable, an event on which the salvation of the world depends.[1]

The bearing of this on the missionary enterprise of the Church is evident. If the missionary went out to proclaim certain general truths, certain eternal moral values, he would in effect only be adding the special Christian ideas and ideals to the common stock cherished by other faiths. He might speak of Jesus, indeed, but it would be as exemplifying something, not effecting something, not " giving His life a ransom for many ". So far, no more than a difference of degree and relative purity separates the sense of spiritual values which the missionary brings and that which he encounters in non-Christian lands. It might well be his part to learn as well as teach. On the other hand, as Dr. Bevan has insisted,[2] in so far as the Christian missionary has to tell of certain events, of things done by God (*imprimis*, of course, the Incarnation), or destined to be done, he gives only and does not receive. This is a point of which Troeltsch takes no account. His type of thought in the last resort is Hellenic, not Hebraic ; " events " for him, therefore, count only as of second-rate importance. But in regard to concrete incidents, either you know of them, or you do not ; it is a plain case of " either-or ". The non-Christian does not know that " the Son of God is come ", that " God has given us eternal life, and this life is in His Son ". These are things which no one could find out by any mere sense of values, but only by actually hearing and believing the witness that records them. For Troeltsch, accordingly, missionary work loses its old motive and acquires a new aim. The task of the future is now to effect an understanding, and, in some form, a synthesis of Christianity with the highest ethnic worships, such as Islam, Brahminism, Judaism.

[1] *Revelation and the Holy Spirit*, pp. 183–4 (abridged).
[2] In the *International Review of Missions* for July, 1919.

§ 5.   JESUS CHRIST, GOD AND IMMORTALITY

In the light of these interpretative ideas the religious importance of Jesus for the modern mind and its construction of human life must be gravely reduced. Troeltsch's early and inherited sense for Christ as somehow bound up with faith in God does indeed keep the thought of our Lord closely related to his argument as a whole. He dismisses the suggestion that Jesus never lived as a " foolish monstrosity ". Christianity, as he puts it in a well-known lecture on the significance of Jesus for faith,[1] " was in its origin not the worship of a new God but the worship of the ancient God of Israel and of all reason in His living, concrete and consummated revelation—i.e. Jesus glorified by the resurrection-faith ". But as the lecture proceeds we discover that in reality Troeltsch is bent on resuscitating the old distinction, familiar in Strauss and Biedermann, between the Person of Jesus and the principle of redemption. His uncompromising relativism in history gives him no choice. In consistency no more ought to be heard of the absolute " Christocentricism " of the older theology, for in the rise of Christianity as such there can be seen at work not the influence of Christ merely, but Hebrew prophetism, Plato, the Stoic philosophy and other popular religious forces that vibrated through the ancient world. Jesus is a great religious personality, and to contemplate Him is uplifting. He may be called a type or symbol whose place no other can fill. Yet, as a symbol, He is relative after all ; as Troeltsch might have put it, He is eternal but not *the* Eternal. Absolute values lie transcendently beyond the whole realm of change ; in the Platonic phrase, they are " laid up in heaven ". Jesus pierced to the highest truth of spirit, and in that sense has primacy. Yet truth can-

---

[1] *Die Bedeutung der Geschichtlichkeit Jesu für den Glauben* (1911).

not be linked inseparably, for good and all, to the person
who first seized it or seized it at its highest point.

We gain the impression that while as a philosopher
Troeltsch felt obliged to make Jesus relative, yet just
as in the case of Biedermann a warmer faith was ever
seeking to intervene. Not, I think, with much success
so far as concerns the doctrinal statement, yet in the
form of what is really an unconscious protest against
relativising negations. More positive assertions, indeed,
are frequent. " The God of Jesus," he writes, " is the
object of faith, and Jesus Himself is transformed into the
historical Mediator and Revealer." And again : " The
whole content of life and faith in Christianity continues
to be related to the prototype found in the Person of
Jesus, and faith in Him is the one unifying bond of the
Christian community." The last clause of the sentence
just quoted points to the new direction in which Troeltsch
is looking. He urges that what could at need be dispensed with by the individual may none the less be necessary for the Church. Each religious fellowship must have
a central object round which its worship gathers, for
adoration and reception ; and if the Christian fellowship or
Church is to persist, it too must have such an object.
Neither feeling nor imagination can dispense with it. We
Christians must worship in each other's company ; but
this is only possible in so far as we come together round
Jesus and submit our souls to the pure influences of
His truth and love. What in itself is logically and historically accidental thus becomes vital from the standpoint
of social psychology.[1] Not otherwise can the Christian
religion keep its power to infect the world with its own
peculiar life. " So long," he declares firmly, " as Christianity exists in any sense, it will involve the centrality
of Christ in worship."

It cannot be said that this is wholly convincing. There

[1] Cf. *Glaubenslehre*, pp. 8, 28.

is a certain spiritual unreality in the attempt thus to divide the interests of individual and fellowship. The mind boggles at the idea of a congregation engaged in worshipping a Person who is felt to be religiously indispensable to the company as a whole, yet in the last resort superfluous for each single member. Apart from that —though this is a point to be considered later—we cannot ignore the scrupulous reserves and qualifications which Troeltsch appends even to so limited an affirmation of Jesus' centrality. Worship gathers round Jesus still, but it may not always be so. We may count upon it for so long as the civilization lasts which sprang up centuries ago in Mediterranean lands, but not, at least not necessarily, for longer. Every historical epoch stands in its own direct relation to God, and we must not stiffly insist on any absolute estimate of Christ. But, though it is forbidden to assert that Christianity will for all time be anchored to one historic personality, our duty for the present remains clear. It is to join with the Church in adoring Christ.

At an earlier point stress was laid on Troeltsch's affinities with Schleiermacher, in general atmosphere and intention ; yet on the subject of immortality Schleiermacher's steady progress to a more positive Christian faith is in strange contrast with Troeltsch's halting and ambiguous declarations. On the question of personal blessed survival, he appears at most to keep an open mind, and the issue may legitimately be raised whether his thought of God permits him to do more. Owing to his dislike for anthropomorphic conceptions of God, he tends to reduce the Divine Love to a mere energy of life—" an energy ", as it has been put, " which is constantly and inscrutably surprising us, confronting us in all the amazing majesty of its activity, an energy which achieves its purpose . . . in stimulating to union with the Divine, in drawing the finite to the Infinite, slowly and with difficulty, but yet remorselessly, as a faintly flickering planet is ' drawn nearer and nearer to the solar fires ' ".[1] The eternity of the soul, in Troeltsch's view, can be nothing more than its eventual re-entry into, and disappearance in, the timeless and universal Divine life. The idea of unending existence is repulsive to him ; the outcome of all must be reabsorption, so that with the culmination of the redemptive process the soul, instead of being saved in Jesus, is lost in God, and with the cessation of individual being the believer drops down into measureless Deity, as a road might terminate by sinking into the gulf.

The first thing to be said of this, as an argument, is that it freely uses terms and conceptions to which it is doubtful whether we can attach a distinct sense. As Leckie has pointed out, when we speak of ultimate absorption, " we are not only exceeding the limits of the Christian Faith, we are also deceiving ourselves with imaginative terms which correspond to no experience of ours and express nothing that has definite meaning for our minds ". He adds, with truth and point, that

the very thought of a timeless state of existence is the symbol of something lower, and not higher, than our present life. Succession, a before and an after, is an essential characteristic of spiritual being. Without it there can be no progress, no service, no fellowship with kindred souls, no hope and no memory.[2]

These are in a sense metaphysical considerations. It is even more important to observe that Troeltsch's representation of the eternal future is definitely at war with the Christian doctrine of God. A Divine life which cannot impart its highest gifts within the limits of personal fellowship, a life to which, as here, the vital impulse of selfhood is no more than an obstacle ultimately to be swept aside, is in no recognizable sense the life of

---

[1] R. S. Sleigh, *The Sufficiency of Christianity*, p. 232.
[2] J. H. Leckie, *The World to Come and Final Destiny*, pp. 321 ff.

Him whom Jesus revealed as Father. Doubtless it is the case that certain types of mind welcome the prospect of personal dissolution, foreseeing in it an escape from endless boredom. But the fear underlying such a revulsion from eternal life springs from what in reality is a Neo-Platonic and not a Christian view of God, and the Nirvana in which not only the believer but Christ and—as in certain passages Troeltsch appears to hint—even God Himself finally disappear, has a much closer resemblance to Buddhism than to Christianity. It is well now and then to read our theology (so to say) backwards, in order that the light of subsequent doctrines may fall on earlier ones. If we do this with Troeltsch, the impression left by his doctrine of " Eternal Life " can hardly fail to excite the gravest doubts concerning the thoughts of God, and of God's relation to His children, which form its presupposition and background. Whatever be the cause, he has lost hold, somewhere and somehow, of the sense of God present in Jesus' argument with the Sadducees. When our Lord uttered the words : " He is not the God of the dead, but of the living ", He was pointing to the Father, Who will not leave in the dust or suffer to pass into nothingness those whom He has bound to Himself irrevocably. They are His, and belong to Him for ever. The denial of this is a denial of God's own nature.

§ 6.   THE FINALITY OF THE CHRISTIAN RELIGION

Troeltsch debated this question not only in a special publication issued for the second time in 1912, but in a lecture written shortly before his death. His main contention is to the effect that no religion, even Christianity, is valid universally or for ever, because each faith is but an individual form of the pure spirit of religion, and has power and authority only within the concrete and

historical conditions under which it first arose. This, we
must observe, is not a form of evolutionism ; Troeltsch
does not try to sweep Christianity under the general
rubric of genetic development. On the contrary, it is
the theory of irreducible and individual vital forms. He
holds that just as " Truth, as apprehended, or even as
apprehensible, by man varies indefinitely from race to
race and from age to age, and does so in *quality* no less
than in quantity ", so it is supremely with religion. As he
states the position broadly in one of his last utterances :
" The universal law of history consists precisely in this,
that the Divine Reason, or the Divine Life, within history,
constantly manifests itself in always-new and always-
peculiar individualizations—and hence that its tendency
is not towards unity or universality at all, but rather
towards the fulfilment of the highest potentialities of
each separate department of life. It is this law which,
beyond all else, makes it quite impossible to characterize
Christianity as the reconciliation and goal of all the forces
of history, or indeed to regard it as anything else than
an historical individuality." [1] What is presented in the
Gospel is but one aspect or facet of the enigmatic Ultimate
Fact.

Not only so. Our evidence for the degree of truth
possessed by Christianity lies, as he affirms, in " a profound inner experience ". But the words that follow
prove how deeply infected with relativism even his supreme
religious convictions had now become.

This experience [he continues] is undoubtedly the criterion
of its validity, but, be it noted, only of its validity *for us*.
It is God's countenance as revealed to us ; it is the way in
which, being what we are, we receive, and react to, the revelation
of God. It is binding upon us, and it brings us deliverance.
It is final and unconditional for us, because we have nothing
else . . . But this does not preclude the possibility that other

---

[1] *Christian Thought*, p. 14.

racial groups, living under entirely different cultural conditions, may experience their contact with the Divine Life in quite a different way.[1]

The Truth concerning God, in other words, is wholly different for different peoples and for different times.

There had been a period when he put things otherwise. Insisting that Judaism and Islam are religions of law, which yet do not redeem, Hinduism and Buddhism religions of redemption, which yet lose God all over again by identifying Him with the world, he had then felt free to claim that Christianity alone meets and satisfies the needs to which both types appeal. " It is thus," he wrote, " not only the climax, but the converging-point of the two great kinds of historical religion." And even in his latest stage, when he regarded Christianity as inseparably linked to a form of civilization that may not last for ever, and contemplated a time when man might grow conscious of needs which the Gospel does nothing to satisfy, he still reasserted that " it is the loftiest and most spiritual revelation we know at all ". Christianity is sufficient ; it is, as we say colloquially, enough to be going on with ; and faith will ask for no more.

We have no cause to disagree with Troeltsch at all events in this, that no proof of the finality of the Christian religion can be led with obvious success in the court of disinterested philosophical or historical thought. Indeed he is altogether mistaken, as I should hold, in supposing that transparent or universally convincing reasons can be given even for the view that Christianity is the loftiest religion so far known to man. How, to take but one example, could anything of the kind be made evident to a Hindu thinker who altogether rejected the assumption, so natural to us, that a personal concept of God is higher

[1] *Christian Thought*, p. 26.

than an impersonal one, and did so in the sincere belief
that personality as such is not good in any sense but
definitely evil ?   It ought by this time to be fairly clear
that no scientific argumentation can either yield or vindicate the supreme standards of value.   All that science,
be it psychological or historical, can say is merely that
such and such beliefs have been held, with such and
such effects on human minds.   But it is never justified
in saying that one set of beliefs is truer or loftier than
another.   Valuation in religion is the prerogative of faith.

Troeltsch's reduced view of Christianity, as a faith
which may be adjudged sufficient in temporary ways,
or as a makeshift for something better but unattainable,
is, it will hardly be questioned, wholly out of touch with
the heroic type of missionary faith which has in the
noblest and profoundest sense made the history of the
Christian Church.   It has no relation to the victorious
conviction which belongs not to sensible men, looking
round for that which, at the moment, may reasonably
be taken as the most adequate form of religion within
their reach, but to the martyrs—to those who believe
that in Christ the holy love of God has been perfectly
revealed, and who therefore are willing to spend and
be spent to the utmost in a cause greater than life itself.
But this type of faith, alive in men like Hannington
or David Livingstone, is Christian faith in its supreme
and most intense form and at its most creative height ;
a view of Christianity, therefore, which can be brought
into no vital relationship to it must be regarded as little
more than a product of academic theorizing.   And indeed
the simplest faith, once it understands the theory, must
repudiate this construction of the Gospel as but a pro-
visory and approximative form of religion.   To say, as an
adherent of Troeltsch's view, if pressed, is obliged to
say : " I find God in Christ, at least up to a point " is
a psychological impossibility for anyone who through the

mediation of Jesus has actually entered into pardoned fellowship with the Father.

The argument that Christianity in its own right possesses the status of the final and universal faith would be rendered much more convincing, I suggest, if we were fully awake to an ambiguity in the chief term. We speak familiarly of the Christianity of the Apostolic Age, of the Middle Ages, of the Reformation, of the twentieth century, meaning by these general phrases the total positive reaction to Christ in different epochs. That this reaction, whatever age be taken, has been profoundly imperfect and in that sense wholly relative, no reasonable person, it may be presumed, could be tempted for a moment to deny. Even an apostle could say : " Not as though I had already attained, either were already perfect." But when serious thinkers raise the question whether Christianity is or is not final and absolute, the real issue is, or ought to be, a very different one. Now we are dealing with " Christianity " in quite another sense. Now it stands not for the reaction of man but for the action of God—for the revelation of God's holy love in Christ, for all that is meant by the Incarnation, the Atonement, the Resurrection, for the great things which the Father has accomplished or promised in the Son for us men and our salvation, for all that God is offering to the world in His declared Gospel. And to affirm the absolute and final character of Christianity in *this* sense merely proves that we understand what Christianity means. Here faith rests on an unsurpassable height, for the sufficient reason that, unless we pass outside the bounds of Ethical Theism, no higher or greater reality than Holy Love can be conceived. Hence the finality of Christ and of what He imparts can justly be called in question only when a loftier fact than holy love has come into view—then, but not till then. What is more, if it be the case that to the sinful Christ offers and conveys a free and pardoned fellowship with God surpassing all we could ask or think, such fellowship with the Holy One is, in point of fact, realized solely within the radius of Christ's influence. Platonism does not possess it, nor Buddhism, nor Islam. Not that in these religious forms God is unsought ; not that eager hands are not stretched out towards His truth. But whatever be attained, it is not apprehension of the Father as only the Son makes Him known, the Father as only the Son gives us, in our shame, the courage to cast our-selves upon Him. Ethnic religion without Christ cannot be the same thing as revelation in and through Christ. " We know that the Son of God is come, and hath given us an understanding, that we may know Him that is true ; and we are in Him that is true, even in His Son Jesus Christ. This is the true God and eternal life."

Troeltsch's life ended, we cannot but think, before it was possible for the onlooker to be reasonably certain what precise direction his development as a theologian would eventually take. It is true that under the sombre in-fluences of Germany's anguish in years subsequent to the Great War he gave expression to what must be regarded as a gravely and even fatally diluted version of Christian faith. Yet this may well have been a passing phase. There have been great believers, as the Psalter shows, whose faith was not always at its strongest and highest, and who could persist in addressing to the Unseen ques-tions full of agonizing doubt. But from many an earlier page of Troeltsch we can glean utterances of a deep and manly confidence in God which, had his life been pro-longed, might well have recaptured the note of stedfast certainty.

In years to come he will probably be accounted less as a dogmatic thinker than as a distinguished historian of religious thought, profoundly interested in translating Christianity into the present social consciousness of man-

kind. To him insight into the development of humanity
belongs only to those who by faith can pierce, through
the crust of concrete fact, to the inner reason of things,
the Divine living ground and source of all. To quote
the moving words that close his comprehensive work on
The Social Doctrines of the Christian Churches :

The Kingdom of God upon the earth can be only approximately realized. Faith is the conquering power in the battle
of life ; but a battle life will remain, ever changing though
never ceasing. After all is said—and this is the all-inclusive
truth—the Kingdom of God is within us. In faithful and
untiring labour it must be ours to let our light so shine before
men that they who see our good works will glorify our Father
in heaven. The final issues of all mankind are hidden in His
hands.

THE THEOLOGY OF PARADOX

SÖREN KIERKEGAARD

§ 1. HIS EARLY LIFE AND TRAINING

NO ACCOUNT of leading modern types of Theology would be complete, or even intelligent, which omitted the work of Sören Kierkegaard. He has been called " the greatest Christian thinker of the past century ", " the greatest of all Christian psychologists ". And such an estimate, in spite of apparent extravagance, is a finger-post it would be unwise to ignore. Prophet as much as theologian—though with a Hamlet-like strain which tormented him till near the end—he stands out on the sky-line for the retrospective eye with the prominence of a Nietzsche or a Carlyle. His teaching, later illumined by intimate diaries, has in it the tragic elements of a deeply shadowed life. His defiance of ecclesiastical convention stamps him as a man of lonely courage ; nor could any man who did not possess singular moral insight and fierce vigour of phrase have come, as he did, to be known as " the accusing angel " of contemporary religion. To him, as to many good men, professors of theology were deeply suspect. By common admission the most original thinker in Danish history, and a writer of classic quality, he extorts from later times the homage owed to " genius ". Yet the description is one he himself would have resented deeply.

In Kierkegaard, it is widely recognized, we have in some degree a precursor of Karl Barth. Barth's words are often quoted : " If I have a system, it consists in this, that always as far as possible I keep in mind what Kierkegaard spoke of as the infinite qualitative difference between time and eternity, alike in its negative and positive meaning. God is in heaven, you are on earth." Readers of Barth, or of books about him, find themselves obliged to become familiar with a new set of terms—existence and existential,[1] incognito (used of Jesus Christ), contemporaneous, moment, offence, perpendicular, tension, decision

---

[1] Existence and existential, in his particular sense, are terms which apply only to men, not to concrete things ; they denote a special quality or attitude of men. In " the existence of the individual " the deepest demands of life, serious and inescapable, are faced and dealt with in grave choice. Only the individual himself can decide his response to these absolute demands, and only so can " existence ", as distinguished from mere " life ", be realized. " Existenz," writes Brock, explaining the importance of the idea for later philosophy, " is an attitude of the individual to himself, which is called forth by such concrete situations as the necessity for choice of profession or a conflict in love, a catastrophic change in social conditions, or the imminence of one's own death. It leads immediately to sublime moments in which a man gathers his whole strength to make a decision which is taken afterwards as binding upon his future life. Furthermore, Existenz never becomes completed, as does life through death. In its different manifestations it is only a beginning which is faithfully followed or faithlessly forgotten. Moreover, Existenz is not real in being known, it is real only in being effectuated, in the remembrance of it, and in resolutions for the future which are taken to be absolutely binding " (*Contemporary German Philosophy*, p. 83–4).
Existential thinking is the kind of thinking which accompanies or constitutes the coming-to-be of " existence ". It is realized through the inner decisions of the individual, who thereby comes in touch with reality at its deepest. It is a mode of thought which concerns not the intellect merely but the whole personality of the man who awakens to it and adopts it. To think existentially, therefore, is to think not as a spectator of the ultimate issues of life and death, but as one who is committed to a decision upon them. " This concerns *me* infinitely, now and here " is its pervading tone, all that is purely theoretical or academic falling away. Kierkegaard would have said that the chief defect in Hegel's philosophy is the definite lack of such thought.

and the like.[1] These words, it may not be unnecessary
to add, are far from being a wilful jargon. They have
an important sense, and are unlikely soon to drop out of
the theological vocabulary, though the use at times made
of them may be more imposing than helpful. In any
case, they all or nearly all derive from Kierkegaard. It
is one mark of his power that, like Tertullian, he minted
a new coinage.

In an exceptional degree, this man's thought was shaped
by his life. For him, as for Hosea, reality was what he
himself had passed through ; and scholars who are working over his ideas find it necessary to start from his personality. This of itself guides us in part to the meaning
of his recurrent adjective " existential ". No thinking *is*
existential save that in which our whole present being is
at stake, in which we are personally wrestling as for life
or death. " Existence " is life at first hand, lived in
deadly earnest. The only truth it is worth while to
know has first to be endured, then thought, and the outcome will have the signature of the thinker's warfare and
pain. In fact, if he is to be understood, Kierkegaard has
to be read with the reverence we bring to lives of great
spiritual agony, like Jeremiah or Dante.[2] To make sport
of him, or shake our heads over his vagaries with a superior
pity, is to shut the gates of understanding.

He was born at Copenhagen, in 1813, the youngest son
of a retired woollen-draper in easy circumstances ; he
died in 1855. From his father, Michael Kierkegaard, he

[1] A passage like the following from E. L. Allen's excellent book
Kierkegaard (p. 144) shows how deeply the older writer had influenced Barth's early terminology : " The ' moment ' at which
the individual stands might be symbolized by the point at which
a descending line impinges on one running horizontally . . . The
moment is not a section of time, but an atom of eternity. It
is *Krisis*—a judgment on time."

[2] See the article " Kierkegaard " in Hastings' *Encyclopædia of
Religion and Ethics,* by the late Dr. Alexander Grieve, one of the
few English-speaking experts in this field.

learnt one lesson which stayed with him to the end—
that faith is responsibility to God expressed in personal
decision. The son was formed, not to say crushed, by
the ascendancy of the father's character. Melancholy had
marked the older man for its own. Once, as a herd-boy
on the moor, overcome by cold, hunger, and solitude, he
had mounted some hillock and deliberately cursed God to
His face. Shortly after he gained a situation in Copenhagen, which eventually led to prosperity and even wealth ;
but, with a morbid remorse and a nearly unparalleled
severity of self-judgment, in this very success he saw
proof that by his youthful curse he had committed the
sin against the Holy Ghost, which has no forgiveness.
Close intimacy with this dark yet lofty spirit graved an
indelible mark upon the son. Sören was a weakly child,
and spent an unnaturally quiet childhood. He relates
how his one recreation was to listen, as hand in hand
they walked up and down the dining-room of the home,
to his father's graphic accounts of imaginary journeys.
Under these circumstances, naturally enough, he too
became the victim of inward gloom. As he puts it, this
was the penalty of being exceptional.

His years at the University were stormy, and for a
time he was on the verge of renouncing Christianity.
Natural science meant nothing to him in comparison with
problems of the spirit. He plunged into the maelstrom
of Romanticism, Hegel most of all ; over Socrates he
brooded with a sense, which never left him, that the
Greek sage and he were blood-kinsmen. " The Concept
of Irony, with special reference to Socrates " is the title
of his thesis for graduation. Here some ideas of central
importance for his later work, such as the infinite and
eternal meaning of the individual, come for the first time
upon the stage. Also the thesis exemplifies, in part, one
of his peculiar literary methods. We have an early glimpse
of the fashion he was to adopt of setting his message forth

by means of what he calls "indirect communication". As Grieve puts it, "he fabricates characters representative of various aspects or stages of contemporary life, letting each work out his own views". Essentially it is a poetic method, with something in it of the Platonic dialogue, still more perhaps of Browning as we see him in his *Dramatic Lyrics*. He has indeed been described as "the *poet* of religion". At first his books were pseudonymous for the most part, though Kierkegaard's name appears editorially on the title-page, with the aim of suggesting that the contents more or less represent his own opinions. Other books came out simultaneously with the usual open acknowledgment of authorship. "Indirect communication", which he somewhere speaks of as "my very nature", is not to be dismissed as a mere eccentricity.[1] Not only does it indicate that the writer is tentatively working out a new view, by trial and error; it is meant to stab the reader full awake, and put him to thought and self-scrutiny. Pseudonymity too has a purpose. It seeks to liberate the reader from idle deference to authority by placing him in presence of a writer whose face he is not allowed to see, and whose ideas on that account will possess just as much value as they are worth. If Kierkegaard often wore a mask, it was because what he had to say could not, he felt, be said otherwise.

Before dying, the father had confided to the son, already sufficiently burdened, some guilty secret of his past life. In consequence of this shattering discovery, the youth resolved to give all his powers to the defence of Christianity in what he felt to be a virtually pagan world. It may be that in the despair following upon his father's avowal he lived riotously for a time. There are elements in his terrible doctrine of sin which may be taken as recalling some unforgettable descent into the depths of evil.

---

[1] These "indirect" books may have been meant first of all for Regine Olsen's eye.

Whatever the precise order of events, a second crisis supervened. In 1843 he was betrothed to a young girl of Copenhagen, by name Regine Olsen, and broke the engagement, as well as his own heart, after a year of tragic inward conflict. The reason for this strange but enriching act was and still remains a mystery, though it is difficult not to feel that he deliberately sought the parting because he could not reveal to her either his father's secret or his own stained record. We may pass from the episode—though it never passed from his own mind and has many echoes in his books—with Dryden's manly comment on Aeneas' desertion of Dido : " Upon the whole matter, and humanly speaking, I doubt there was a fault somewhere."

His sense of guilt over breaking with Regine—whom to his last hour he held in most loving honour—was such that, notwithstanding a conviction that he could not have acted otherwise, he thenceforward lived as a penitent. Oppressed yet sharply challenged by the feeling that he was not as other men, he gave himself up to a passionate crusade against unbelief. If it should mean that he perished in the battle, this too befitted his guilty but dedicated lot. He was to be a " solitary ", called and set apart from above to demonstrate to men " what it is to be a Christian ". He must cry aloud and not spare. Truth, he had begun to learn, had meaning only for the temper of true inwardness ; we have to face God as lonely souls in whose individuality no other can have a share. In that character we must place ourselves in His hand, with no reserves. Our one duty is to give our life over to the Most High, unquestioningly and irrevocably—for obedience, if need be for rejection and annihilation.

§ 2.   SOME FUNDAMENTAL PRESUPPOSITIONS

Two assumptions, important for Kierkegaard's general point of view, are to be noted here. First, the principle of spiritual inwardness, or, as it is often called, subjectivity, has a determinative influence on all his thinking. By inwardness is meant the personal appropriation of Divinely presented truth, its apprehension with or through *passion*. As Brunner puts it, interpreting Kierkegaard with true insight :

Faith is a *suffering* . . . a shaking of the whole existence which can be compared only to what we call passion. In fact, it is a curiously mixed passion or suffering ; it is even, as the classical Christian expression puts it, a death, the death of the old self, the autonomous Ego. And at the same time it is a joy ; it is the resurrection of a new Ego.[1]

Truth, Kierkegaard declares, is subjectivity, as subjectivity is truth. This, however, is by no means equivalent to the denial of given or objectively encountered reality, for it is on the objective that the soul feeds. His point rather is that the coldly objective counts for nothing by itself ; or, as he expresses it in familiar words, " only the truth that edifies is truth for thee ". Religious insight, that is to say, is higher and more veracious in proportion as it includes and, as it were, glows with that " infinite passion " through which alone our right relation to God comes into being. There is no such thing as spiritual truth not fused with personal experience that costs. At every point the one question worth asking is, " What does this truth signify for my tragically real existence ? " Knowledge of God's truth becomes ours only in the act of deciding for it with all our strength. Decision is no mere consequence of recognizing truth, it is a living and essential factor in apprehending it. To think subjectively —and no other kind of thinking matters here—is to act

[1] *The Word and the World*, pp. 71-2.

upon a risk. Cool detachment is an atmosphere in which
we cannot believe, as the New Testament accounts believing. " Thou art the man " are words which must sound
in our ears perpetually if, in Kierkegaard's special phrase,
our thought is to be " existential "—i.e., carried on with
the unfailing consciousness that we stand before God,
guilty and blind, awaiting His judgment and mercy.

A mind so gravely realistic could never have been
touched or tempted by the subjectivity of " religion
without an object ". On the other hand, two prominent
forms of so-called objective thinking in religion awakened
his bitter and scornful censure. One is the cold and
futile objectiveness of speculative divinity, which dissolves
the Gospel in ideas, rejects the unique incarnation of God
in Christ, robs men thus of a commanding spiritual authority, and shirks the imperative duty of calling upon
them to make up their minds for God. This is the unpardonable sin of thinking dispassionately about God and
eternity. The other is the tepid objectiveness of conventional Churchmanship, which lives at peace with the world,
atrophies the sense for spiritual heroism, and displaces
personal concern about salvation by decent or prosperous
membership of an institution. When Kierkegaard said
that truth is subjectivity, then, he bade men recollect
that personal Christianity without *decision* is nothing
better than a phrase. We are set, each of us, in the inescapable presence of God ; and to live and think as if
it were not so, is in fact not to think or live at all.

The second underlying principle for Kierkegaard is the
rooted distrust of Hegelian philosophy in which, after
years of storm and stress, he had ended. He now rested
in an immovable conviction that Hegelianism, with its
serene objectivity and optimistic acceptance of the actual,
is the worst possible framework in which authentic Christian
belief can be set. Hegel stood for the royal autocracy of
human thought, the exclusive supremacy of the so-called

T.M.T.   Q

creative reason of man ; but to Kierkegaard nothing could
be more falsely and sentimentally out of touch with the
sombre facts of life as lit up by the flash of revelation.
Here are all the materials for a great controversy ; and
the balance of forces in the fight changed when Kierkegaard stepped into the arena. " The beginning of the
new apprehension of the problem of God," writes Karl
Heim, " dates from that moment in the nineteenth century
when Kierkegaard, in conflict with the Hegelian philosophy,
rediscovered the way back from abstract thought to the
actually existing reality." [1] Hegel stood for the world as
a closed system ; his antagonist pointed to grim factors
in life and thought which are incalculable. Hegel, with
a higher naturalism, dissolved the individual in " bloodless
categories " ; the other proclaimed the sheer individuality
of conscience as it listens to God. Hegel found it possible
to approve of Christianity as at all events a first sketch
of the all-inclusive metaphysic ; the other announced the
paradox of God's self-revelation, by its nature an offence
to reason, and only to be grasped through the infinite
passion of faith.

Such a philosophy as Hegel's, it follows, is inwardly
and unavoidably at odds with Christian religion ; it will
pass the wit of man to bridge the gulf. The Gospel asks
of each man the question : Wilt thou be made whole ?
But philosophical idealism, taking its own characteristically frivolous view of sin, recoils with distaste from a
query so intrusive : for its chief purpose is not to cleanse
or cure, but to explain. In Kierkegaard's concise words :

Speculation can have nothing to do with sin ; in fact, it
ought not to have anything to do with sin. Sin belongs to
the sphere of ethics ; but ethical and speculative thought are

---

[1] *Glauben und Denken*, I, p. 93. Kierkegaard's criticism of the
Hegelian philosophy is now widely recognized as one of the two
or three really important examinations made of that system in
the light of positive principles.

moving in opposite directions. The latter abstracts from reality, the former makes for it. Hence it is that ethics operate with a category which speculation ignores and despises —viz., the individual.

Action is more than philosophical perspicacity. " The highest is not to understand the highest but to do it." What supremely kindled his anger was the Hegelian notion that all contradictions can be ironed out in a higher synthesis, the dialectic process moving forward in smooth and unbroken continuity from one point to the next.

Yet Kierkegaard had a dialectic of his own and ascribed to it crucial importance.[1] This method he styled a "qualitative dialectic"; it consisted in the sustained effort to bring out absolute distinctions, each aspect of which calls the other in question. Such pairs of ideas, each negating yet resting on its opposite, are holiness and love, grace and responsibility, eternity and time. These antagonistic aspects of experience came in contemporary speculation to be sponged out in a cheap and shallow reconciliation; Kierkegaard dwells on them with subtle vigour, protesting against the eager hunt for idyllic harmony. The idealist philosopher, he urges, is playing with life and religion; he stands off with the detached curiosity of the theatre-goer to whom the issues of the drama on the stage matter much less than that he should catch his train. He is a spectator of history, but hates taking sides. For him the selves by whom history was lived are scarcely more than things indicated by neuter nouns. All the time he is shirking the crucial relationship by which human life is constituted—that of *me* to *you*. The success of this evasion would be death to

---

[1] Brock writes suggestively : " It is due to his works that the two leading philosophers of the last decade, Jaspers and Heidegger, attained to their fundamental principle, and thus contemporary philosophy, like Protestant theology, received from Kierkegaard its decisive impulse " (*Contemporary German Philosophy*, p. 73).

Christianity. Hence the formula " both—and ", on which
Hegelianism thrives, must be displaced by " either—or ".
The true thinker will not try to have everything about
him just a little clearer than it is, for his business is to
make difficulties. Rationalism is the enemy. In the
actual world of personal life where destiny is at stake,
antinomy rules. " There may be a system of logic ; a
system of being there can never be."

Kierkegaard revolts especially from the Hegelian doctrine which, if words mean anything, teaches that the
human spirit is identical with the Divine. It is blind to
the truth that man, as one whose being is derived from
elsewhere, must clearly rest in faith on Him by whose
Will he exists. It is a comical thought, he sarcastically
observes, that the poor philosopher (or theologian) who
just after setting down one of his profoundest sentences
must turn from his desk to sneeze, should confuse himself
with the Infinite Spectator of all time and all existence.
If moral disease betakes itself for cure to speculation, it
will come empty away, for a tempted man gains nothing
by being told that sin and virtue are members of a transparently logical sequence. The reconciliation of which
Hegel speaks perpetually, and which indeed forms the
unvarying pattern of his argument, is no more than
logical or verbal ; to be reconciled, at bottom, is simply
to awaken to the truth that by the nature of things we
are reconciled and were formerly deluded in believing the
opposite. Thus the Hegelian harmonist misses both the
awfulness of the Gospel and its glory. Revelation has
come to mean only man's discovery of his own latent
powers. The offence of the Cross has been done away.

§ 3. THE SUCCESSIVE LEVELS OF HUMAN LIFE

In the first years of his writing life, we have seen, it
was Kierkegaard's practice to try out his ideas by putting

them in the mouth of imaginary characters. In 1843 appeared the book *Either—Or*, and for three years more pseudonymity was maintained. In this book, as in two others, *Fear and Trembling* and *Repetition*, published a few months later, he worked out the distinction between morality and religion, elucidating it in *Fear and Trembling* by a detailed study of the experience of Abraham and Job. After the interval of a year, two books more definitely theoretical were issued—*Philosophical Fragments* and *The Conception of Dread*. The first largely consisted in an impressively conceived dialogue between Socrates and Christ, centring in the question how eternal salvation can rest on a historical event; the second was a discussion of the meaning of sin, original or actual, which has dread as its psychological presupposition. In 1845 there came out what has been thought the most remarkable of all his books, *Stages in the Way of Life*; and after no long time it was followed by a treatise entitled *The Concluding Unscientific Postscript*, where Kierkegaard gives a full statement of what, in his view, is involved in being a Christian. Some good critics consider his *Practice in Christianity* (1849) as in a theological sense his masterpiece. Its main topic is the pervasion of Christian life and thought by paradox. Much space is given to the difficulties felt by the contemporaries of our Lord's ministry " in interpreting the Sign whose distinctive characteristic it is that It can be spoken against with a fair show of reason ". Yet we all of us are His contemporaries in a like sense ; the Christian is one who is content to recognize the love and personal visitation of God in a form that evokes doubt, refusing to judge according to appearances. During this period of intense literary activity, lasting about twelve years, in order (as he says) " to keep in telegraphic communication with religion ", he printed a large number of devotional addresses.

Before long these books made him famous. George

Brandes, the eminent literary critic, declares there had been nothing like them in Danish prose. He comments on the author's ill fortune in having been born in one of the lesser European countries ; had he used one of the great languages, the world must have rung with his name. Kierkegaard was aware of his own powers, and indeed puts forward one of his own works as the modern counterpart of Plato's *Symposium*. The history of systematic thought has rarely, if ever, seen so astonishing an example of a writer coming late into his kingdom. From an early point, it is true, his name had been well known in Denmark. But thirty years ago few outside that country had heard of him. Then the wider world awoke to his importance. Like a river that for a space flows underground, then rises, full and brimming, to the upper air, his work has come to the surface with an imperious claim after nearly two generations of neglect. To-day, books dealing with either his life or his thought, or with both in their indissociable connexion, pour out almost unceasingly.

What, in general terms, are the leading ideas he thus flung down before the world ?

He begins by insisting on the three main stages or levels at which men live. There is an inevitable progress or pilgrimage, yet it is made clear that the individual's transition from one stage to the next is no automatic natural process, but the outcome of impassioned decision. What drives men on, as it were, to leap perforce from one dimension to another, is the unchanging presence, in the background, of God before whose eyes we live. The silent pressure of this elemental fact urges men forward in a self-chosen development that issues in the consciousness of sin. We have every reason to believe that much in his exposition is imaginatively treated autobiography. He depicts what he had passed through and left behind, but the poison of which was still a torture ; for in him, as in Faust, two souls grappled with each other.

The first stage is the æsthetic. The æsthete, as viewed here, need be neither artistic nor lustful; in general terms he is rather the natural (not necessarily sensual) man whose maxim is : *Carpe diem*, savour the joy of life, and with all thy getting get pleasure. Enjoyment is the thing, and it scarcely matters whether it be enjoyment of spirit or of body. The æsthete is the uncommitted man, who looks on but declines to take a hand, and more than anything else hates boredom. The extraordinarily graphic nature of his psychological description suggests that Kierkegaard felt it incumbent on him to win men of the world by the fidelity of his presentation, in the hope that they might trust him the more readily when he spoke of religion. It is an existence without unity or meaning that he pictures —an existence libertine throughout in quality, devoid of interest in duty, or in the formation of a home by marriage. As he puts it vividly, the æsthetic life is like a stone thrown across a pool which for a time sustains itself by dancing lightly from wave to wave, but instantly sinks in darkness when the dance is over. So, by an inward necessity, this form of human experience changes presently into despair and damnation. Once this point is reached, all depends on *how* the man despairs. Let him betake himself for help to the finite, and nothing can save him. For Kierkegaard, æstheticism thus understood takes on its most imposing form in the philosophy of Hegel, with its neglect of the basic realities of existence. In the higher secularity of Hegel's thought we see the connoisseur of life turned reflective.

Ethical experience is the second stage. Here there is nothing *blasé*, no cool or cold detachment ; wholesome concrete interests have their place ; all is open and above board ; life is shared with others, as in a happy marriage ; there is a development (if only partial) of personality. Through real choice we now rise into moral being, above and beyond mere imagination, which treats only of possibilities. Authentic personality is not to be handled, as in Hegelianism, with the tools or methods merely of acute observation ; we know persons only as we *are* persons, and persons come to be in moral decision. In the new world thus opened, where the æsthete could find only vain tedium, an endless beauty and promise come to light. This, let us not forget, is the life for which Kierkegaard himself had longed, and whose climax and fruition, marriage, he had put away in tragic renunciation. Yet in that process of inward struggle where his hopes had suffered martyrdom, he had made the discovery of that which is higher than ethics. One fact there is, he now saw, on which the merely ethical life goes to wreck, and is broken up—the fact of penitence. In penitence there is something that takes all heart out of a man, and, so long as he remains within the purely moral sphere, condemns him to the fruitless pains of remorse. It absorbs and exhausts the force of action. When Fichte said that he had " no time for penitence ", he betrayed the typically ethical temper. From the point of view of authentic moral idealism, penitence is both a waste of time and a menace to energetic action. Not only so ; once it has begun, it has an ugly way of leading a man downwards into ever more hopeless depths of evil within himself. It proves irrefutably that even true morality is beyond us ; in the last resort, it points beyond itself, whether it be regarded as a despairing signal for help or a believing gesture towards a higher refuge. In brief, penitence marks the transition from ethics to religion.

Thus religion, the third and last stage of life, while by no means hostile to morality or denying its value, is not itself morality in any sense. Consider, urges Kierkegaard, how in the exclusively moral life we encounter no final problem, no incurable conflict, no spiritual agony ; we are not yet face to face with the Will behind all things that perpetually demands our decision. We have still to make the awe-inspiring discovery that there is such a thing as *faith*—the deepest passion, the most audacious and incredible paradox in which the human spirit can ever be involved. It is a favourite idea with Kierkegaard that the meaning of faith is best exemplified in the story of Abraham. He received the command to slay Isaac, a morally wrong act ; and, by what may be called a temporary suspension of the ethical, he obeyed in virtue of his personal relationship to God. Such a relationship, to be real, must baffle reason and outstrip all interpretation ; for what is faith, except a leap of despair ? [1] As finite things sink under us, we spring to the arms of God, obediently, blindly, by grim compulsion. " The absurd ", for Kierkegaard, virtually becomes a technical expression for the conviction that with God all things are possible. " In the power of the absurd," he writes, " Abraham clung to the certitude that he would receive Isaac back again, and he thereby gained anew the whole sphere of time."

To this Biblical instance he never wearies of returning. He sees in it the crowning proof that faith is wholly opaque and irrational—something given, something done to us, by which our whole being is convulsed. Purely ethical categories fail to embrace its meaning : indeed, it has no meaning of any kind till we utter the word " God ". Upon His absoluteness we can lay hold only through the struggle of faith, in which (to take one example) the No of doubt and fear evoked by His felt holiness is overcome and absorbed by the Yes of trust engendered by His love. As he writes in a more than usually characteristic passage :

The strongest emphasis a man may dare to lay upon himself—saying to his neighbour, as it were, With me hast thou to do—is to demand that the other shall believe in him ; but

---

[1] Despair, as it has been put, is the condition of latent melancholy and doubt so impossible to endure that a man is driven back by it into the refuge of belief.

the sole Subject, the one and only Self, Who in face of all the inhabitants of time can and does so accentuate His Ego as to say, Believe in Me, is God.

Kierkegaard's thinking starts from the real self, in presence of the real God, as though the man stood out before the Most High alone in empty space. No other sort of thinking, he would persuade us, is fully personal or relevant.

He proceeds to argue, chiefly in the book entitled *Philosophical Fragments*, that the believer may be defined as one who once for all has renounced the hope of reaching a logically congruous or speculatively transparent view of life. So far from solving the enigmas, faith has only begun to see what they are. None but the forgiven man perceives the incredible nature of forgiveness. Looked at from either within or without, faith is purely paradoxical, a *coincidentia oppositorum*—from without, for no kind or amount of reasoning can bring you there; from within, for the joy that constitutes its innermost being can only arise from incessantly renewed pain.

It was a well-known jest of Sidgwick of Cambridge that he never could distinguish between the kind of contradiction that was just a contradiction and the kind that was a vehicle of the profoundest truth. This is a shrewd caution against the loose employment of words, or the timid retreat from open argument into the convenient thicket of mystery. Yet surely room must be made for antinomy wherever we are bringing a finite intelligence to bear upon any aspect of an infinite reality. Paradox in Kierkegaard, it must be remembered, is far from being nonsense. It is indeed part of faith to hold that for God the paradox is resolved. In one passage he actually translates the word into terms that had long been familiar : " What I am accustomed to express by saying that Christianity hangs on paradox, philosophy on mediation, Leibniz brings out by making a distinction between what is above reason and what is against reason." But he insists that whereas the philosopher can only make headway by utilizing at each step the notion of continuity, it is on discontinuity that faith rests, so that every attempt to exhibit, analyse, or prove the objects of saving trust by means of the pedestrian categories of the understanding must, in the nature of the case, fail utterly. The understanding works in an atmosphere of detached unconcern ; Christ and His benefits cannot be apprehended otherwise than by intense and passionate interest, of which wonder, with its awareness of the astonishing grace of God, forms a large ingredient. Thus I should argue that Kierkegaard's general contention is sound because indissolubly involved in the nature of faith as such.

Like a rod in water [Brunner has written] God's Word is broken in the element of the world ; just as Christ could only reveal the glory of God through the form of a servant, so all speech concerning God, if in the sense of this revelation, is necessarily " paradoxical ". It is only by means of the contradiction between two ideas—God and man, grace and responsibility, holiness and love—that we can apprehend the contradictory truth that the eternal God enters time, or that the sinful man is declared just. Dialectical Theology [he proceeds] is the mode of thinking which defends this paradoxical character, belonging to faith-knowledge, from the non-paradoxical speculation of reason, and vindicates it as against the other.[1]

To hold that God can be known " directly ", Kierkegaard urges, is to think as the heathen do. When the Word of God passes into and takes shape in the inadequate medium of human idea and speech, it is unavoidably refracted in antinomy.

§ 4.   HIS READING OF THE CHRISTIAN RELIGION

By a long and difficult approach we have arrived at the gravest problem of all—most fully treated in *The*

---

[1] *The Word and the World*, pp. 6–7.

Concluding Postscript—on which Kierkegaard concentrates his whole powers. This is the problem how to become and be a Christian. With scarcely any exaggeration we may say that he regards it as incumbent on him to make its solution as difficult as possible. Nothing else, he is persuaded, befits the exacting idiosyncrasy of our religion. Christianity, too often victimized by the spirit of accommodation, must for once be set forth in the interest of God rather than man. Before the Eternal, we men are always in the wrong.[1] To become Christian we must win from ourselves the unreserved confession that our best needs the Divine pardon no less than our worst :

> Suffice it if—my good and ill unreckoned,
> And both forgiven through Thy abounding grace.

To say from the heart, " Before Thee we are but dust and ashes," means suffering, ever-renewed and poignant—not only the pain of breaking with the easy life of nature, but the still deeper pain due to the consciousness of sin and guilt. That consciousness can never be removed by any general, humane or cultured experience of religion, but only by our entering the fateful region of revelation —of revelation on God's side, and of faith on ours.

Kierkegaard's view of sin is marked by the infinite gravity found in the Bible and in the Reformers. Sin is the category that singles out the individual and puts him sheerly by himself, unconfused with God, or with his fellows, or with the encompassing world. This is not a doctrine to suit thinkers, he adds with a wry smile, for the sufficient reason that it is unthinkable. The matrix of sin is fear ; as a psychological event it springs from dread or anxiety. Despair, taken by him as the virtual equivalent of sin, is a universal condition. Men fear or

---

[1] To Kierkegaard this is no sad conviction. What he insists on is " the *blessedness* of the thought that we are always in the wrong as against God ".

dread when they hear the challenge of eternity, the call
to be spiritual ; they despair when they refuse it.

As doctors could tell us [he writes] that there is perhaps no
man living who is completely sound, so a real knowledge of
men would compel us to say that there is no living man who
is not in some degree the victim of despair ; no man in whose
inner life there does not dwell an unrest, a dispeace, a disharmony, the dread of something unknown, of something on
which he dare not look, a dread of the possibilities of his own
being, a dread of himself.

Sin, he proceeds, is qualitatively the *salto mortale* of freedom. Original sin is a fact, and a guilty one. We come
in a sinful context and bring ever new sin to birth, for
there is in sin an inscrutable combination of conscious
volition and inability to act otherwise. Between God
and the sinful lies an infinite abyss : as he puts it, " If
the distance is infinite between God, who is in heaven,
and thee, who art on earth, infinitely greater is the distance between the Holy One and thee, the sinner." He
justly points out that the distinction between God and
man has never been so sharply fixed as by the Christian
doctrine of sin. On this he has some striking words.
" Sin is the one thing that cannot be predicated of God,
whether by the *via negationis* or the *via eminentiæ*. If,
in the same way as one says that God is not finite, one
were to add that He is not a sinner, it would be blasphemy."
All this is convincing enough ; yet there are certain passages where Kierkegaard is on the brink of representing
the gulf created by sin as being merely an aggravation
of that which is due to finitude. He can definitely be
quoted for the view that our whole existence in time,
the relativity in which we live as creatures who are not
God, is *per se* guilty. Such a position could be distinguished only by the narrowest margin from downright
Manichaeism ; and it has been held, with less justification,
that traces of a similar hyperbolical aberration can be

detected in earlier statements of Karl Barth.[1]   Yet even
in Kierkegaard the culpable passages, which are few,
remain as but a negligible fringe upon his profoundly
searching and evangelical estimate of sin, which for him
forms the decisive presupposition of the whole idea of
redemption.   It is sin that drives men to God.   " Take
away the alarmed conscience," he exclaims, " and you
may close the Churches and turn them into dancing-halls."

It is sin, then, that opens our eyes to the cardinal fact
which, in Kierkegaard's judgment, underlies all true
theology and forms the major premise of every sound
argument it contains.   This is the absolute dualism
between God and man.   Here the satirist pours out his
scorn on those who, in pride or folly, persist in thinking of
God as only man in a superlative degree.   God is holy
and sublime ;   when we face ourselves we know, without
reasoning, that in us there is no such thing as either
sublimity or holiness.   It is not for us to make charges
against Him.   If we are ever to understand Christianity
or have a part in the new life it offers, we must learn to
keep our distance from the Most High.   The dualism is
such as no form of ratiocination can mitigate or resolve ;
it can only be overcome in *act*, the act of faith, and for
a moment.   Only for the twinkling of an eye, convulsively
as it were, can the individual spring by faith into a positive
relationship to the utterly Transcendent.   Man must dare
the leap of pure passion if the gulf is ever to be crossed.
True, there are dialectical considerations by which the
dualism might seem to be alleviated.   The qualitative
absoluteness of God seems to forbid the possibility of
a positive relation between God and man, yet on the other
hand man's inner subjectivity is in point of fact dominated
by that Divine absoluteness that apparently cancels it,
for the very existence of a *created* and *finite* being presupposes a Being that is absolute.   Hence the innate

[1] On the whole subject, see W. Künneth, ·*Die Lehre der Sünde*.

trouble of human life : the Absolute, by which alone man can live, is a burden to him—God is his malady. As Kierkegaard writes in anguish of soul : " That a sparrow can live, is intelligible ; the sparrow knows not that it is there, there before God. But how can man know that he is there, and before God, and not that very instant go mad or sink in nothingness ? " The Eternal is at once the sheet-anchor of our being and its torture. The only escape for human personality, held captive by its very constitution in the endless tension of antithesis, lies through the strait gateway of ever-renewed decision for God. At each successive point the relative must be sacrificed to the Unconditioned. For us the alternatives are self-immolation or nothing, for by intrinsic nature the two beings, God and man, stand wholly apart.

It is hard to believe that, as a general conception, this reproduces with fidelity the teaching of the New Testament. Plainly enough, in proportion as Kierkegaard sternly declines to avail himself of all aid in characterizing God which may be derived from the predicates of human life, even at its best and purest, he incurs the risk of leaving Him wholly unnamed and indescribable ; and as this self-denying ordinance is taken to be determinative of the very *definition* of God, it follows that not even His self-revelation in Christ, evocative as it is of human faith, can lighten our darkness. The result is what might have been expected. Kierkegaard, desiring to speak of God, must of necessity name Him somehow ; but, in a measure disconcerting in a Christian thinker, the chosen forms of designation are predominantly negative. Thus to him God is " the absolutely Unknown ", the mere " Limit ", the " sheerly unqualified Being "—all of them terms with a disagreeable resemblance to the well-known phrases of pantheistic mysticism. At times we are actually reminded of the famous mediæval dictum, *Deus propter excellentiam non immerito Nihil vocatur*—God so exceeds our measures

that we may well designate Him as "Nothing". He is
the Ineffable; and this epithet is to be taken so strictly
that we cannot fitly apply to Him even the concept of
existence. We have travelled far from the tender words
of the Psalmist : " Like as a father pitieth his children,
so the Lord pitieth them that fear Him."

I do not myself see why we should be challenged in the
name of Christianity to accept this as the only version
of the matter which is compatible with authentic faith.
That God is unfathomable is a basal element in all true
theology; that God is the " absolutely Unknown " is a
position separated from the other by the whole diameter
of being. Scripture gives it no support. Despite its
superficial resemblance to the language of the Hebrew
prophets, it is in fact at variance with their explicit teaching. What the prophets declare is, on the one hand, that
God cannot be known except in so far as He reveals
Himself, and on the other that God thus self-revealed is
God as He really is in Himself. In the classic words of
A. B. Davidson : " There is no trace in the Old Testament
of the idea . . . that His revelation of Himself is meant
merely to be regulative of human life, while what He is
in truth remains far away in the transcendental background
out of which it is impossible for it to advance, or into
which it is impossible for men to penetrate." If God is
unknowable by nature, the possibility of revelation of
course falls away. But the argument of Kierkegaard
perpetrates the fallacy of turning the actual into the
necessary. It is the case that *actually* the unbeliever does
not know God, and that for him while he remains un-
believing God is unknowable; but neither faith nor reason
justifies the conversion of this into the statement that
necessarily, or *per se*, God is such that He cannot be known.
The knowledge of God by man is something man can
never bring to pass, but it may be, it perpetually is, brought
about by God. It may indeed be suggested that in his

argument about the dualism existing between God and
man, Kierkegaard has not been dialectical enough. The
teaching of the Bible on the subject surely is just of that
twofold and paradoxical kind on which at other points
he so much insists ; it is that man is unlike God, yet also
like Him. The image of God in man is broken, yet not
utterly destroyed. What remains of it is not kept in
being by man himself—a view wrongly ascribed to their
opponents by those who contend that the *imago dei* has
been utterly obliterated by sin. It owes its being, of
course, simply to the patient and infinitely merciful grace
of God, Who " in His mysterious humility tends the
last smouldering lamp in every rebellious heart ". But,
in whatever diminishing fragment, it remains as the secret
door of entrance which God keeps for Himself in the
soul. Human qualities may therefore be so far a parable
of the Father. Could the man who had never encountered
love among his fellows, and for whom accordingly the
term " love " had no recognizable content, put any real
meaning into the message of God's " love " in Christ ?
If familiar kindness is in no sense or degree whatsoever an
index of the Divine being, what value can belong to
Christian nurture ?

It is not of course to be forgotten that Kierkegaard's
vigorous denial that the character of God can simply
be read off human nature, is both sound and opportune.
His solemn emphasis on the majestic transcendence of
Deity corrects and refutes all feeble anthropomorphisms.
But a transcendence so defined as to forbid all contact
with earth is not that which stands behind the teaching of
Christ. The truth is—and this Kierkegaard as a theologian tended to ignore, though as a tender-hearted preacher
of God's love he knew it well—that while we in our sin
are infinitely distant from God, you do not state the whole
truth, or even its more important side, by laying down
that He is infinitely distant from us. He is near as well

as far. But Kierkegaard sets forth so extreme a doctrine
of transcendence that we can see it to be trembling on the
verge of the old monastic misapprehension which felt the
world to be God-forsaken and fled from it to the desert.
The Christian view is that the revelation in Jesus is decisive
for the *whole* of God's nature and puts what He really is
within our reach. It is not that of ourselves we have
scaled the height; He has come to us. Nothing still
hidden in God can be incongruous with what has thus been
made known. He dwells in light unapproachable, but
of His own initiative He has made approach to us in
Christ, and has come the whole way to where we sinners
are. If this be called in question, Christianity sinks to the
plane of a nature-religion.

In virtue of this unqualified dualism the relations of
God and man take on, for Kierkegaard, an aspect which
is not merely obscure but sinister. Human life is in any
case a synthesis of eternity and time, a meeting-point
at which there prevails a nearly total pain and darkness.
But let the Gospel come upon the ground, and at once
—so argues Kierkegaard in his eagerness to make
difficulties—the darkness thickens. For one thing,
Christianity forces a man to look with open eyes at his
own sheer sinfulness, hounding him out of the petty
enumeration of particular offences and confronting him
starkly with the fact that not merely is he a sinner because
he sins, but—which is a graver truth—he sins because
he is a sinner. Earlier, he had stood as finite under the
shadow of the Infinite; now he kneels in guilt before the
Holy One, " the fiery limit of all human endeavour ".
He has made the ultimate discovery that sin and human
nature are one and the same, and that redemption, to be
more than a phrase, must be conceived as a fresh beginning,
which carries on *nothing* from the past and breaks all
continuity with the man's old self. Perplexity deepens
—here we are " dazzled with excess of bright "—when it

transpires that the Holy One, in unimaginable love, is seeking fellowship with the guilty. Now we stand upon the very peak of truth. It is the essence of Christianity that eternal Truth once came forth in history, a personal presence in the God-man. Christ was not the effulgence of human nature, but the breathing of Eternity into time.

Critics have pointed out that, in distaste for the lust for historical detail, Kierkegaard more than once plays with the doubtful notion that even if we possessed no more than believing witness to the *fact* of the Incarnation—" that in such and such a year God showed Himself in the humble form of a servant, lived among us, taught, and thereafter died "—this by itself would have sufficed. This, which has all the weakness of hypothetical theology, is a position to which he occasionally leans ; yet it is not characteristic. On the contrary, his strongly marked doctrine of the *incognito* [1] in which the Son of God appeared—as a mere man to all not in the secret, confounding reason by His obscurity and lack of splendour and omnipotence, and thus making it possible for Him to be misinterpreted with a fair show of reason—invites him to make much of the historical Jesus. He can even reproach Luther for reading the story of the Gospel through Pauline eyes ; the Figure drawn by the Evangelists, he urges, must ever be at the centre of our thought. The signature of Jesus' glory is this, that it is veiled in lowliness.

None the less, it is precisely in his Christology that Kierkegaard's special doctrine of paradox assumes its most baffling form. The Incarnate Person, he insists, is

---

[1] It has been suggested that this application to Christ of the idea " incognito " is the outcome of " Kierkegaard's own love of disguise and shrinking from self-revelation ", of his feeling himself " to have a secret which it was impossible to communicate to any ". This may and does cast some real light on the uprising of the idea in one particular mind ; it hardly explains the serious use he made of the idea, or the valuable meaning later thinkers on the revelation present in Christ have found in it.

alike the object of saving faith and a mortal affront to human reason. *Credo quia absurdum est*—the famous words of Tertullian might be his own. The Person of Jesus flouts intelligence by the mere fact that it is an earthly phenomenon with eternal Godhead at its heart. The other incredibilities latent in the Gospel—such as the dependence of salvation on a historical event, or the Divine justification of the ungodly—are crowned and sealed by the supreme paradox that in Jesus the eternal God enters time. It does not merely *happen* that at this point tension reaches its maximum ; Christ is *constituted* by sheer essential contradiction. He unites in Himself two elements or aspects which unconditionally repel each other ; and we know it as we utter the fateful words, " This Man is God ". Thus the Person of Jesus Christ is a logically preposterous entity against which, in Kierkegaard's vivid phrase, " reason beats its brow till the blood comes ". Yet the absurdity is fact, and with it the Gospel stands or falls.

It is not to be thought of that a man of Kierkegaard's supreme ability could revel in mere nonsense for its own sake, like a perverse child. Arguments which, on the surface, have a provocatively extravagant sound may yet be significant of what is true and vital. He was well aware of the dangers involved in a Christology so para-doxical—the danger, above all, that the Incarnation might come to be thought not astonishing merely, but impossible, and the Fatherhood of God thus be lost all over again—and against these dangers he sought to guard himself. But he was resolved to make two points clear. First, by the irrationality of the Gospel he means some-thing which evokes a sudden glory in the mind, a specific sense of wonder.[1] To put it so, the Person of Jesus is not

[1] Part of the wonder, as Kierkegaard rightly urges with great power, is that this Person far off in history is *contemporaneous* with us, and we with Him. When He speaks to us, when we

absurd or irrational for God, but only for us. Even for
us it is not absurd in the ultimate sense, in so far as it has a
meaning upon which we can reflect to good purpose, provided the reflection be done in faith. And secondly, by
insisting on irrational paradox he seeks to bring out the
indubitable element of provocativeness in the Gospel—
what the New Testament calls " the *offence* of the Cross ".
In the Gospel as apostles preached it there is to be found
something which, as we say familiarly, is more than
nature can bear. It scandalizes both reason and moral
common sense. If we are left to ourselves, we undoubtedly
recoil from the idea that Christ is wholly different from us,
not merely separate from sinners but distinct from the
saints. We resent His power to force us into a personal
interview with Himself, in which matters of life and death
are in the balance ; this, for natural feeling, is an unpardonable invasion of personality. Or again, one to
whom man is the measure of all things must hate the
thought of being forgiven, and forgiven by such a one as
Jesus. Pardon, to his mind, is in any case impossible,
and that it should be offered freely to those who do not need
it is a fresh insult. Now, says Kierkegaard, remove this
distinctive feature of the Gospel that it *offends*, and its
savour is gone. The safeguard or antiseptic of the Christian message lies in the fact that it involves stumbling-
blocks for mind and heart of a kind so formidable that
nothing less than Divine power can enable men to sur-
mount them. " No man can say that Jesus is Lord but
by the Holy Spirit." Kierkegaard, with the New Testament behind him, bids us recollect that any form of the
Christian gospel which has parted with the element of
wonder, or become altogether inoffensive to those who

decide for Him, the limits of time and distance disappear. The
idea is not one peculiar to Kierkegaard, but he has given it a
new prominence in the Christian thought of our relation to Christ,
the same yesterday, to-day, and for ever.

hear it, is fatally untrue to type. For beings such as we are, in presence of such a being as Christ is, the only alternative to offence is adoration. It is in the main from Kierkegaard that modern theologians have learned to regard paradox as part of the staple or essence of Christian thinking rather than as merely a sporadic and disconcerting accident, like a rock in the sky.

True, there are not a few pages where his approach to Christ is made from a different angle. Assuming that by nature man is in a state of falsehood or untruth, he can argue, like others, that the Teacher who is to lead him right must not only give the truth itself but also empower man for its appropriation by effecting an inward trans-formation of the soul. But since such transformation outgoes the powers of a merely human teacher, He who teaches redemptively must Himself be God. Here we are in touch with the impression Christ actually makes on the believing mind.

But elsewhere, more characteristically, he adopts a different line, and tends to invest the dogmatic formularies of Christology with a value or function they were never meant to have. He persists in declaring that the inward-ness of our personal relationship to God positively depends on our blind acceptance of a Christological paradox, which is insoluble because intrinsically it is paradox and nothing else. In no other way can we give proof of willing sub-mission to " the offence of the Cross ". Sacrifice of the intellect is imperative ; we must simply own that although God and man are pure opposites—with no affinity of any kind or degree between them—yet in the God-man they become one. On this showing, the mediæval fancy that God *might* have been incarnate in an animal would not be so unreasonable as it sounds ; for so far as kinship with God is concerned, man and animal are upon an equal footing. Or, to take another point, if by definition God and man are sheer contraries, if there exists no good reason

why the ideas of God and man should vary together
(as in the history of theology they have done uniformly),
then to accept the idea of a " God-man " is much the
same as accepting the idea of a " round square ". Nor
can we escape the difficulty by pleading the difference
between God's standpoint and ours. If things are as
Kierkegaard states them, they are so also for God.

It is of course true that at a certain level of thought the
presence of antinomy, of unresolved tension between
concepts, may be a mark of depth rather than shallowness.
But here the explicit contention is this, that in personal
religion the value of different stages of spiritual attainment
can definitely be measured by the degree of paradox
accepted at each stage, and that at the highest stage of all,
faced by Christ, we believe against *every* counter-reason.
Faith on these terms is blind defiance.   The way into the
Kingdom lies through the simple crucifixion of intelligence.
Reason is stunned—rendered unconscious, as it were—
by the logical enormities thrust upon it by the Gospel.
The *creative* action of Revelation upon reason and conscience will presumably be acknowledged by all who
take Revelation seriously ; it is another matter to describe
this action as of a wholly negative and destructive kind.
There is surely a sad irony in the fact that this man who
could write of the inwardness of faith so memorably,
urging with a force which recalls Luther himself that
spiritual truth must be our own possession, should thus
in the end place a compulsory theoretical assent at the
centre of the religious act.[1] For the paradox in question,
though incomprehensible to reason, is none the less
theoretical ; and Kierkegaard drives it through with an
all but Roman intransigence.   But we must not so misuse

---

[1] " Few men have offered to God such a sacrifice as he did,
yet surely that he gave was that one sacrifice which God does
not ask of His children, for it was the quenching of the Inner
Light " (E. L. Allen, *Kierkegaard*, p. 22).

the method of antinomy that instead of religious sense it yields only logical nonsense.

We have seen cause to doubt whether the absolute and unrelieved dualism attaching to Kierkegaard's view of God and man is in harmony with the teaching of Scripture. His general argument is curiously out of touch, in particular, with the picture of Jesus Christ in Gospel and Epistle. " The presence and work of Jesus in the world," writes Denney, " even the work of bearing sin, does not prompt us to define human and Divine by contrast with each other : there is no suggestion of incongruity between them." When we ask how the disciples wakened, slowly or swiftly, to the personal presence of God in Jesus, plainly such things as His holiness, His love, His infinite forgiving patience, His power over men had a share in bringing them to faith. These human qualities or manifestations were not, as on Kierkegaard's terms they logically ought to be, a merely obscuring screen ; they became, as used by the Spirit of God, a transparent medium. Men saw the light of the glory of God in the face of Jesus Christ. Occasionally we can see that Kierkegaard himself felt he had gone too far. His violent and exclusive emphasis, in Christology, on the canon *finitum non est capax infiniti* —the finite cannot contain the Infinite—began to trouble him, and seemed to call for supplementation by the positive *finitum capax infiniti*. Uncompromising minds have too often read the latter formula as if it implied that the finite is capable, *of itself*, of grasping or holding an infinite Divine content, and in that sense have rightly rejected it. But the question may be raised whether what is impossible and unthinkable from below may not be possible from above. God may take the finite life and *make* it able to receive and exhibit His boundlessness. It is not for us so to assert the incapacity of man as to limit the power of God.

The element of unmitigated paradox also suffuses Kierkegaard's teaching on forgiveness and regeneration. On the amazing character of forgiveness—to which many Christian thinkers appear more than half blind—he writes with an imaginative and spiritual power which, once felt, can scarcely be forgotten. But his study of regeneration is marred by excesses which recall his Christology. Human nature as it stands, he believes, shows no point of contact for renewing grace; God's gracious action, accordingly, can take no form but that of infinite supernatural force. When He recreates a man in and by faith, the thing is done by breaking all ties with the past and calling into existence what, not only in figure but in fact, is a wholly new personality. Discontinuity is all, continuity has nothing to say. The question is not raised whether what the actual Christian life discloses may not be the paradoxical combination of both. Much of this, it need scarcely be said, is altogether out of line with Kierkegaard's initial principle of inwardness or subjectivity, which means nothing unless man is made for truth and, under God, sensitive to its appeal. It will not do, first to destroy the very conditions of a saving change by abstracting man utterly from God, in a sense which denotes that God has completely withdrawn Himself from all unregenerate lives, then, in the second place, to impose upon God a mode of saving action which is totally irrelevant to the nature of a created spirit made in the image of the Creator and not wholly bereft of its traces. Reasoning of this kind can be vindicated only on the ground of an absolute, intrinsic and impenetrable dualism as between God and man; and this, it has been argued above, we are bound to reject, less perhaps for its thought of man than for its restrictive and unworthy thought of God. It denies that God in boundless love has the power of keeping touch with man though man has lost touch with Him. Yet this is the real paradox of the sinner's life, which Kierkegaard should have been the last to overlook. Throughout the

initiative is with God—before regeneration, in it, after it.
It is by God's patient provision, not man's poor virtue,
that even in the fallen there remains that to which the
Holy Spirit can fasten the appeal of the Divine Word.
As it has been put concisely, " On the one hand, the
effect of sin on human nature, and especially on the human
will, must be such that man needs a Redeemer ; on the
other hand, it must only be such that he remains susceptible
of redemption ".   This second aspect of truth Kierkegaard
wipes out impatiently ; and from such petulance neither
religion nor theology is the gainer.

There are times, as we have seen, when a careful reader
is tempted to expostulate with Kierkegaard for not being
sufficiently paradoxical.   Thus, to recur for a moment
to Christology, he errs, as I should judge, in selecting the
two-nature doctrine of Christ's Person as the supreme
example of paradox.   If taken simply as asserting the
co-existence of deity and humanity in Christ, the two-
nature doctrine may be read as an immediate utterance
of faith, a conviction to be found in every genuinely
Christian mind.   But the doctrine takes on another and a
different aspect if we consider how it has actually func-
tioned in the history of theology.   There it is hardly a
paradox, but rather the rationalization of one.   The
mystery of Christ is explained or smoothed out, for
example, by the tenet that His human nature was impersonal ; or, to put it otherwise, the manhood thereby is as
it were curtailed in order that it may be adjusted to the
Godhead.   Similarly, the two-nature doctrine becomes
a rationalization of the mystery of which faith is conscious
when, as by Anselm, the experiences of our Lord are
distributed between the two aspects of His being in a
fashion that makes everything only too perfectly clear
and simple—the miracles being achieved by His Godhead, the sufferings undergone by His manhood.   But we
best keep the paradox or mystery by saying that in Jesus

Christ, the man, God is personally present; or, more briefly with Luther: "This Man is God."

§ 5. THE LAST PHASE

In order to survey the main body of Kierkegaard's teaching in a single view, I have so far made no allusion to the episode which led or misled him to interpret personal Christianity, in its moral aspect, as essentially a form of suffering.[1] By some fatality of temperament he had provoked a public dispute with a satirical weekly journal of Copenhagen. For many months the paper held him up to the city's scorn, poisoning his life with bitterness; all the more that, as he felt, his friends forsook him in his hour of need. Through this incident, he tells us, God by direct action opened his eyes to a deeper truth than he had yet perceived. He learned now that the authentic secret and token of being a Christian is to suffer.

Kierkegaard's intensified belief that to be in personal relation to God, to follow Christ, is equivalent to suffering owes its poignancy, we may surmise, in part to his conviction that all real religion is a lonely business. As he puts it, to seek for company in faith's pilgrimage is mortal sin. It is pure pain to stand alone before God, to feel our whole life exposed and sentenced as His eyes rest upon the infinite guilt of each least offence. Nor is this sense of guilty pain removed, or even mitigated, by forgiveness. On the contrary, a man's newly apprehended relationship to God, with its heightened responsibility, sharpens the inward anguish from one day to the next. Pascal was right when he declared that pain is the Christian's normal state. Suffering, as it is expressed in one of

[1] We must not confuse "suffering", as Kierkegaard uses the word, with pain or disaster simply. At bottom it is religious— the inward agony of finite man pressed down under his sense of the infinite God.

Kierkegaard's most imaginative passages, is the sea 70,000
fathoms deep, over which the believer hangs suspended.
Doubtless we may be reconciled with Christ, but only by
absorbing His agony and humiliation as our own. Inwardness is good ; but a Christian may keep his religion
to himself so completely, may so shut it all up within, as
to be indistinguishable from a worldling. Suffering
within, persecution without—these are the conditions of
warfare from which no believer may seek to be excused.
They spat upon Christ, they always do ; and we too must
go forth to Him without the camp, bearing His reproach.
Truth is known for truth in direct proportion to the pain
it costs. It follows that conventional Church life and the
following of Christ are as different as water and wine.
The true Christian is a martyr, not necessarily by violent
death or because he hunts for misery, but because in a
society like ours he is made the offscouring of the world.

It is from this point of view that he pours a fierce broad-
side upon the Church as he knew it. Its members may be
called to be saints, he protests, but they do not fulfil
their calling. The saints are the people of God, who
carry His colours and suffer shame for His name ; but it
is idle to speak of Church members as a *communio
sanctorum*. They are no such thing. Church life, rather,
represents a flight from passionate subjectivity to a cool
and as it were professional objectiveness, for which the
Gospel is something to be as calmly taken for granted
as the second law of thermo-dynamics. The assumption
underlying all is that you are a member of the Church
just as you are a citizen of the State, and you are both by
birth. There is no passion here, no sharp and tragic
decision ; there is nothing but a simulacrum of Christian
faith. Between the claims of the Eternal and the world's
affairs no tension now remains. Instead of the " comforted
despair " in which Luther found the essence of Christian
living, the Church as it is breeds a temper of naïve com-

placency, of compromise and hypocrisy. It encourages a
man to believe that Revelation from a transcendent source
can be dispensed with ; all we need is already within us,
latently, and we have only to bring it out.

This strain of unrelenting asceticism is absent, or only
faintly present, in Kierkegaard's earlier teaching. Then,
possession, not renunciation, had been his last word in
ethics. The ascetic note, no doubt, is never completely
silent ; how could it be, if the right Christian attitude
to the world, its culture and civilization, is one neither of
acceptance nor of hostility, but of criticism ? Finite things
must be held with a loose hand ; the Christian ought to
have the world as though he had it not. At that stage,
Kierkegaard could summarize his ethical doctrine in the
saying that at one and the same time we are called to
take an absolute attitude to the absolute *telos* or en , and a
relative to the relative. But with the lapse of years, and
a lengthening series of embittering disappointments, a
new tone crept into his language.

At last he began to preach openly the negation of life.
He felt a growing sympathy with Schopenhauer—a fact
surprising in one whose belief never wavered that the
world is the good creation of a loving God. His sense of
grievance against the Church was fed by the dark suspicious
mood in which he now rejected the thought that religion
is meant to hallow every aspect or incident in human life.
It had come for him to be an unpardonable sin in the
Church that it actually kept up some kind of positive
contact with the world. For the world is there simply
to be negated. Apparently he had by now thrown overboard the fundamental conviction of other days that
Christian thinking, practical no less than theoretical, is at
every point suffused by paradox. There is living paradox
in the contention that believers, men as they are, must
strive to be on God's side—that they are called to accept
the world, while none the less putting it in its place under

God. But paradox has vanished in a wholly unreal and evasive simplification once the position has been adopted that the world, the self included, is good for nothing except to be obliterated, as if all that is not identical with God were for that reason His enemy, or as if the relations of men to each other were irrelevant to faith. The problem of being a Christian, it is certain, can never be solved by any purely exclusive attitude to life, as though it were sin to be alive. Not to deny life, but in daily trustfulness to receive from God the opportunities of life and through them render thankful service to Him and our fellows— this is the appointed task. When the formula " either— or " is driven to the limit, as Kierkegaard drives it, the tension of experience is lost in stagnation.

Thus his interpretation of Christianity appears to terminate, so far as explicit argument is concerned, on a note of shrill defiance. And yet even this defiance becomes the vehicle of an austere and sombre message which does give us something to think about. The Gospel is never to be explained, much less defended ; far from being its judges, we ourselves are summoned to bow beneath its judgment, confessing that the sinful are without excuse. Let it be so thrust upon men categorically that they have no option but to take sides. God, the Eternal and Holy One, is too majestical to abide our questioning ; He will give no answer to our " Why ? " Nothing remains but to cast ourselves in the dust before Him, as the great challenge thunders in our ears.

As we look back, some features which make Kierke-gaard's mind and temper unusual rise into prominence. Thus he· was a man of striking self-confidence. It was more than the confidence of a strong, original thinker, and resembled rather the great prophet's sense of mission. He proposed to name his diary *The Book of the Judge*. And for *The Concluding Postscript* he foretells a great future ; it represents, as he is well aware, a novel and peculiar reading of Christianity, yet he feels no doubt whatever that in the long run his interpretation must prevail, even though he himself, the pioneer, should fall in his tracks and be forgotten. In this belief he was not wholly mistaken. After two generations of comparative neglect, his name once more is in the mouths of men, while his uncompromising rigour and vigour have been received eagerly, as it were with cries of relief, by many to whom a soft and idyllic version of the Gospel had become abhorrent.

It must not be overlooked that the arresting exaggerations in which Kierkegaard indulged so freely were put forward, often, with a quite clear and conscious intention. Newman was once asked why his attack upon Kingsley had been so violent. " Had I said these things in ordinary tones," he replied, " no one would have taken the least notice. I was obliged to speak at the top of my voice." If a boat is on the point of capsizing, it can only be trimmed by leaning far over to the other side ; and Kierkegaard looked upon his own theology, he expressly tells us, as " a corrective to things as they are ". An age of flat and craven rationalism must be stung into wakefulness ; in the circumstances of the hour no place was left for timid impartiality ; the crisis called for didactic hyperbole which by its sharp edge pierced to the vitals. Not for him, accordingly, to strike the balance nicely between God and man, transcendence and immanence, the Gospel and the culture of the age. Like a prophet he cried to his generation that God is absolute and the world is evil. The Church must cease to " count God a fool ". Yet he was less blind than we might suppose to the value of factors in the problem which, in the interest of his message, he ignores almost ruthlessly. If truth is stated unconditionally, we may trust the average man to supply all the conventional qualifications. Life for him was contra-

dictory throughout ; why then, in construing the majestic
Revelation of God, should we indulge a taste for smooth
and puny reconciliations ?   Logic, everywhere, is at odds
with experience, reflection with faith ; let us therefore
face with open eyes all the implications of this and confess
that to pass from the domain of reason to the last and
highest Reality we must dare a blind leap of the soul, a
secret passionate resolve, a mysterious inward fiat that
brooks no obstacle.   So desperate is the leap " through
the fires of an agonized conscience ", so vast and painful
are the renunciations by which alone citizenship in that
higher Kingdom can be won, that Kierkegaard holds no
one would fling himself across the gulf were he not driven
on by the insupportable tortures of a guilty mind.   In a
significant passage, he once made the admission that
his view of the Gospel had little to offer to the child.

The chief value of his work, it is permissible to think,
lies not so much in the detailed or systematized exposition
of Christian belief as in the clear, even if occasionally
strident and hysterical, note of warning which he sounded
for theologians as a class.   He is one of those thinkers
who indignantly resent all efforts to bring faith and speculative philosophy into agreement, urging with vehemence
that the apologetical vindication of Christianity betrays
the very genius of our faith, and that the only legitimate
form of defence is frontal attack.   And even if we feel
that it is something more and better than intellectual
ambition that compels us to do our utmost, in Christ's
service, to think things through and think them together,
still we cannot merely stop our ears when men of Kierkegaard's mould insist on that element in Christian faith
which is none the less certain that it defies satisfactory
explanation.   Above all, he put forth his powers unreservedly in teaching the world that God, the Eternal
and Unsearchable One, is not man.   Religion has too often
declined into a temper in which we inspect God, are

on easy terms with Him, or employ Him as a theoretical
hypothesis. On this sort of humanistic folly, we may
affirm with confidence, Kierkegaard has said the last word.
He tears in rags all religion which is utilitarian and
anthropocentric. He gives voice to that sense of creatureliness which overwhelms us as we worship, and stops every
mouth before God. He brings home to the awakened soul
those factors in life which express the Divine sovereignty
in its sublimest form. Across the page he writes, in letters
of smoke and fire, the critical truth that God is holy
and we are sinners—sinners, not because as creatures we
have been made finite, but because we have thrust the
will of God aside and rejected Him to His face. There
is no need to consider this the whole of Christianity. None
the less, the man who fails to discover in prophets and
apostles something of which Kierkegaard's strong words
are an index—something real and august at which he
is pointing, though with one-sided emphasis—appears to
me to read with a veil upon his eyes.

Yet his effects have been purchased at a price too
great for the faith engendered by Jesus Christ. The conclusion is unavoidable that, in his efforts to alter the
balance of contemporary religious thought, Kierkegaard
induces new distortions of belief so violent and perverse
as gravely to imperil our hold on the New Testament
conception of God and of the life His children are called
to lead. Thus, to recur to one salient example, his individualism is of so extreme a type as largely to disqualify him from understanding actual religion. There
is no sense of any kind, he asserts roundly, in which
faith can pass from one life to another. Here fellowship
counts for nothing; the Church, even the family, except
in a purely external fashion, has no relation to the interior fact of piety. The knight of Christ rides out on a
lonely quest. Whatever its momentary impressiveness,
this, if taken seriously, is a caricature of Christian disciple-

ship as the New Testament pictures it. Also it is a direct contradiction of his own earlier and sounder views. Formerly he had perceived clearly that the religious life of the individual is threatened by society only so far as society is tainted, not by society as the family or community of God, i.e. the Church. There is a form of social influence—that of the public, the majority, the crowd—which robs a man of free responsibility before God ; there is none the less a form which nourishes and brings to maturity the sense of higher obligation, and is constituted by God a living instrument whereby men learn to know sin and grace. The contagion of living faith is a reality ; and the persistent imperfection of human faith is no ground for doubting that it can be used by the Holy Spirit for the great purposes of grace. It must be confessed that we are all tempted, in our exasperated moments, to think with indignant scorn of the company God has given us within His Church ; and the temptation to this sin is one which Kierkegaard has not wholly escaped.

The same utter dualism between God and man, eternity and time, which led him, especially in his later years, to disparage the social or corporate aspects of discipleship,[1] rendered him also more than half blind to the movements of God in history. Kierkegaard's language on this point is a good deal more sweeping than is necessitated by the wholly sound position that faith cannot be based upon historical research, that such an " event " as Jesus Christ breaks the limits of what we usually call " history ", or that it is only from the standpoint of faith itself that a genuinely historical interpretation of human life becomes possible. In his later and most characteristic moods, he holds with Emerson that from history faith has nothing

---

[1] He raises the question whether the apostles may not have gone wrong at the very outset, by administering baptism after Pentecost to thousands, and so giving their imprimatur to mass-conversion.

to learn, and that to gain anything worth the having
the single soul must sink more deeply into its own inward
experience, the only fruitful source.   God is the Eternal,
history the field of limitation and temporal sequence ;
in very nature they are sundered by incomprehensible
distances.   Kierkegaard indeed felt obliged to exempt one
event in the past from this summary judgment—that
infinite and creative moment when " the Word took flesh
and dwelt among us ".   But he derived no wider principle from this special interposition.   Brave champion of
faith though he was, for the most part and most of all
in later years, he persisted in regarding the world of time
as a sphere of chaotic darkness ;   he read its meaning
otherwise than by positive faith and, because man cannot
rise to God, forgot the greater truth that God can reach
and redeem man.   He knew that God was in Christ,
he traced providential guidance throughout his own career ;
but he failed to discover any vast movement of the Divine
purpose traversing the generations.   To his lonely thought
the prophetic reading of history brought no conviction.
History gives no revelation of God ;   even from believing
eyes its meaning is completely hidden ;   if meaning there
be, only God can know it.   Kierkegaard will not see the
promised Kingdom of God looming through the past,
beckoning into the future, finally triumphant over human
failure.   For him only two realities are luminously visible
—the God-man and his own soul.

On a review of all the data we are justified, I think,
in concluding that two conceptions of God (as of the
Christian's relation to God) were at war within his divided
mind—conceptions which it is impossible to reconcile, not
simply because the problem of combining them defeats
us for the moment, but because we see clearly that
they cannot be combined.   On the one hand is the thought
of God as Holy Love—a conception evoked by the whole
redeeming fact of Christ, and made good to faith in every

age. This personal revelation, it need hardly be said, Kierkegaard acknowledges and utilizes to the full for much of his theological construction. "Before Christ," he writes, "God has indeed been communicated to creation, but as an invisible sign, like the watermark in paper. But in the Incarnation, creation is completed by the fact that, over and above, God has now come to be present Himself." Alongside of this, however, stands a thought of God totally different from it in character, which no synthesis, however dialectically comprehensive, can unite with the other. Here what is still called the "love" of God appears as a purely formal attribute, involving pain and even torture for its objects. It is well to affirm an infinite qualitative difference between God and man if what we are thinking of is the absolute distinction that separates majestic grace from guilty sin; but in the later phases of Kierkegaard's reflection we encounter a sheerly metaphysical contrast between Eternity and time, between a featureless Absolute Substance and the nothing-ness of man. Obviously for God and man, as thus defined, there can exist no possibility of union or communion of the kind known as personal fellowship, and this not merely in virtue of what man is but definitely in virtue of what God is. Hence, in his attempts to force a union, Kierkegaard is often led to depict man's approach or assimilation to the Godhead as tantamount to the dis-solution of finite personality in the boundless Whole.

The harshest figures, at this stage, are deliberately used to indicate the destructive impact of Christianity on human life. It is asserted that the influence of God, revealed in Scripture as a purely transcendent Being, must act upon us like the all-devouring heat of the tropical sun as it scorches and kills vegetation. Again, the Christian message has the effect of embittering our lot to the uttermost, for the relation even of a believing man to God implies, or consists in, a slow torment that extinguishes joy and corrodes his very nature. The design of such extravagances, one need not doubt, was to rid the Christian life of all comfortable security and put in its place the humble and thankful assurance of faith. His final position in all likelihood would have been that faith is both things—uncertainty about ourselves but a deep and strong certainty about God. Yet it is possible to become so absorbed in exposing the weakness of man as to have no time to bring out the glory of God's redemptive power. Denunciation may overleap itself and fall on the other side. In darker moods, Kierkegaard can represent even forgiven sonship as only a vestibule leading into the Christian life, but nothing specifically Christian in itself. He can protest, unintelligibly, that the Gospel is not invitation but pure demand. He can depict the Christian's moral task not as the conquest of sin through the hallowing of all life in fellowship with God, but solely as the mortification of our nature.[1] He can argue that man possesses God only in isolated moments, so that, to escape annihilation within the Infinite, he has no option but ever anew to seek relief in the finite. If this be so, and if the underlying reason for it is the sheer antagonism of God and man, it is difficult to understand why this indescribably painful tension should not last on, beyond death and for ever.

There is no way of bringing these two conceptions of God together in a mind which has submitted trustfully to the Christian revelation. In a sense, the conflict between them in Kierkegaard's theology represents one phase in an internecine struggle which has persisted in the Church's thought from the second century onwards.

---

[1] Von Hügel quotes the following from the *Concluding Unscientific Postscript* : " What the conception of God, or of man's eternal beatitude, is to effect in man, is that he shall remodel his entire existence according to it ; but by this remodelling *man dies to his entire immediacy.*"

It is needless to labour the point that by choosing the latter way of interpretation, which not seldom Kierkegaard was tempted to regard as the nobler of the two, we make Christ's revelation of the Father of none effect, and lapse once more into pagan uncertainties concerning the "unknown God". By what the New Testament calls a "wilful humility" we refuse to consent that the disclosure given in Him who was both Son of God and Son of man should rule and direct all our thoughts of the Eternal, and perversely insist on viewing His relation to His children in a light which differs *toto caelo* from that of New Testament faith. But this, in the ancient phrase, is to make sad those whom the Lord has not made sad. It is an effort to teach God how large is the proper scope of His own severity and to improve on His ineffably gracious ways with men. The ground of such error lies, after all, not in the fact that the conception of God is inevitably paradoxical, but in the abnormal psychology of Kierkegaard—the man, as he has been called, of "extraordinary intelligence with a sick imagination". In that brave, tragic life of faith and genius, impulses were moving for all of which we must not claim Biblical sanction. We repudiate his error, while yet we find no cause to doubt the truth of his impassioned affirmation that for him also the certainty of God's fatherly love in Christ was "the Archimedean point". Under his theology, so piercing in insight, so mixed in quality, we may fitly inscribe the words of Pascal: "In great men everything is great—their faults as well as their merits."

VIII

THE THEOLOGY OF THE WORD OF GOD

KARL BARTH

THE LATEST important phase of Protestant theology is to be found in the teaching of Dr. Karl Barth, which, if we consider the grave needs of to-day, is vastly more modern than Modernism itself. In him we have incontestably the greatest figure in Christian theology that has appeared for decades.[1] Wordsworth has observed that " every great or original writer, in proportion as he is great or original, must himself create the taste by which he is to be relished ; he must teach the art by which he is to be seen ". This is particularly true of Barth. In a large degree he felt it incumbent on him at first to choose a new language in which to set forth doctrines which in his judgment were as old as Scripture and the Reformers. Without this, it seemed, people could not understand his positions, let alone make up their minds about them. His language has become considerably simplified with time. There was a stage when an admirer could own that " Barth strides along clad in a scientific terminology which is hard, intricate, and every way exacting—one which at the start (and even in many points for long) makes the impression of oracles and speaking with tongues ". Simplification has come, in part, as the result of his discarding, amongst other things, the " existentialism " which perplexed his earlier readers.

---

[1] Creevey's words about Lord Grey come into mind : " Take him all in all, I never saw his fellow ; nor can I see any indication of him on the stocks."

Recalling the first edition of his *Dogmatic* he now writes :
": To the best of my ability I have cut out in this second
issue of the book everything that in the first issue might
give the slightest appearance of giving to theology a
basis, support, or even a mere justification in the way
of existential philosophy." [1]

In spite of ever-recurring rumours that his influence
is waning, there is every likelihood that it will increase,
and that the problems he has compelled the Church to
face will more and more engage attention. Not many
years since it might have been said of the Barthian group :
" Concerning this sect, we know that everywhere it is
spoken against." But at all events it has forced men
to take Revelation seriously, with revival of faith as a
consequence. Thus the feeling of grateful recognition has
spread ever more widely. Barth always confronts Revelation with a sense of wonder, awe, and solemn responsibility ; and here the Church has been willing to learn
of him.

Impressive as Barth's work has been, it is far from
being beyond the reach of criticism. Some camp-followers
of the movement have inclined to forget this, but the
master himself leaves us in no doubt. He criticizes his
own statements, often, by modifying them. " To live
is to change, and to be perfect is to have changed often,"
it has been said ; and one fact which makes comprehension of his thought so difficult is that in detail it
changes constantly. He warns us vehemently against
canonizing his results up to date. He offers clear principles, definite assumptions, but never a closed system.
Theology on the wing, it has been called. His thought
moves ; it does not crystallize. Of him as of Dostoievsky
we may say that he is not interested in tepid notions ;
there is a dash of the spirit of Heraclitus in him, every-

[1] *Church Dogmatic*, I. (English Translation by Professor G. T.
Thomson), p. ix.

thing is heat and motion, opposition and struggle. Fitly, therefore, he exhibits a most rare and excellent combination of humility and humour. " It is a real question," he has suggested, " whether there is as much joy in heaven as there is on earth over the growth of the Barthian school." Far from being an oracle, he is simply a servant of the Church, with no thought of forming a party. He would perhaps not object to my saying that if I succeed in giving a clear account of his thinking, that will prove that I have not been successful after all. Life is not simple, hence theology cannot be simple either ; and Barth's thought is not, in any ordinary sense of the words, easy or transparent.

The group around him has received various names. It has been called " the Swiss school ". Geographical titles give little help, and this one need not delay us ; though it is perhaps not wholly fanciful to note how frequently mountains and abysses figure in his language. He can speak of " the impassable frontier of death, the unbridgeable chasm before which we are called to halt ", or of man as " standing on the edge of a precipice daring the swing into the uncertain, the bottomless, and there, suspended over the gulf, taken hold of by God's hand ".

It has been called " the Theology of Crisis ". Crisis, as is frequently pointed out, means both things—the climax or turning-point of an illness, and a change of direction in a movement of thought. Both significations must here be kept in mind. And crisis, at its profoundest, means judgment. Man, the world, religion, the Church— all for this theology are under the judgment and demand of the Word of God, which the New Testament describes as " piercing even to the dividing asunder of soul and spirit ", as " scrutinizing the very thoughts and conceptions of the heart ". To understand Revelation man must listen with the consciousness of standing at the bar of God.

Again, it has been called "the Dialectical Theology ". And for this title there is still more to be said. Barth contends that so long as we are here on earth, we can do no otherwise in theology than proceed by using the method of statement and counter-statement ; we dare not pronounce absolutely " the last word ", at least if we are not to incur the guilt of presuming to identify what as sinners we say of God with " the dogmatic of the saints in heaven ". The Word of God itself cannot be broken or refracted. But our human word about God *is* broken, and only in this " brokenness "—this absence of limpidly clear self-evidencing terms—can it bear witness to the truth of God. " We know that we are unable to comprehend except by means of dialectical dualism, in which one must become two in order that it may be veritably one." This is the inevitable consequence of our bringing Infinity within the range of concepts fitted only for the apprehension of the finite. In the light of God every assertion of what we are must and does contain as a constituent opposite the thought of what we are not. In an early passage this is exemplified vividly. " Men can grasp their unredeemed condition only because already they stand within the redemption ; they know themselves to be sinners only because they are already righteous." Or, to take a wider range :

We can only speak of the glory of God in creation as we bring out the complete hiddenness of God for our eyes in Nature ; of the image of God in man only as we give warning once for all that the man we know is fallen ; of sin, only with the reminder that we should not know sin, were it not forgiven us ; of the justification of the ungodly, only as we recall that it is the ungodly who is declared just.[1]

Paradox is no accident in Christian theology ; it belongs in some sort to the staple of doctrinal thinking. As Luther says, God in His revelation is hidden *sub contraria*

[1] *Das Wort Gottes und die Theologie* (1925), p. 172.

specie; we have to utter such internally contradictory propositions as that the timeless God enters time, the sinner is pronounced just, eternal life is a present possession, it is the revealed God that is known to be hidden and unfathomable. Even the name " Jesus Christ " has its dialectic; the two words composing it belong each to a sphere alien to the other, the first to history, the second to the Divine realm. " If you ask me about God," Barth once wrote, " If you ask about *God*, and if I am really to tell about Him, dialectic is all that can be expected of *me*. Neither my affirmation nor my denial lays claim to being God's truth. Neither is more than a *witness* to that Truth which stands in the centre between every Yes and No." The task of theology is to interpret the Yes and the No, and the No by the Yes.[1]

To many this manner of speaking has seemed no better than a jumble of organized nonsense; but one or two suggestions for a stay of judgment may be offered. To begin with, it is the dialectic of Kierkegaard, not of Hegel. Barth has never meant that we can elicit the Yes merely by logical manipulation of the No, as if, for example, the need of man made God's self-revelation inevitable. The positive, countering and abrogating the negative, is given not by reason but by Christ. Only faith can see the opposites, or see them as belonging together. Again, the Yes is not in turn displaced by a deeper No; for the Yes of God in Christ—the " Yea and Amen "—is final truth. Once more, when the opposites appear contradictory, this is for us, not for God. In Him the No is dissolved in the Yes, for the synthesis we seek is in God alone, and in Him alone can we find it. Such dialectical language plainly tends to bring men sharply to their bearings and compel them to ponder what is said. Truth taught in paradox cannot be committed to memory.

Dialectical thought follows from Barth's fundamental

[1] This use of " No and Yes " goes back to Luther.

view that God is always Subject, never object.   By this he means that God is not one unit in the world of objects ; He is the Infinite and Sovereign One who is known only as addressing us.   He cannot be explained, as an object can ;   He can only be addressed, and that because He first is addressing us.   Just for this reason, theology, forbidden to measure Him in direct or unilinear thinking, and seeking to speak of Him, not to Him, necessarily falls asunder into dialectical aspects, or statements that wear the guise of contradiction.   We cannot call Him near except as we call Him far ;   we cannot describe His mind towards man except as one of judgment and mercy.

When Barth discarded " existentialism ", it was evidently with the sense that even as a temporary intellectual apparatus it had been dangerous and wholly inadequate. We cannot say that similarly he has got beyond dialectical or paradoxical thinking.   True, the word " dialectic " has no place in the Index of his last great work, the first volume of his revised *Dogmatic*.   But this appears to be less because its usefulness had wholly vanished than because it bade fair to become a new fashion, practised indiscriminately.

The Word of God alone [he there writes] fulfils the conception of paradox with complete strictness, whereas in all other thinkable " paradoxes " the opposition between communication and form is such that it can be dissolved from some superior point of vantage.   Therefore it is to be recommended that in theology more sparing use should henceforth be made of this concept now that it has done its part, not without causing all manner of confusions.[1]

Accordingly, the name Barth's thought is now acquiring, and much the best, is " The Theology of the Word of God ".   The content of prolegomena to theology, indeed the chief content of theology as such, is that Word.

[1] *Church Dogmatic*, I, p. 189.

Theology springs out of preaching and tests preaching; but, as he puts it, " the presupposition which makes proclamation to be proclamation, and the Church therewith to be Church, is the Word of God ". His Word attests itself in Scripture in the word of the prophets and apostles, to whom it was originally and once for all uttered through God's revelation. Believer and theologian equally are concerned above all to know whether God has spoken, and *what* He has spoken. *Deus dixit*, answers Barth, with all the fathers of the Protestant Church ; then let us listen on our knees to what He has said and is still ever saying. God is God, and must be given His right name, and known as He wills to be known. " We do not seek God elsewhere than in His Word, we do not think of Him save with His Word, we speak nothing of Him save through His Word." The understanding of that Word, accordingly, is the chosen task of this theology and fixes its proper title. All other titles or descriptions are secondary in character. We have the less need now to dwell on this that it will be our central interest throughout this brief study.

It is because a widely influential Modernist theology had become indifferent to the Word of God, replacing it by the word of man, that Barth resolved to speak out, to utter his " warning cry ", to suggest his " corrective ", to make his " marginal observation ". Typical of the temper and presuppositions to which he found himself in unqualified antagonism is the view that the Reformation proper arrived only in the days of eighteenth-century Enlightenment, when the doctrine of the sinful nature of man fell away, and man was declared capable of finding his own way to the God Who had made him. It is a mood which unconsciously has affected many who in set terms would disown it. Barth holds, not unjustly as I think, that the all but openly professed purpose of much contemporary theology has been to satisfy the human intelligence—its religious, moral, and even æsthetic assumptions—rather than to understand, obey, and set forth the Word of God. Roman and Protestant alike have found the supreme criterion of preaching, not in Scripture, but in the mind of the living Church. The Romanist can speak of the " dead word " of the Bible in contrast to the " vitality " of Church tradition. The liberal Protestant, bent on expressing man's thoughts of God, not God's thoughts of man, can become wholly oblivious of the truth that the Church and its mind stand perpetually under the authority and judgment of God's Word. In the name of Christian liberty it is contended that the Church possesses the inherent capacity of determining how far she will let herself be judged by the Bible. She is the autonomous judge in her own cause. So Modernist Protestantism lost the proper criterion for Church teaching, the standard set over against it. The conscience of the preaching Church was gone, and other criteria derived from immanentist philosophy, science, or the conception of sound civilization, put in its place. Now Barth's only purpose is to let it be seen that no other criterion can be a substitute for the Word of God. All Churches profess to accept the Word of God as the supreme rule of faith and life. Shall we not, he asks, make an effort to take this profession seriously ?

Here lies the reason why Barth renounces all sympathy with the thought of Schleiermacher. His own line of ancestry goes back through Kierkegaard, Luther and Calvin to St. Paul and Jeremiah—all of whom taught that man is made to serve God, not God to serve man.

With all due respect to the genius shown in his work [he writes] I can *not* consider Schleiermacher a good teacher in the realm of theology because, so far as I can see, he is disastrously dim-sighted in regard to the fact that man as man is not only in *need* but beyond all hope of saving himself ; that the whole of so-called religion, and not least the Christian religion, *shares* in this need ; and that one can *not* speak of God simply by speaking of man in a loud voice.[1]

Just because to Schleiermacher human culture as such was holy, not sin-pervaded, he was blind in principle to the positive truth that, under God, culture is a parable full of promise. In short—and in theology this is the unpardonable sin—he makes only what may be called a quantitative difference between man and God, thereby suggesting that the revelation of God in Christ is merely a more excellent way than others, instead of proclaiming that it is the true and only way, all other ways being dross and illusion. Nothing, Barth finds, is more characteristic of Schleiermacher's ultimate attitude than his tendency to make a fetish of " continuity ", and therefore to gloss over man's worst troubles with a veneer of immanentism. The dogma of continuity might be called the real foundation of the more recent European pantheism, consisting as it does in the assertion of the homogeneity and the continuous connexion between all parts of the universe. In the last resort, there is an unbroken line of development from matter to life, from life to mind, from man to God. Thus in religion the measure of all things is man, not the sovereign God who has spoken in His Word.

The main facts of Barth's career are now well known. He was born at Basel in 1886 as the son of Professor Fritz Barth, author of a familiar and useful book on the chief problems of Jesus' life. He studied at the universities of Berne, Berlin, Tübingen and Marburg (he later speaks of Herrmann as " my unforgettable teacher "). For twelve years he held a pastorate in Switzerland. It is no accident that his theology has the closest ties with preaching ; like that of others in association with whom his systematic work began, it sprang out of the felt mys-

[1] *The Word of God and the Word of Man*, pp. 195 f.

teries and perplexities of the preacher's task. In 1921 he was called to fill the chair of Reformed Theology at Göttingen ; four years later he moved on to Münster in Westphalia ; thereafter for a few years he held a chair in Bonn, and not long ago was dismissed from his post for political reasons. Now he teaches theology in Basel, his birthplace. Amongst his early allies were Thurneysen, with whom his theological comradeship has always been most intimate, Brunner, Gogarten and in some degree Bultmann, the well-known New Testament scholar of Marburg. Here, however, we shall study Barth on his own account. In the preface to his *Dogmatic* of 1932 he requests that his work shall be read just as it stands, not as the exposition of any particular movement, tendency, or school. " The communion in and for which I have written this book is the communion of the Church." He serves a cause and not a party. There have been differences of such moment between Barth and Brunner on the one side, between Barth and Gogarten on the other, largely in both cases respecting the doctrine of man, as would make a synoptic view of the three virtually impossible. It ought to be noted further, that he no longer wishes his " Epistle to the Romans " to be taken as an authoritative source of his theology.

§ 1.   WHAT IS THEOLOGY ?

Theology is *ministerium verbi divini*—service of the Word of God. It is the attempt, by means of human thought and human speech, scientifically to clarify the question that must arise as to the basis and norm that govern the Church and its preached message. Its task is to scrutinize the proclamation of the Church relatively to its agreement with the Revelation witnessed to in Holy Scripture, and to correct it where it has gone astray. As Calvin puts it, all right knowledge of God is born of obedience, and Dogmatic (the theological discipline with which we here are most concerned) is an act of obedient faith, done in the sight of God. No technique can make a teacher of it sound or effective. We know divine things only when and where it pleases God to make us know them. Only in the attitude of prayer can dogmatic work be done. In theology, then, the Church tests itself, bringing its own teaching to the tribunal of God's Word.

Dogmatic, as much as the confession or creed itself, is human acknowledgment of the reality of God in His revelation. It lives solely by the truth God has given, and is obedient to God's sovereign decision to reveal Himself, a decision over which man has no power. The special feature of Dogmatic is that it is the act of faith striving to understand and explain itself, seeking to think and say after God what antecedently He has said in revelation. While not itself confession, it is explication of the confession of faith already present, as well as preparation for a new one. It can be taught only by a teacher commissioned by the Church. His function is a public and responsible one ; he teaches within the Church community and for it. Dogmatic is not research for research's sake, but rather discharges the task of the faithful watchman, facing errors of his own time, and displaying a flexible adaptation to present needs which the older confession might seem to lack. Like Church preaching, it may err and make others err ; but also it may call the preacher to order and recapture touch with Scripture. By the very existence of Dogmatic the Church acknowledges that in her service she has good cause to show humility and vigilance.

Exegesis comes before Dogmatic in order of birth ; Scripture must first be interpreted before its teaching can be organized. In other words, Dogmatic does not create or embody its own standard of reference. The theologian is not there in his own right to judge the message preached by the Church, as though in his private philosophy he possessed the supreme norm of truth. The proper and only judge here is the prophetic and apostolic witness to Revelation, as through the Holy Spirit that witness speaks to our spirit. Only faith can appeal for faith, and in her confession the Church placards her faith before the world ; but in Dogmatic she undertakes to explain this confession for which she stands. Theology might be described as the confession itself speaking more exactly, now and here, to meet the needs of the actual present. It strives to exhibit the confession as deriving from Scripture an inner connexion and intelligibility of its own. Briefly, it is an elucidating expansion of the confession in the sense of Holy Scripture.

Dogmatic, therefore, starts from the message preached and taught by the Church, and finds the materials of its discussion there. When the Church speaks of God, it claims to be declaring His Word. And for Dogmatic the central question is this : how far is the Church's language about God, in its intention and content, fit to serve and express the Word of God ?

But for all its high function and responsibility Dogmatic is still no more than a human enterprise, with limitations only too easily ignored. It cannot guarantee the right proclamation, but only try to secure it. The sacraments are there to remind the Church that all her words, even her correctest, can do no more than *point to* the event,[1] the event of revelation, in which God in His reality addresses man. They mark the boundary between what man can say concerning God and God's own unfathomable reality. Not only so ; Dogmatic is limited by the nature of human life—its weakness and strength, its confusion and clarity, its sin and its hope. The Church is

[1] An event may be loosely defined as " a happening at a specific time ".

obliged to speak of, and take aim, at human life, while conscious all the while that her words fail to hit the central white of the target. Her language has the task of placing men under God's judgment and God's grace, yet is inadequate for its purpose. And finally, Dogmatic is a thing of time, not of eternity. We know in part, we speak as children, we see darkly in a mirror, not yet face to face. When God is all in all, its function will have ceased.

The only volume of his large doctrinal work so far published Barth devotes to Prolegomena. Prolegomena, he explains, is that introductory part of Dogmatic in which it is our business to explain its particular path to knowledge. What assures us that we are on the way to truth ? Where is the measure by which we are to test that Church proclamation which, despite the Divine commission behind it, is none the less a word spoken by man ? The test can only be the Word of God. " Prolegomena to Dogmatics," writes Barth, " in the sense of coming to an understanding about its path to knowledge, must therefore consist in expounding the doctrine of the three forms of the Word of God, as revealed, as written, and as proclaimed." [1] God's Word is first revealed ; it is then witnessed to in Scripture by prophets and apostles ; it is proclaimed in the uttered message of the Church.

§ 2. THE CHRISTIAN VIEW OF REVELATION

To the revelation of God, the coming of His Word, we must listen in the attitude of awe, trust, and obedience. Not for us to subject it to man-made presuppositions about God, or man, or their relations to each other. To accept it is to accept " what man is to believe concerning God, and what duty God requires of man ".

[1] *Church Dogmatic*, I., p. 284.

Revelation, in essence, is an event which has taken place in Jesus Christ and still takes place in Him; our thought of it is subservient to Him, gaining from Him its freedom from every other authority. In Him alone, the Word of God made flesh, does the really new enter human life—not a mere best, emerging in an otherwise familiar-sequence of development, and not the supreme realization of a general potentiality, but what is new in the strict sense, something hitherto unknown because wholly concealed. Jesus Christ, in whom revelation is present and operative, is a concrete reality, to which there are no analogies. Revelation is simply once for all.

Just as a man can have only one father, is born once and dies once, so he can only believe and know one revelation. It is possible to collate and compare a number of religions, not a number of revelations. He who says revelation says— a revelation which is unique, taking place once for all, irrevocable and unrepeatable.[1]

Jesus Christ is indeed the manifestation of the eternal wisdom of God; He is not the vindication of the *a priori* insight of man. One who dreams that he possesses a standard by which to measure Him, or some principle by which to determine beforehand what He ought to be, simply betrays thereby the fact that he knows nothing of Jesus Christ, and therefore nothing of revelation.

We become aware of His utter newness because we recognize in His person the Eternal Word of God made flesh. It is not that here we are guided by general considerations and reflections; we cannot recognize Him in that character at all except as we perceive that Revelation means *grace for sinners*. Had it not been for God's free compassion and condescension to man, the Eternal Word would have been eternally hidden from us. Once we have apprehended the revelation of God in Jesus Christ,

[1] *Offenbarung, Kirche, Theologie,* p. 18.

as pure grace, it is impossible to imagine ourselves receiving a disclosure of God elsewhere which was direct and unmediated, or indeed any indirect revelation other than that contained in Him.[1]

Barth gives no place to Natural Revelation; but precisely what he means by this must be carefully observed, for in some degree the question is one of terminology. He is speaking of the Christian believer—not of the detached spectator, not even of the anxious inquirer—and elucidating that which, through the persuasion of the Holy Spirit, has become for *him* an irrefragable conviction. If I receive grace, and thus perceive that I need grace and that I am the object of God's pure compassion, for me the question is closed.

Such a man [Barth declares] will acknowledge to himself that the same Eternal Word that became flesh is audible also in creation as God's primary work, audible therefore in Nature, in History, in his own heart, conscience and understanding. But he will go on and to his own shame acknowledge that as a matter of fact he has never heard the Word there, and neither can or will hear it.   Not on the ground of some theory of cognition will he make this acknowledgment to himself, but because he knows that Jesus Christ is the Word made flesh, that it has pleased God for the revelation of His Word to adopt this wholly other way, and that he personally has received grace, and therefore needs it.   In the light of this knowledge he certainly will not claim for himself the ability to apprehend God's Word in creation.   As one whom grace has brought into judgment, he will rather confess that always what he has heard there, what he will hear in the future, is only the voice of the gods, i.e., the created elements of this world—the voice of the earth and animal life, the voice of the seemingly infinite heavens and, embraced therein, the voice of his own seemingly inescapable destiny, the voice of the blood in his own veins derived from parents and ancestry, the voice of the genius and hero in his own breast—all these invested

---

[1] Which is witnessed to also in the Old Testament, for there too the Word of God is uttered.

with a false divine value and authority, all these, but just *not* the eternal Word of God. Knowledge of grace in point of fact destroys the idea of an indirect revelation in Nature, in History, or in the consciousness of our own existence.

Barth thus urges—and surely his argument has weight— —that revelation is far too great a name for the faint and ambiguous suggestions of God which are all the sinner can detect in creation. Objectively, no doubt, they are present ; the heavens declare the glory of God. But, for one thing, they are audible solely to faith, which is evoked only by true revelation in Christ ; and secondly, they are definitely not such as lead man into reconciliation with the true God. It is by no means a novel doctrine. " Apart from Christ," said Chalmers, " I find that I have no hold of God at all." And although it may be objected that on such terms atheism becomes the only right creed for those who have never apprehended Christ, is the doctrine more than a believing echo of the words : " No man cometh unto the Father but by Me " ? There is no real revelation which is not a Divine unveiling of *grace to us*, to me, the sinful. This, once we recognize it, strips us bare of that pride which would lightheartedly and self-confidently cast round for revelations in other quarters.

Revelation in the true sense is just the Incarnation. For God to reveal Himself is to descend into our depths, to meet us as a man amongst men, in all the distance and the nearness of a human form. The true manhood of Jesus Christ is one aspect of revelation ; the other is (for Christ is the grace *of God*) the fulness of His deity. We are not here dealing with vague and shapeless thoughts of " the Divine ", but with God as the Unchangeable and Almighty Maker of heaven and earth. Jesus Christ is Lord of all ; He who encounters us is the Creator, for except as we are brought face to face with God in the fulness of His glory man would be left to himself ; revelation there would be none.

Above all, Jesus Christ is the revelation of God because in His existence He is the Reconciliation. Only as we know God to have reconciled us to Himself by His Son do we know Him at all. Anything that man may imagine he knows about God otherwise, i.e., in his natural position as a rebel against God and consequently under His wrath, is only the idol of his own heart. The gulf yawning between is bridged by God stepping into the place of sinful man and, conversely, sinful man is set in the place of God.

It is in this context that we gain our clearest look at Barth's interpretation of Atonement. Reconciliation must not be thought of as something supplementary to, or following upon, the revelation of God in Christ; His reconciliation is itself revelation. There is an utter interchange of parts between God and man. God steps into the place of man. But as man like ourselves Jesus Christ acts quite otherwise than we do.

In His humiliation, His suffering, His death He espouses the lostness of humanity, He acknowledges the righteousness of the Divine wrath and judgment, He submits Himself to the baptism of repentance, He confesses God to be right as against Himself, He calls upon God out of the depths in praise. Nowhere is His sinlessness so manifest as in His bowing, as we do not, under the judgment of God. Thus innocently He bears our impurity with the punishment that ensues, making it His own. And because it is He, the eternal Word of God, who does this, it is no more ours; rather it is His impurity and punishment, and there has happened once for all what had to happen for the expiation, covering, expunging and forgiveness of our sin. Once for all He has borne it to the Cross and to the grave.

But the counter-position also holds good—sinful man is set in the place of God.

Jesus Christ is true God. But just as true God He does not keep the majesty of His Godhead to Himself. In that

majesty He espouses man in His lowliness, in His suffering
and death, in His standing under judgment, in His subjection
to death, in His sheer need of grace. This man, this " flesh ",
it is that the eternal Word of God in the person of Jesus Christ
has accepted and raised to unity with Himself. But this very
unity means, also, the exaltation of this man, once for all
accomplished in Jesus Christ's resurrection and ascension. In
Jesus Christ, Who is true God, man is snatched away from
the ordinances and necessities of his mere humanity, made
partaker of the free, transcendent, eternal life of God Himself.
In Jesus Christ the glory of God, without ceasing to be His,
has become ours.

This change of parts between God and man is the
reconciliation ; it is at once our justification and our
sanctification, the forgiveness of our sins and our regeneration to a new life. It is triumph over the gulf between
God and man, abolition of the darkness which keeps us
from knowing God ; it is the Truth and thus the revelation.
And because in Jesus Christ this exchange is accomplished,
He truly and solely reveals God.

These are wonderful things to be found in Jesus Christ,
but it is by no means obvious that we recognize them.
We have no power of our own to do that. To have faith
is to have a living interest in the existence of Jesus Christ,
to refer all to Him, as the one ground on which we stand.
Such faith is our own free choice, and yet we know that
before we choose, we are chosen. The reconciliation, in
other words, has come to us from elsewhere, from the
grace of the Holy Spirit. Thus the Christian apprehension
of God self-revealed inevitably reaches its climax in the
perception that such apprehension, when it takes place,
comes to be through revelation. Or, to put it more
precisely still, the apprehension is itself revelation ; for
as such it is the outpouring of the Holy Spirit.

Two points here are noteworthy. In the first place, for
God to reveal Himself is *eo ipso* to reveal Himself as Triune.
He makes Himself known, when He does so, as Creator,

Reconciler, Redeemer.   Always in revelation He is Father, Son, and Holy Spirit.

Secondly, revelation explicitly includes the bestowing on man of the gift to recognize and believe it.   The imparting of the Spirit, creating faith within, is an essential element in revelation itself.   The event called revelation in the New Testament is both things—a happening *to us* and *in us*.   " The Spirit guarantees to man, what man cannot guarantee to himself, his personal participation in revelation.   The act of the Holy Spirit in revelation is the Yea to God's Word, spoken through God Himself on our behalf, yet not only to us but in us." [1]   In other words, revelation *is* revelation only when by the Spirit it " gets through " to man.   This is an attractive position, yet one with difficulties of its own ; for we are led to ask how the " once-for-allness " of the event of revelation in Jesus Christ is to be harmonized with the contention that revelation, as complete, includes man's believing acknow-ledgement of its reality.   Is the " givenness " of revelation in Christ quite real and unconditioned if after all, to be fully realized, it must be apprehended by man, even if that apprehension is wrought in us by the Spirit ? Is not God's gift of Himself in Christ fully real whether it be received or not ?   These are questions I may ask without attempting to answer them.   That there are strong considerations on the other side is obvious enough, but at least the problem is a sufficiently difficult one to demand a more careful study of it than I have hitherto found in Barth's pages.

We have seen that for Barth revelation is an event whose Subject is and remains God Himself.   But it occurs on earth.   It is amidst the context of natural and historical occurrences that revelation takes shape and appeals for faith.   Jesus Christ, in one aspect, is a human fact which, though not itself revelation, points to its presence, is a

[1] *Church Dogmatic*, I., 578.

sign or *token* that revelation is actually there. Under that rubric we may place, above all, the words and deeds of Jesus, as presented in the Gospels. But, be it noted, these are not themselves revelation, for many who heard His words and beheld His deeds did not believe in Him. True, we may comment; nothing is revelation except as God makes it to be so, not even the cross of Christ or His resurrection; but if these may be instruments in the hand of God through which He makes Himself known, why not also words that Jesus spoke, or actions done by Him? Is it incredible that when the Fourth Evangelist wrote: "We have seen His glory, seen it to be full of grace and reality ",[1] he was thinking precisely of what our Lord had actually done or said before men? Was Jesus' behaviour to the woman that was a sinner no true revelation of the Father's mercy, but only a sign of it? But this opens up the large question, how far Barth's thought makes room for the Jesus Christ described in the Gospels as having companied with men; and to this problem, as crucial as any, we must return.

Other signs of revelation are the Virgin Birth at the entrance of Jesus' life, the Empty Tomb at its close. They point to His existence as identical with that of God Himself, not of themselves compelling faith, though it may well be asked whether faith is possible except as they are apprehended. Or again, Holy Scripture, comprising documents derived from prophets who looked forward to the great event of Jesus Christ, or from apostles who looked back, is not as such the revelation; it is as it were the permanent possibility of revelation, if and when He speaks to us through the prophetic or apostolic witness. Here again unbelief is possible even when the Bible confronts us; it is but a sign, a means for God to use; yet no faith in true revelation is to be found that passed by this sign indifferently. Once more, to the series of signs belong

[1] St. John i. 14 (J. Moffatt's Translation).

the proclamation of the Word and the Sacraments, through which Jesus Christ acts as present from moment to moment. Preaching and sacrament, that is, are mutually explanatory signs of revelation, pointing to it as that which is both once-for-all and also present. It is solely the revelation which they attest that gives them efficacy now and here. Other correlative signs are the congregation of believers and the ministry.

Once more, the Christian's experience is a sign or token of revelation. There can be no faith without experience. This experience, by which the life of the believer is changed and shaped, though not unambiguously or directly perceptible to the man himself, is a reflex of his faith bestowed by the Holy Spirit, serving to confirm him in his faith and thus in the revelation that evoked it. Experience of itself cannot give such confirmation, but Jesus Christ can so use it as a confirming sign. So, too, the manifestations of faith in his outward life may to others—not to himself—form the index or sign of revelation as having been given him by God; for though he cannot *make* himself such evidence, through Jesus Christ he can *be* it, and indeed it would be impossible anywhere to find a believer who did not owe his personal faith to having encountered this Christ-given sign that revelation is a reality—the presence of faith made manifest in other lives.

All these signs of revelation may be subsumed compendiously under the fact of the Church, which may be described as the sum-total of them all. The primary token is the manhood of Jesus Christ, taken by the Eternal Word into union with Himself; the secondary is the Church, which is His Body; and outside the Church so conceived there can be no such thing as faith in revelation or any understanding of it.

Students of Barth will not miss the striking change of tone he here displays with regard to the character of faith as an experience. Earlier he had expressed a deep distaste for any accentuation of the experimental realization of Divine truth, as though content alone mattered, not inward form. Faith, he had held, was a vacuum, a void to which the Eternal gives Himself as content. Or again, faith is " the leap into the unknown, into the dark, into empty air ". We must ignore all inward processes, and think only of an event Divinely wrought on and in man. Even so Barth invited sympathy by his contention that faith cannot be directly observed ; it is not to be psychically localized or exhibited by scientific analysis of mental process. It was another thing to deny outright its experimental character, as though grace could not be present in the inward life because that life is human. Indeed, there are early passages in which Barth comes near to teaching that when we believe savingly, it is not we who believe at all, but the Spirit in us ; which is more than saying that faith is " no mere awareness of God as an object, but a veritable functioning of the consciousness of God within the mind of man ".[1]   In the New Testament, however, the Spirit possesses but does not (as in essential mysticism) displace the human self. In his recent *Dogmatic*, however, Barth carefully makes room for experimental fact. " Faith," he there writes, " is certainly also a human experience. And this experience likewise has corresponding to it a definite human attitude, and this human attitude also will find expression in definite human thoughts." Or, to quote one of his most significant passages : " In faith men have an actual experience of the Word of God ; and no *finitum non capax infiniti*, nor any *peccator non capax verbi divini* ought now to prevent us from taking this affirmation seriously, with all its consequences." [2]   But he still insists, and rightly, that whether experience has the character of true faith is to be decided by its relation to the believed Word of God. In

[1] Camfield, *Revelation and the Holy Spirit*, p. 249.
[2] *Church Dogmatic*, I., p. 250.

short, that experience is right and true which God calls
forth in us by His Word, not such as we manufacture for
ourselves. It is Christ, on Whom faith lays hold, Who
gives Himself thereto as object, that makes faith to be
faith and thus *real* experience.

The revelation, then, that is Jesus Christ, is the work or
action in which God re-establishes the broken relationship
between Himself and man. Except when apprehended as
thus restorative, revelation is not apprehended at all.
Extraordinary as it is, and inevitably as it offends the
human mind, it shatters the false order of sin with a view
to re-establishing the true order which God had made and
meant.

All true thinking about revelation gives the glory to God
alone, for it rests on and perpetually circles round the
Divine sovereignty. True, revelation takes place in the
sphere of nature, of history, of man's personal life, but it is
always the outcome of absolute Divine freedom, neither
concurring nor competing with other forces or originating
causes which operate independently in their own right or
prescribe antecedently the lines on which the self-unveiling
of God must move. At each point the free dispensation
of God is in command. *He speaks* ; it is for man to hear
and obey as God opens his heart. If God's revealing
action—for all is His *act*—is free viewed *a tergo*, it is no
less free *a fronte*. In other words, His revelation once for
all given is not thereafter merged or absorbed in finite
processes ; in particular He does not as it were hand it
over to the control of the Church or Church officials, as
though by a delegated authority it passed into the possession of believing men to be " managed " or " distributed "
by them. The insignificance and frailty of all Christian
experience and all Christian activity forbid the man to
whom revelation has come to ascribe to either a righteousness or intrinsic efficacy which God must acknowledge.

In revelation, as posited by God's free and sovereign

act by Jesus Christ within the human field, a new Divinely restored order is announced; but the restoration is announced only, not yet made perfect. We live in a time which is neither the time of the prophets and apostles nor the time when God shall make all complete. Remembering the fulfilment God gave in Jesus Christ, and taking comfort from its promise, we await the fulfilment also of our time. It is in hope that we share in the revelation once-for-all bestowed in Him. Announcement marks this as the time of Divine forbearance, in which God gives truly those signs or tokens of revelation named above, which answer our deep need. Thus the work of revelation, as operating fully on man and his world, is a future work; but in that fulness it will still be the work of Jesus Christ. We expect the full redemption; none the less, we live in joyful and confident hope, for God's announcement in Christ is authentic and sure. Our time is the time between the Ascension and the Return of Jesus Christ.

Here again, in these statements concerning the End to be anticipated, we appear to find an important modification of Barth's original eschatology. From the outset, it is true, Barth had set eschatology at the very centre of his interest. He rightly insisted that theology is eschatological in temper and outlook not merely by accident; on the contrary, its whole thinking must be done in the light of the End. Thought which is mundane, secular, absorbed in the " here " to the exclusion of the " yonder ", is theology only in name. Eschatology confronts us when eternity breaks into time, and the Word of God replaces the word of man, i.e., when what we men can tell ourselves is displaced by truth which only God can speak. But now and then the New Testament conviction that " the End is near " seemed to be robbed of one half of its meaning. The apostles did not merely look up, they looked forward to the close of history. Barth inclined to drop out the temporal element in this, and to translate their thought of a temporal nearness of the End into terms of a permanent relation.   Eschatology largely became an emphasis on the ever-abiding transcendent or eternal relations of the Now ;   each moment has infinite significance, but the thought of a Divinely caused climax of time, such as the New Testament designated when it spoke of the Return of Christ, was somewhat obscured.   The eschatological character of revelation seemed to mark the quality of truth rather than the expectancy of faith.   The question after all concerns only the distribution of accent ; if Barth earlier read " eternity " mainly as a timeless, over-shadowing present, imparting to every moment of existence its own critical relation to God, he now stresses equally the forward-looking aspect of revelation.   It still remains true that eternity overshadows time, now and here ; it is no less true that at the completion of God's revealing work time will be replaced by eternity.

§ 3.   THE WORD OF GOD

Barth envisages the Word of God in two main aspects. Primarily and originally, it is the Word " which God speaks by and to Himself in eternal hiddenness " ; [1] a truth which is developed in the doctrine of the Trinity, for Jesus Christ is the Word of God from all eternity. In a distinct though not different sense it is the Word addressed to man, in a threefold way, in preaching, in Scripture, and in revelation.   How precisely Barth conceives the relation of the Word of God to revelation is not quite easy to determine, and his insistence on the fact that we encounter the Word in three distinguishable forms does not make the problem easier.   From what has just been said, the eternal Word is obviously the *prius* of revelation. Elsewhere he describes the revealed form of it, or revelation,

[1] *Church Dogmatic*, I., p. 218.

as the "independent and unsurpassable *origin* for the Word of God ", and speaks of it as having " its origin in revelation ". I do not mean that here Barth's thought is opaque, but only that now and then his varied terminology is difficult to follow. At all events, a special discussion of the relation between these two ideas would be welcome. Perhaps we may take it that the *coming* of the Word is revelation. The Word comes, first, in the Incarnation, the existence of Jesus Christ within the created realm ; next, the Word comes when it makes contact with the spirit of man through the Holy Spirit and brings itself home to faith. Revelation, which is always an event, comes to be in these two ways—first, in the once-for-all form of Incarnation ; second, in its ever-repeated apprehension of individuals. God spoke in Jesus ; through Jesus He ever and anew speaks to men. Thus the two great concepts are the same, yet not the same.

We have seen that the criterion by which Dogmatic has to try Church proclamation, and must itself be tried, is the Word of God. Preaching rests on the given Word, which it cannot supersede ; it is an act demanded and controlled by the Biblical witness ; and Dogmatic has to inquire whether such fidelity is actually shown. Modernistic thought completely misses the point that man must let himself be told by God that which, of himself, he does not know. Neither Modernism nor Romanism feels the ultimate necessity for a declared Word of God, to be heard with faith. Yet apart from this relation of Word and faith, grace has no meaning.

There are three forms of the Word of God. It meets us, first of all, as something *proclaimed* in the Church, and proclaimed as that which has its source beyond the Church itself. Preaching is the event in which God is speaking through the speech of men. The Word is the commission under which preaching is done ; it is the object that stands over against the preacher, given by God to control his service under it ; it is the criterion of his message ; but it is more. Above all—and this is decisive—it is that which constitutes a man's word the very Word of God ; and God, the Creator and Lord, can make it to be this, when and where He will. This does not and cannot imply the submergence or obliteration of human thought and will, any more than the manhood of Jesus Christ was obliterated because God dwelt in Him.

Secondly, the Word of God is *written*. The Church's message is spoken both in recollection of something and in expectancy of something. It is spoken in the expectation that God will reveal Himself to those addressed, but also (and this chiefly concerns us here) in recollection that already God has spoken once for all in Jesus Christ in the great event of the Incarnation, which is in history, but not of it. We cannot too carefully signalize the fact that in preaching the Church does not draw her message from the hidden deeps of her own consciousness ; she speaks as the Canonical Scriptures, witnessing to a unique event, guide her to speak. As witness to the revelation in Jesus Christ, the Bible is the written Word of God, declared by prophets and apostles.

Scripture must not be thought of as the creation of the Church, much less her private possession. In it the Church is not—as in her tradition—speaking to herself ; she is being spoken to. Exegesis is there in order that the Bible, all veils of misinterpretation removed, may be left free to tell us what the Word of God really is. The Bible is the canon or rule of preaching for the definite reason that it imposes itself as such, in virtue of its content. Thus we can say that the Bible is God's Word in so far as He speaks through it ; and this He does—for the thing always is *His act*—when a portion of it lays hold of us in God's name and by the working of His Spirit. In that concrete happening it becomes God's Word to us, and He makes it so to men ever and again. The Bible *becomes*

T.M.T.　　　　　　　　　　　　　　　　　　　　U

God's Word in this event, and it is to its *being* in this *becoming* that the tiny word ' is ' relates, in the statement that the Bible *is* God's Word." [1] It does not become God's Word because we accord it faith, but because by the act of God the Bible has reached out to us and become revelation for us, here and now.

In the third place, God's Word is *revealed*. As we have seen, the Bible is the concrete means through which the Church is reminded of His past revelation, is called to expect revelation now and in the future, and is thereby challenged, empowered, and guided to declare her message. Speaking to us and heard by us as God's Word, the Bible attests past revelation ; to attest is to point to something else, in a definite direction and beyond ourselves. The Bible gives authoritative witness inasmuch as it lets something else be the authority, viz., God's revelation thus attested. *It must never be identified with the revelation itself.* The revealed Word of God is the Word He spoke to prophet and apostle in Jesus Christ, and speaks through their instrumentality ever anew to men.

We have seen that as so much printed matter the Bible is not identical with God's Word. But at any moment God can make it identical. And this actually happens whenever and wherever the word of the Bible really functions as a witness, and whenever and wherever by means of it we also are brought to see and hear what was seen and heard by those to whom God spoke of old. *Deus dixit*—that is revelation ; *Paulus dixit*—that is witness ; and these two are not, directly or of themselves, the same. But God can make them the same, and when He does, then in what Paul speaks we hear God speaking. This happens in virtue of God's decision that " here and now " it shall be so.

The Word of God meets and addresses us, then, in this threefold form.

---

[1] *Church Dogmatic*, I., p. 124.

It is one and the same, [Barth explains in an important passage] whether we regard it as revelation, as the Bible, or as proclamation. For so far as proclamation really rests upon recollection of the revelation attested in the Bible and is therefore the obedient repetition of the Biblical witness, it is no less the Word of God than the Bible. And so far as the Bible really attests revelation, it is no less the Word of God than revelation itself. By *becoming* the Word of God in virtue of the actuality of revelation, the Bible and proclamation *are* also the Word, the one Word of God within which there can be neither a more nor a less.[1]

The first form, revelation itself, is the form that establishes the other two. But each is known only through the others. The sole analogy which Barth can find for them, in themselves and in their mutual relationships, is that of the three " Persons " in the Trinity.

It is a mistake, Barth urges, to ask the question : What then is the Word of God ? as if a general and universally applicable answer could be furnished. " God and His Word," he points out, " are not presented to us in the way in which natural and historical entities are presented to us. We can never by retrospect, and so by anticipation, fix what God is or what His Word is : He must always repeat that to us and always repeat it afresh." But at least we can say that God's Word means " God speaks " —where " speaks " is not merely a symbol, for no other concept could properly designate His free act in speaking. Moreover, His speaking means that God's Word is primarily spiritual ; it is a rational and not an irrational event, as Otto has suggested. " The form in which reason communicates with reason, person with person, is language ; so too when it is God's language." The Word does not belong to the realm of natural or corporeal things, though it may and does clothe itself in a natural or corporeal vesture. The power it possesses is pre-eminently the simple spiritual power of truth. Here we must perpetually

[1] *Church Dogmatic*, I., p. 136.

be on our guard against slipping back into the sphere of
the natural or mechanical, where there is no longer speech
and answer, knowledge and decision, but only impersonal
movement, pressure and impact.

The one way to escape from a doctrinaire and static
view of the Word of God is at each point to recollect that
the Word is Jesus Christ.   It is not a thing to be described
and catalogued, nor is it a concept to be defined.   It is
not " a truth " in some general sense, but God Himself
speaking, *Dei loquentis persona.*   " Where My Word is,
there am I."   Let us fill our minds with Jesus Christ if
we wish to bar out the old Protestant idea that Scripture
is a fixed total of revealed propositions to be systematized
like the sections of a legal *corpus.*   God is the Lord of His
Word.   " He is not bound to it, but it is bound to Him.
He thus has free disposal of the verbal character of Holy
Scripture, He can use it or not use it, He can use it in
one way or another." [1]   Nowhere is God so manifestly
a Person as in His Word.

Not only so, but the Word has a purpose or direction ;
we only recognize it as we perceive it to be something
addressed *to us.*   " To every man from time to time it
has something quite special to say, something that comes
straight home to him, and only to him in that way.   The
real content of God's speech, or the real will of the speaking
Person of God, is thus never to be conceived and repro-
duced by us as a general truth."   Continually it confronts
us anew, in stark majesty.   We can never say : " There,
that is the Word of God," except as we know that God is
aiming at us.   When He speaks, it is to tell us what we
could not tell ourselves, what touches and pierces our
personal life, what is needful for the restoration of the
original relationship between Him and us, what is absolute,
final, and covers all the future.   Each time His Word is
made audible, it is a unique act of God.   It is indeed His

[1] *Church Dogmatic,* I., p. 157.

characteristic act thus to make His Word contemporaneous with us, so that what was spoken by prophets and apostles is spoken directly to ourselves. Thereby He tells each man that he is not his own but belongs to God, and lays on him the hand of authority from above. It is thus that God's Word makes history, sovereignly causing itself to be received as promise, as claim, as judgment, as blessing. God in His Word is always on the ground first ; His Word descends upon us, not depending for its Divine validity on our faith, but presupposing the absolute power of Jesus Christ as Lord, and manifesting from first to last His power of disposal over man. " Long before he can adopt an attitude to God, God has adopted an attitude to him. Whatever attitude he may assume, it will take place within and on the ground of God's attitude to him."

Or again, we are perpetually being tempted to conceive the coming of the Word as an event which may be classified with other events, and we look round for the category under which it might find its appropriate place, the syllogism by means of which its reality might somehow be demonstrated to our satisfaction. This is to forget that *the Word is God speaking*, and that by preferential action. Once we are compelled to recognize it as a deed of His free choice, to think of it as an occurrence subject to any higher necessity becomes impossible. He speaks it in His own unconditioned freedom. Though as a human event it takes place in history, yet still more and supremely it is an event springing from His choice beyond all history, which effectuates itself in this way and no other, concerning this or that particular man. There is ever a Divine decision, becoming operative on and in a decision —be it for faith or for unbelief—in the man to whom it is uttered.

Since the Word is God's, not man's, we could not *a priori* prophesy one poor syllable about its nature. To prescribe how it shall come, to delimit it from other homogeneous

entities, would be to make of God an object, a member
of the measurable and calculable world of objects. We
bow before it as His mystery, acknowledging that we cannot master but only serve it, guarding ourselves reverently
from any theology that presumes to assign its place amongst
other more or less co-ordinate realities. Mystery here
signifies not simply the hiddenness of God, but His manifesting Himself in such wise that His Word always meets
us clothed in garments of creaturely reality, in a vesture
belonging to this world, so that what He declares to us is
known not directly, or to normal human inspection, but
only to the faith He has created in the heart. The Word
of God is *unveiled* just because (in the humanity of Christ,
in the Bible, in preaching) it is *veiled* ; the form here so
shrouds the matter that the matter reaches us through a
form which does not mirror it simply or directly, but, so
to say, opaquely screens it from sight. Thus there is a
twofold indirectness in God's communication, due not
merely to the creatureliness of man but also to his sinfulness. Put summarily, the fact is that " *God Himself veils
Himself and in the very process unveils Himself*". Well
for us that He does so ! It would be the end of all things
were God to address us directly. " Thou canst not see
My face and live." Thus, while it is true we cannot hear
or know the Word of God except as in faith we pierce
through the veiling form to the unveiled content and interpret it, this we cannot do of ourselves ; the interpretation
also must be given us by God. What God has joined, man
must not seek to put asunder. " The worldly form without
the divine content is not the Word of God, and the divine
content without the worldly form is also not the Word of
God." But these two, implying and implied in each other,
we cannot see transparently as one. God wills to lead us
now through form to content, and now through content
back to form, and in both cases to Himself. Thus in the
Gospel according to St. John, faith is led at times from the

known Son to the unknown Father, at times from the known Father to the unknown Son.

Nothing is more characteristic of Barth, or more rewarding, than the insistence he places on the fact that God's self-unveiling and His self-veiling are so closely interrelated that neither can be understood without the other. Where would be the goodness of God's Word but for its severity ? How should we know the glory of God in Jesus but through His lowliness, His power but through the weakness in which He was crucified. In sober truth, it is only the man who knows what grace is that can tell what wrath and judgment are. By being seriously put under law, man comes to the gospel, and by coming to the gospel through revelation and faith he is seriously put under law. " The Word of God in its veiling—its form—is God's demand upon man. The Word of God in its unveiling—its content, is God's turning to man." [1] No systematic or logical conspectus of the two is possible. We can only listen to the one or to the other, and faith alone can see each in its counterpart. Everywhere in the Bible we come upon these great " onesidednesses ". When the Synoptic picture of Jesus fills the mind, we cannot simultaneously take in the Johannine ; when our thoughts are intent on the Cross of Jesus and its shame, we cannot at that very moment look up to His Resurrection and its glory. Faith, but nothing else, can see threat in the promise, promise in the threat.[2]

[1] *Church Dogmatic*, I., p. 204.

[2] I have found no more enlightening comment on this than some words of Dr. Campbell N. Moody. " The soul moves," he writes, " from the faith that the Lord died for us to the faith that He lives in us, and ever back again to the assurance that He who deigns to dwell in us has given Himself on our behalf. For, as Barth has observed—and this is one of the most illuminating of his observations—God never permits us to see both aspects of a truth at the same time. Barth selects a sermon by Martin Luther on the Syrophenician woman to show how this is so. We

There was a time, ten or twelve years since, when Barth's expressions on this subject might not unreasonably have been characterized as misleading. The idea of the *Deus absconditus*—the hidden God—filled a place in his argument that at times seemed to overshadow the *Deus revelatus*. Readers might then ask, without obvious absurdity, whether that in God which is unrevealed even to the believer might not conceivably be hopelessly out of keeping with what has actually been disclosed in Jesus. Was the veiled aspect of God spiritually homogeneous with the unveiled ? Were we to lose the Fatherhood all over again ? They recalled how Luther had charged it upon the Mediaeval Church as the gravest of religious faults that Scholastic theology had set the unknown deity of the pagan philosophers once more in place of the God and Father revealed in Jesus. Magical sacraments, saints' intercessions, expiatory penances—all had been justified by being referred to that dark hidden region of God, of which Jesus was no index, but where, for all that was known, cruelty might consort with love, caprice with faithfulness. Various readers of Barth's *Romans*, like myself, confused by paradox and seemingly deprived of the guiding-thread of a recognizable historical revelation,

seem, like the woman, to encounter nothing but blank refusal. This very refusal becomes a means of blessing. For Faith, kindling here, wins victory. When all is black as night, when God tells us that we are sinners, and have no ground to look for mercy, just then we seize on the very fact that we are sinners, and plead His grace for such ; thus out of despair we gain peace. Yet we are not allowed to remain at this point ; we do not pass from triumph to triumph, from joy to ecstasy. We do not sit aloft on the dreamy heights of the mystic ; but presently we are back at the battle of faith. We move from finding to seeking, from the wealth of spiritual experience to honest and acknowledged poverty. Our life is ever in transition from struggle to triumph and back to a sense of failure ; or, it may be, from Law to Gospel, and back to Law once more, or from the Letter to the Spirit, and back to the Letter again. God lets us see but one side at a time " (*Christ for us and in us*, p. 68 f.).

must have asked themselves whether the Scholastic error was not being repeated, as in the sharp emphatic words —" God is pure negation ".[1] But these misgivings, excusable as they may have been, turned out to be based on misapprehension. Barth's point rather is, not that what is veiled is at variance with the unveiled, but that each involves the other. Neither would be itself but for the meaning imparted to it by its obverse. We cannot synchronously envisage the grace and the wrath of God, nor can we demonstrate their transparent connexion with each other. But take either away, and the other disappears. To Barth the statement that God is the unknown God means three things : (1) He cannot be known save as He reveals Himself, (2) He is apprehended, not by direct inspection, but by faith alone, (3) even to believers, nay, precisely to believers, the God discerned by faith in Christ is for that very reason unfathomable, with depths the human mind cannot sound, and such that the different aspects of His action towards and upon us cannot be adjusted in a logical unity. All this is a sharp reminder at every moment that the Word of God does not give itself over into our control or mastery. His truth, if it did so, could not be the *theologia crucis*. We have not the revelation under lock and key, to do with as we choose. When God speaks, when in the event of revelation His Word comes home to the human soul, it is an event in which the Word is not only revealed to man but also believed by him. " The Lord of the language is also the Lord of our listening to it. The Lord who gives the Word is also the Lord who gives faith."

In his earlier forms of exposition Barth gave us, it may not unfairly be said, considerably less help than was desirable in identifying the content of the Word, in distinguishing what it was from what it was not. There was at that stage a certain justification for the complaint that

---

[1] *Epistle to the Romans* (E.T.), p. 341.

his conception of the Word had a vague and indeterminate outline, and at times seemed to be little more than a compendious expression for some transcendent communication, no matter what, from beyond the limit of all human potentialities. In recent works he has made it plain— what no doubt was present by implication from the first, though wrapped in clouds of difficult phraseology—that the Word of God is Jesus Christ. In Him for good and all God speaks His judgment and His grace. We shall later have to inquire whether the meaning attached by Barth to the words " Jesus Christ " are such as wholly to satisfy the believing student of the New Testament.

§ 4.   GOD AND CHRIST

Barth's mind is dominated by the thought of God which emerges from the Bible. In the service of that thought he finds perfect freedom. God is the " wholly Other ", incognizable by man, from whom He is removed by a wholly impassable difference, except as He comes forth almighty in self-revelation. Human thoughts of God have a place in the philosophical system, but the Bible supersedes them all. To speak, as advocates of immanentism do, as if the highest human life shades off into the Divine, and God were the superlative of man, is to turn theology into psychology and seek vainly to ward off contact with Ultimate Reality. The true God, far from being humanity at its loftiest, stands over every concrete human fact in radical judgment—" the negation of this world in which is included also the god of human logic ". We learn to think rightly of God—so far as men may— only when He has spoken to us, in severity and grace. In His place, times innumerable, has been put the No-God or idol of the human soul, wherein is mirrored our own inward disorderliness. In truth He is the Holy One, the Light which dawns upon us from beyond the limit of all that is temporal and comprehensible. To put all in a word : God reveals Himself as the Lord. In Creation, in Reconciliation, in Redemption He is Lord, and that absolutely. Yet, transcendent as He is, He becomes ours in the Incarnation. " Through the knowledge of God which is in Christ, He whom men name ' Despot ' is known and loved as the eternal, loving Father."

In this context, Barth has been charged with teaching a radical dualism which divides God from the world by a gulf which in the metaphysical sense is absolute. Certain ill-advised phrases had made the charge a colourable one, as when in his *Romans* [1] he had spoken of " the misery of our createdness ". But this must not be pressed. On the same page stands a noble passage which blows all Manichæan notions sky-high.

> In our apprehension which is not-knowing and in our not-knowing which is apprehension, there is shown forth the final and primal unity of visibility and invisibility, of earth and heaven, of man and God. In that duality, which now and to the end of our days is alone accessible to our perception, is announced the ultimate unity, which is the glory of the children of God and our hope.

It is because man is fallen, not because he is finite, that man is incapable of God. The dualism follows upon sin.

In his full doctrinal discussion of what revelation is, Barth expounds at length his interpretation of God as Triune. That is the point at which his doctrine of God *begins*. The Trinity is no mere appendage to, much less an inference from, the Gospel ; *ab initio* God is revealed as Father, Son, and Holy Spirit. If we are to expound the thought of revelation, we must begin (not end, as most theologians do) with the doctrine of the Triune God ; we must prefer the *ordo essendi* to the *ordo cognoscendi*. This is done in Chapter II of *Church Dogmatic*, the first volume of Barth's second edition, just rendered into

[1] p. 321.

English by Professor G. T. Thomson,[1] of Aberdeen University, whose courage and skill have put the Church under a debt. Of the exposition given there (pp. 339–560) the translator has said, I believe with justice : " The original is undoubtedly the greatest treatise on the Trinity since the Reformation, by one whose faith has been put to the touch and come out the stronger ; I have read nothing like it except Martin Luther and John Calvin." The problem of the Trinity, as I have said, Barth takes as the first part of his doctrine of God. When in the light of Scripture we think upon the self-revealing God, three questions are seen to be involved. First, Who reveals Himself ? Secondly, how does it happen that this revelation is given ? Thirdly, what is the effect of this event of revelation on the man whom it befalls ? Scripture leads us to answer : the veiled God is unveiled and imparted ; the Father is disclosed in the Son and communicated in the Spirit ; and in these three characters the one God is made known as the Lord. This is the doctrine in its initial, Biblical form, which must be regarded as springing out of and, as it were, of one substance with the revelation itself.

Space fails us here to develop Barth's fully articulated doctrine of the Triune being of God. We are studying his fundamental dogmatic principles, not analysing any one of his doctrines in detail. Suffice it to note the vigilant care with which, even in the minuter parts of his exposition, he keeps the whole discussion close to the actual revelation in Jesus ; and again, the deeply religious insight which at every point guards him against the most distant suggestion of Tritheism. God in Himself is the Love that in the mystery and miracle of the " new birth " makes itself visible to us. It is a Love unbeginning and primordial. " In God Himself this Love is the love of the Father to the

[1] [Now of Edinburgh University as Professor Mackintosh's successor.   Ed.]

Son, of the Son to the Father. This eternal love within God Himself is the Holy Spirit." [1]

A few words, however, ought to be said regarding the doctrine of divine Immanence, on which Barth has so often been supposed to write without a proper degree of understanding. He has been charged—and incautious phrases are not lacking—with so crying up the transcendence of God as to negate all moral relation between God and men, and to remove Him, somewhat after the Deistic manner, from positive contact with the created world. But what Barth rejects is not Immanence, but the wholly unscriptural philosophy known as Immanentism, a product of the autonomous human reason untaught by revelation. God the Creator, Barth teaches, upholds all things by His power. The universe has a reality He has willed, still wills, accompanies and guides. It can never be a world He has abandoned, yet He is not merged in it, or captive to its fatalities. The world exists together with Him, with a reality of its own beneath His eye, but the relation between Him and it is irreversibly a one-way relation. He has absolute primacy. The Creator must be unchangeably " above ", the creature " beneath ". The world as such can have no " divinity ". Immanence, construed as the Christian must construe it in the light of Creation, means simply God's free and almighty presence and rule within the world He has made. True, God does not become the world ; the world cannot become God, but is for ever " over against " Him. None the less, in this world God is present, " not distant only, but also near, not only free as He confronts it but bound to it by His sovereign choice, not transcendent only but also immanent." This is an idea of immanence not to be excogitated by the logician but humbly acknowledged by the man who knows God as his Creator. So, too, there is a presence of God at every point in history, though

[1] *Credo* (1935), p. 119.

a presence not to be co-ordinated or confused with His
special presence in the Incarnation. All must be viewed
from the summit where God places men when He gives
them faith in Christ, never from the level still un-
enlightened by revelation.

If we knew nothing of the once-for-all and sheerly *special*
immanence of the Divine Word in flesh, how would or could
we dare—in face of sin, evil, death and devil—to believe and
live by any *general* immanence of God in the world? Far,
then, from our being compelled or bound to deny the first
on account of the second, we must acknowledge the first in
order rightly to believe and teach the second.[1]

All that God does in this world, He does by injecting
eternity into time and space. The Unknown and Inaccessible puts Himself within our reach by descending
to us in Jesus Christ. We must utterly reject the view,
always flattering and always widespread, that if we are to
see God with the deepest assurance of His presence we
must look within ourselves. No one could believe that
who perforce had come to acknowledge that we men are
immersed in a life of corruption and relativity, a world
separated from God by the grim line of death. We
inhabit a sphere divided in its alienation from God by
a gulf of such a kind that our whole being is arraigned
and called in question by the Holy One. But the good
tidings is that the gulf between " yonder " and " here "
has been crossed by God in Jesus Christ. From man to
God there is no way ; this is certain, but all the more
certainly there is a way from God to man. In history
there is an advent of God laden with eschatological or final
significance. The presence of the Maker of the world,
His presence in the world unknown to the world—this is
the key to the understanding of history. Jesus Christ is
an event not in secular but in divine history—a real
historical fact but not one which gains its character

[1] *Credo*, p. 37.

from its historical connexions. He came into the world,
He did not come out of it.   His existence is a discontinuous
insertion in the web of happenings within space and time,
and one that laughs immanentist " continuity " to scorn ;
for neither is He to be explained by the previous trend of
earthly events, nor is His abiding redemptive power
capable of being interpreted as the normal continuous
influence of the past on all that follows.

In Christ the new Reality dawns.   Yet here more than
ever we have to confess the indirect character of faith's
apprehension, for God dwells in Christ *incognito* ; men can
see and hear Him without discovering the secret.   Apart
from faith, God's proper gift, His outward appearance
can be read in two ways.   He can be hailed as the Son
of the living God, but He can be rejected as " a gluttonous
man and a wine-bibber ".   No such blinding glory appears
in Jesus as we naïvely predicate of Godhead, no power that
strikes down opposition there and then.   He does not
strive or cry or make a sensation.   In all that came under
external observation, Jesus simply was a man.   Within
or beside all in Him that was familiarly human there goes
what is totally incompatible with natural assumptions.
He is at our side, yet infinitely above us—and different.
Something is here to shock and puzzle men, a veil only
faith can pierce.   And when it pleases God to reveal His
Son to us, the effect is like that of an earthquake.   Everything in our life that appeared secure is shaken critically
to its foundations.   God has encountered us, and thereby
compelled us to leave the judgment to Him.   We know
ourselves in the presence of the Word made flesh.

It is here that Barth's famous mathematical figures are
applied.   Jesus Christ is the sheer perpendicular from
above, coming plumb down to touch our world as a tangent
at this single point.   Or otherwise, in Him two planes
intersect, one known, the other unknown.   The known
plane is God's creation, fallen out of union with Him ; the

unknown plane, now making itself known, is the world of the Father, the world of grace for sinners. But, to repeat it once more, " the line of intersection is not self-evident ". The point on that line at which the relation between God and us becomes observable and observed is Jesus of Nazareth. The single point is a most definite point. " The years A.D. 1–30 are the era of revelation and disclosure." Then the coming of the Word happened once, and happened once for all.

Critics are not lacking who hold that Barth's attitude to the historical Jesus is of such a negative and distant character that it would make no vital difference to his faith were it proved that Jesus never really lived. This, taken at its face value, appears to me almost grotesquely mistaken. I have just quoted his words, as old as his *Romans*, to the effect that " the years A.D. 1–30 are the years of revelation ". Again, readers of his *Credo* [1] who observe the stress he lays on such things as the Virgin Birth, the suffering of Jesus (*passus*) as pervading His entire life and not merely His last days, and most of all his emphatic insistence on the clause " suffered under Pontius Pilate ", can feel no real doubt on the subject. These things made it plain that the historic Jesus forms an integral and crucial element in his whole theological outlook. Once more, in his *Dogmatic*, he makes it clear beyond all question that

it belongs to the concept of Biblically attested revelation, to be a *historical event* . . . By the thing it calls revelation the Bible always means *a unique event, one occurring in that place and at that time* . . . The fact that Cyrenius, the governor of Syria, cannot be left out of the story of Christmas, and that Pontius Pilate genuinely belongs to the Creed—all that asserts the Bible's claim, in its account of revelation, to relate history . . . The divine unveiling of which it tells is imparted not simply to man, but to such and such men in a perfectly definite

---

[1] An Exposition of the Apostles' Creed.

situation. Each time it is a quite special event, and as such incomparable and unrepeatable.[1]

So far all is tolerably transparent, and the suggestion that Barth in the last resort is indifferent to the historical existence of Jesus Christ must be unconditionally repelled.

The situation, as a whole, however, is far from simple. In the first place, Barth rightly insists that in this context the word " historical " must be closely scrutinized. In modern usage " history " is a radically equivocal term, and we cannot assume that it is capable, in its current meaning, of supplying the framework into which God's revelation must fit. Two ordinary and secular meanings may be distinguished. Historical, first, means that which can be vouched for by scholarly research, working on universally accepted scientific rules. And secondly, historical means that which is apprehensible by a neutral observer, devoid of faith. In neither sense is the Jesus Christ in Whom God's revelation comes to be described as " historical ". For history in this detached sense, Jesus can be no more than a problem or a myth. Faith must pierce deeper ; " though we have known Christ after the flesh, yet now we know Him so no more ". The ultimate basis for faith is behind and beyond externally perceptible history, the individual facts of which might well be got by heart yet have no revealing power of God vibrating through them ; it lies rather in facts that happened, facts witnessed to by prophets and apostles, and now in my own present sent home to me by the Holy Spirit. Much of this, which seems to me manifestly sound, goes back to the argument of Kähler that it is idle to seek, behind the testimony of the apostles to Jesus, a scientifically reconstructed picture of Jesus as He really was. Their preaching, accordingly, must remain the final court of appeal by which the truth of the Church's

[1] *Church Dogmatic*, Vol. I, pp. 373–5.

message is sanctioned. Their witness is confirmed and made actual in my present experience.[1]

In the one word Resurrection lies the whole of Christianity; so Barth declares in a hundred turns of expression. Here too faith rests upon what is history and more; Christ rose from the dead a conqueror, yet the event is wholly outside the range of the detached historian. Eternity has pierced the dreams of time. The Resurrection is the turning-point of the ages, the divine Moment when time stands still as charged with infinite significance; and from this point of view Barth can say it means the same as the Parousia. It marks the divinely provided swerving of the No to the Yes, from judgment to grace, from death to life. The limits of human possibility have been broken through, and the impossible divine possibility has become fact. But Resurrection is a truth of wider range than the event of the first Easter: it stands for the fact that God gives new life (for example, in the transforming words of forgiveness spoken by Jesus to the sinful) to all broken and rejected human things, breathing His Spirit into all we are and have and do. Barth's entirely right emphasis on the Pauline doctrine that by faith we partake in the power of Christ's resurrection has betrayed him, as I think, into some misleading observations concerning the Resurrection itself. " The Resurrection," we are told, " is the non-historical relating of the whole historical life of Jesus to its origin in God." [2] Still more roundly he declares, in a controversial passage, that the Resurrection is no historical occurrence, because " if it be brought within the context of history, it must share in its obscurity and error and essential questionableness ".[3] Only a failure to enter sympathetically into Barth's

[1] [From this point onwards the contents did not receive a final revision at the hands of the author. Ed.]

[2] *Romans*, p. 195.

[3] *Ibid.*, p. 204.

convoluted thought can take these words to mean what they say upon the surface. In part, they are infected by the radical doubleness of the word " history "; in part, we cannot but feel that, like many a Hegelian, Barth frequently tends to say " A is not B " when his real meaning is " A is not merely B ". He does fuller justice to the idea he is expounding, when he speaks of " the victory which has occurred, does occur, and will occur in Christ ".[1] Supremely in Christ's rising from the dead, but mediately also in believers, the creative and transforming powers of God break into time. In the Resurrection the new world of the Holy Spirit touches the old world of the flesh, but transcendently.

The note of joy over the free Divine invasion of grace in Christ resounds everywhere in Barth, that supposed pessimist. The sovereignty of God is not caprice, it is liberty to interpose in judgment and mercy as He pleases.[2] In an early essay we find a passage where Barth rises to a great height in extolling the sheerly supernatural character of pardon.

The highest expression of the *totaliter aliter* announced in the Bible [he writes] is the preaching of the forgiveness of sins. Now that we are on the point, I feel as if this word " FORGIVE-NESS " compels our amazement even more than the raising of Lazarus. It is an inconceivably new factor in our practical reckoning. This constituting anew of the moral subject, in the very midst of moral and political realities, by a man's being set in the order of the Divine King—and being reckoned as belonging to God; this spectacle of the beginning of good there at the very heart of evil; this establishment of his kingly freedom through the kingly freedom of God—man in his captive, limited, provisional life which yet is simultaneously stayed on God alone, disturbed by God yet borne up by God

[1] *Ibid.*, p. 498.
[2] Sovereign election means that we are *all* the subjects of " double predestination ". We are all rejected in that we are condemned, we are the elected in that we are received in Christ.

—is this anything which we can deduce psychologically, or prove, or visualize ? Is it not rather something outside all history, a sheerly new thing, an absolute datum ?

We cannot overcome sin by moral enthusiasm or the spirit of adventure ; not till the grave and creative word " forgiveness " is spoken, and spoken by Him who is Lord, is the problem solved—by God, and for Him. This, and only this, makes an end of the attempt to build the Christian life upon ideals, instead of God's pardon. Nothing remains for any of us to do but take our place on the same bench with publicans and sinners, willing to live penitently from moment to moment by the grace of God. Thus, for Barth, study of the Christian life of obedience is not a second chapter supplementary to that which spoke of reconciliation, election, faith and hope ; it is still the same unconditional attack upon the natural man, the same attitude of utter dependence on God. To the *soli Deo gloria* there answers on our side *sola fide*. After all, they mean the same thing.

The mark of the Christian life is not assurance but hope. It is hidden, not so far openly manifested, with Christ in God. We have heard the Word of God out of eternity, but we live in time, " not yet " ever sounding in our ears. We shall never in this life have the right to count the dangers past or to behave ourselves as those who have attained. We are pilgrims, and the vision of God still lies before us. In the Christian life, which believers seek to make a life of obedience (though, as they themselves know best, with poor success), God does everything that is real, and He does it through the forgiveness of sins. From moment to moment we are summoned to do the will of God, as ever afresh He makes it known. At this point of view it becomes clear to Barth that it is truer to say that God lives the new life within us than that we ourselves do. And since all Divine action is hidden, and apprehended by us only indirectly, it follows that our sanctification by the Spirit is not something we can detect and register, but something we believe in, solely in dependence on the Word of promise.

§ 5.   THE CHURCH

The Church, as Barth sees it, is as questionable and equivocal a fact as religion itself.   The gusto and emphasis with which at first he set out this view misled certain of his critics, needlessly yet not altogether unnaturally, into supposing that he despised the Church.   But we shall see how mistaken this is.   More in sorrow than in anger his early work called attention to the fact that the concrete Church, the institution we know, belongs like all earthly things to the present age, the æon of flesh and sin.   From this point of view it is simply a more or less effective organization whose aim is to promote certain valuable human interests.   Hence, like the world, of which as a visible undertaking it forms part, it stands in absolute opposition to God.   As it is put in words that leave nothing to be desired for clearness : " In the Church the hostility of men against God is brought to a head ; for there human indifference, misunderstanding, and opposition attain their most sublime and also their most naïve form." [1]   Thus, supremely among human things, the Church stands under the Krisis of God. [2]   Bring it into relation to God, see it in His light, and there is nothing whatever to be said for it.   Far from being the Kingdom of God, it is the Tower of Babel.   Not that the separatist conventicle is sounder or worthier : " Better with the Church in hell," we are told, " than with pietists of higher or lower type in a heaven—which does not exist ! "   How can we ignore the fact that the more " up to date " and " efficient " the Church becomes, the more it is the object

[1] *Romans*, p. 418.
[2] " You only have I known of all the families of the earth ; therefore I will punish you for all your iniquities " (Amos, 3, 2).

of God's judgment and rejection ? It was the Church, not the world, that crucified Christ.

Now the one thing we must not do with this is to repudiate it as if spoken by one who sits in the seat of the scorner.   Barth is no bitter or triumphant critic, prepared in the pride of superior knowledge to lead the Church in the right way. He is himself deeply and sadly involved in the Church's imperfections, and utters a brother's warning. Moreover, on this point as on others, we must hear Barth out to the end.   It is true, he writes, with one-sided dogmatism : " The work of the Church is the work of men ; it can never be God's work," [1] but this somewhat noisy emphasis is far from being his last word. What he intends to say is that in proportion as the Church becomes self-deifying, galvanized and complacent, it has lost touch with the purposes for which Christ by His Word gathers round Him a fellowship of faith and love.   Men, as such, however much they " get together ", can never from their own resources heal the hurt of even one soul ; for God and God only can heal and bless. The Church, as we not only observe but share its life, is in itself utterly unworthy, and for that reason perpetually confronted with the possibility of rejection. If it be ignorant of the meaning of repentance, it cannot be the Church of God. But to stop there is faithlessly to forget the mercy of God. He has not cast off His people. In and by His grace, the possibility of rejection is unceasingly being overcome. Doubtless here also the victory of life over death is hidden from us at every moment of time ; it is victory only in hope.   But it is none the less sure.   " In any case, we are His, for it is on Him that we are broken in pieces, and for this reason we also participate in His people's victorious and unconquerable hope." [2] Existentially, that is in ultimate Divine reality, the promise already fulfilled in Christ holds good for all the Church's future.

[1] *Romans*, p. 353.   [2] *Ibid.*, p. 393.

If, therefore, those who have only considered the darker side of Barth's picture turn upon him with the question : " If this be the Church's character, why do you not leave it ? " his answer is unhesitating. " It would never enter our heads to think of leaving the Church. For in describing the Church we are describing ourselves." [1] The man who abandons the Church must have forgotten that it is a company of justified sinners. If we will but cease to censure others from a spectator's point of view, as though we possessed a store of private merits that made us fit judges, if only we accept God's point of view, to Whom alone vengeance belongs, nothing can be said concerning the Church which is too glorious or lofty. We should then see clearly that " regarded from the invisible standpoint of God, the operation of the Gospel of Christ cannot be distinguished from the operation of the Church ".[2] We should then feel free to say : " The Church is the place of fruitful and hopeful repentance ; and it is nothing else." The concrete Church " under the Cross " is also the Church of the Holy Spirit. Whatever the faults or tribulations of the Church, we may still boldly say that the real and true Church is that which is strong enough to recognise its weakness in the presence of God. Therefore, participating as we do in its responsibility and sharing the guilt of its inevitable failure, we should humbly accept it and cling to it. So to think will preserve us who make up the visible Church from setting ourselves pharisaically over against *any* of our fellows. Be our neighbour never so abandoned, we cannot avoid the grave question whether in him, precisely in him, Christ may not be confronting us with an inexorable call for service.

Thus Barth's final estimate of the Church has all the gravity and all the grandeur of Reformation thought. He is as sure as were the Reformers that through its instrumentality there takes place that movement from

[1] *Ibid.*, p. 371.   [2] *Ibid.*, p. 418.

death to life which is the only hope of man. He would join *ex animo* in the great words of Calvin concerning the body of believing people and their place in the life of faith :

Let us learn by the mere name of mother how profitable, indeed how necessary, is the knowledge of her : since there is no other entrance into life unless she herself conceive us in her womb, unless she bear us, unless she foster us at her breast, unless she guard us under her care and government, until we put off this mortal flesh and become like the angels.

For him, as for the greatest minds in the evangelical tradition, it holds true that outside the Church there is no salvation.

The theology of Barth is eschatological from end to end, but not perhaps in the ordinarily accepted sense of that word.[1] As he has put it recently : " Eschatological does not signify what is not properly or really meant, but what is related to the ἔσχατον, i.e., to that which for our sight, for our experience and thought, is still outstanding, to the eternal reality of the divine fulfilment and execution." [2] " Eternal reality " gives the keynote. Eternity is first, then time ; the future is first, then the present. We have seen that he tunes all his Christian thinking to the truth of Resurrection, and builds everything on hope. We are those who wait ; we have been reconciled, but we still have to be redeemed ; and " redemption is invisible, inaccessible, impossible, for it meets us only in hope ".[3] In the light of Christ the frontier of our existence now is not death but the new promised land. Exaggeration here also is too often a mark of Barth's language. There are not a few passages in which he goes the length of teaching, contrary to the New Testament, that even faith itself is not actually the beginning of a new life, but only the beginning of yearning for the new life reserved for

[1] See T. Ellwein, *Evangelische Lehre*, p. 169.
[2] *Church Dogmatic*, I, pp. 486-7.   [3] *Romans*, p. 314.

" heaven ".   But the same apostle who wrote " we are
saved by hope " wrote also " we have peace with God ".
Still, allowing for such intelligible hyperbole, we shall do
well to listen to Barth as he expatiates on the place of
forward-reaching hope in the business of being a Christian.
What the Bible speaks of as the Return of Christ is not, in
his view, a second thing in addition to His resurrection ;
it is the finally emergent manifestation of that same power
of an endless life which came to sight when He was raised
from the dead.   Until then, we live in a transition stage
—between the Ages.   As things are now, God rules the
world, but, as Luther puts it, not visibly or publicly, but
in some such way as the sun shining behind a cloud.
We see the light, we do not see the sun.   One day we shall
see both, and see them as one.   Till then we await the
great light that lies behind all history, the day when death
—the climax and epitome of all in the world that is against
God—shall be dissolved.   To that point all God's acts are
moving on.   If these things are so, theology is not eschatological by accident ;   on the contrary, its whole thinking
should be done from the standpoint of the End.   Barth
rightly declares that theology which is mundane, secular,
occupied with the " here " to the exclusion of the
" yonder ", is theology only in name.

§ 6.   SUMMARY AND CONCLUSION

Before we register some of the greater aspects of Barth's
teaching which have issued in the enrichment of the whole
Church, I should like to fix attention on one or two
matters on which we may reasonably demur.   It must be
admitted that Barth has not made things easy for his
critics.   By that I do not simply mean that, in the staple
of it, his thought is profoundly Biblical, and therefore
unassailable ;   though this is part of the truth.   I mean
rather that his writing, so often, is temperamental.   He

states this or that absolutely, when what he really means
is that it is an indispensable part of the truth. You will
find the complementary truth, formulated with equally
absolute emphasis, a few pages later. Hence to anyone
starting on his works we may tender the advice : *Respice
finem.* Take his first sweeping or iconoclastic utterances
with a pinch of salt ; wait till the argument is complete
before you arrive at a verdict. He may begin with shattering negatives ; but there is little doubt that he knows
perfectly well they are one-sided exaggerations, indulged
in by him for the praiseworthy purpose of rousing the
complacent or the conventional, and shaking them into
real reflection. His theology, as he himself would have
it understood, is a warning cry, with much of the element
of ejaculation ; and those who have to warn their neigh-
bours use great plainness of speech. Barth's style of
writing is that of a speaker, a rousing orator or herald.
This comes out in the immense number of rhetorical
questions to be found on his pages ; no theologian has
ever used so many interrogation marks ! Luther too was
a speaker, a speaker of genius whose brain and heart God
had touched ; and like Luther, Barth by his spiritual
exuberance gives himself away to his critics with both
hands.

One point at which the most sympathetic student
finds it difficult to give assent to Barth's argument is
his excessive *actualism.* By this I mean his persistent
tendency to stress what may be called the dynamic aspects
of Christian faith and life at the expense of the static.
The whole idea of a " state " appears to be distasteful to
him. Thus his predominant thought of creation is *creatio
continua*, the ever-renewed calling into existence by God
of the whole world of finite things. It is as if created
things did not " stay " created, but at every moment fell
out of existence again. At each instant of time their
being has to be restored. This is a familiar idea in the

theology of the past, but when made commanding or all-inclusive it has never gained the assent of the best Christian minds. That the conception of perpetual creation is part of Biblical thought, no careful reader of prophets and apostles will deny. But it is never employed so as to blanket the conviction that there was a Divine creating of the world once for all. If the Bible be our guide, our faith has to make room for both aspects : that God created the world, set it in a created *state* by the word of His power, and that within it He is still constantly creating.

Similarly, his aversion to the idea of a *state* of personal Christianity is unconquerable. Faith and regeneration are not conditions into which grace brings men, but bestowals from moment to moment. As he puts it in *Romans* : " Faith cannot be a concrete thing, that once began, and then continued its course. Faith is the Beginning, the Miracle, the Creation in every moment of time." [1] Or again : " Rightly understood, there are no Christians : there is only the eternal opportunity of becoming Christians." [2] The motive at work here is clear enough. Whatever happens, we must be rid of the notion that faith is our independent possession, become ours once for all like the colour of our eyes or the name we received at baptism, something in short that we can own and enjoy quite apart from God. Holding this, as all right-minded Christian thinkers must, to be a fatal error, Barth conceives that the only method of securing the opposite truth against negation or corrosion is to urge that faith is only real *in actu*. It is by its very nature an event, an occurrence perpetually renewed. It exists only in the form of momentary decision, in the ever-repeated leap from despair to certainty. Here again we can only say that both aspects of truth must be included, as Scripture undeniably includes them. In the New Testament there are " believers ", who, as St. Paul says, " have peace with

[1] p. 499. [2] *Romans*, p. 321.

God ", or in St. John's phrase " have eternal life ". They
have this inestimable boon not of themselves. They are
in a certain state or condition, but this state is not self-
produced or self-propagated ; God, and God only, *sustains*
them in it. And to them, in this condition, God perpetually ministers new faith. They do not cease to be
" believers " because their faith temporarily is overcast ;
but when their trust is renewed, the renewal is God's gift.
To strict Barthians we can say, as we recommend a fuller
scripturalness of teaching : " These things ye ought to
have done, and not to leave the others undone."

Other topics on which we may well seek for further light
are these : the conception of the Church which lies behind
Barth's recent dogmatic work. We have a right to know
precisely what Barth understands by the Church for which
he is writing. More important still, there is that fundamental subject on which he and Brunner disagree somewhat
seriously—the *imago Dei* in man. Briefly, we may say that
in Barth's judgment this *imago* has been totally lost and
obliterated by sin, while Brunner contends that it is still
represented even in the sinful by their humanity and
personality. It is interesting to observe that in his earlier
thought Barth took a position which, it might have been
supposed, left room for ultimate agreement between the
two thinkers. Thus (in *Romans*, p. 170) he wrote :

In all the negativity there is no point which does not bear
witness to the summit. There is no relativity which does not
reflect a vanished absolute which can never be wholly obliterated, since it is this absolute which makes relativity relative.
Death never occurs but it calls attention to our participation
in the Life of God, and to that relationship of His with us
which is not broken by sin.

But we must turn from these undeveloped hints of
criticism to the more congenial task of signalizing the
greatness of the theological work done by Barth, and its
promise of what is even greater. No true-blue Barthian,

I suppose, will ever admit that his views can be stated even by a friendly observer without some degree of caricature, but it is to be hoped that no radical injustice has been done above to the chief principles of Barth's thought.

We owe to him, to begin with, the most serious theological effort of this generation. He rightly rejects the plea that Christian men would be better employed in keeping to practical religious tasks and leaving theology alone. If you have to preach, must you not first clarify your mind ? Must you not decide what you stand for in contrast to Rome, to secularism, to all theology whose centre after all is in humanity or the single Ego ? No better starting-point can be found than universal doubt with regard to all previous systems. To be fundamentally sure, we must first become wholly unsure. Barth is emphatic that the charge made against him of obscurity is misleading.

If our thinking is not to be pseudo-thinking, we must think about life ; for such a thinking is a thinking about God. And if we are thinking about life, we must penetrate its hidden corners, and steadily refuse to treat anything as irrelevant. To be sincere, our thought must share in the tension of human life, in its criss-cross lines, and in its kaleidoscopic movements. And life is neither simple, nor straightforward, nor obvious. Things are simple and straightforward and obvious only when they are detached from their context and then treated super-ficially . . . It is not " complicated " thinking which is doctrinaire, but that much-praised " simplicity ".[1]

It is mere justice to say that Barth has faced more directly than any other Christian thinker of our time the menace to Christian belief presented by Humanism. To a Humanism which understands itself, the ideas of God, sin and death have lost all importance, except as symbols which proved of temporary advantage in the past. Barth replies that there is a living God, and that God has spoken. With a volcanic vehemence—feeling that passion alone is

[1] *Romans*, p. 425.

suited to the occasion—he is endeavouring to draw the
Christian mind of his generation back to the truth in
which all other truth that counts is embraced, viz., that in
the Bible God has uttered His absolute and ineffably
gracious will.   There is an objective revelation, which
puts every religious idea of man at its bar.   This is
supremely true of theologies, and from the Divine testing
and the risk of utter rejection Barth, as he tells us explicitly, would not exempt his own.   In theology we must
think as well as ever we can ;   that is our duty.   But—
and this we must never forget—the end of all theologies is
that every mouth is stopped before God, lest any flesh
should glory in His presence.

The inexorable repudiation of modernistic Humanism
involves him in a constant but wholesome and good-
humoured polemic.   He exposes all attempts to think of
God simply in terms of man, to climb to a knowledge of
God by the resolute exercise of reason or the technique of
mysticism, to conceive God as a compound of the best
things in our own nature, or to say genially that the
presence of God in Jesus and in ourselves is of much the
same kind.   It is plain that one who has learned from
Scripture the illimitable difference between God and man
will have much that is overwhelming to say concerning
fashionable modern ideas of immanence, of evolution as
an all-embracing category of reflection, of inevitable
progress—above all, of Pelagian notions of sin.   His
works are a treasure-house of strong and incorruptibly
Christian convictions on all these and related themes.
In his controversial practice there is no ill-temper ;   and
a sense of comedy is never far away.

So far from Barth having no ethical outlook, it is a
question whether it is not from his standpoint alone that
the true approach to the moral interpretation of actual
life can be made.   No one can contrast so profoundly as
he the righteousness of God and the unrighteousness of

man without the most fruitful consequences for the serious study of good and evil. He takes his point of departure in justification by faith ; that is to say, he makes it clear that righteousness—i.e., being right with God—is the beginning of everything, not the hard-won goal of interminable but sisyphean effort. The really good man is the man whose conscience has been comforted and his will fortified by submitting to have his sins forgiven for Christ's sake. Not ethical autonomy is the watchword, but obedience to the Word of God, speaking in a man's heart to disclose to him his duty for the actual or existential moment through which he is living. This is what dependence on God means, rather than ethical programmes, or assorted moral precepts, or even the effort meticulously to imitate Jesus. Once we have grasped the reality of sin, we shall cease to be easy optimists ; once we have seen God in Christ, and have looked up to His eternal Kingdom, we shall have done with pessimism.

The theology of Barth, criticize it as we may, is the Christian thinking of a great Christian mind, explosive and often unduly emphatic, but none the less of incalculable import for the Church of our time. Even those who reject many of his detailed results will not deny his unrivalled power to wake up the sleeping intelligence of the Christian society and to insist that theology shall be Biblical in its essence from end to end. He is compelling us to face again the problems of life and death. He thrusts upon us those terrible questions that are rampant in the world. He bids us seek the answer to them on our knees before the Lord, to listen that we may obey. At the moment he stands in the midst of his theological work, which cannot but take years to complete. Nothing more enriching for the whole Church could be thought of than that the time for completion should be given him, if God will, and that more and more his living influence should pass from land to land.

INDEX OF SUBJECTS

INDEX OF PERSONS

Strauss, D. F., 118 *seq.*, 130,
131, 133, 137, 207

Taylor, A. E., 113, 136
Tennyson, Lord, 141
Tertullian, 220, 244
Tholuck, F. A. G., 138
Thomas Aquinas, St., 9
Thomson, G. T., 264, 300
Thurneysen, E., 272
Troeltsch, E., 181 *seq.*

Underhill, Evelyn, 145

Wehrung, G., 41
Weiss, J., 183, 184
Wendland, J., 43
Windelband, W., 188
Wordsworth, W., 27, 263
Wrede, W., 183

Zinzendorf, Count, 13, 32

Printed by the Replika Process in Great Britain by
PERCY LUND, HUMPHRIES & CO. LTD.